OUTER SPACE

Curriculum Consultants

Dr. Arnold L. Willems
Associate Professor of Curriculum and Instruction
The University of Wyoming

Dr. Gerald W. Thompson
Associate Professor
Social Studies Education
Old Dominion University

Dr. Dale Rice
Associate Professor
Department of Elementary and Early Childhood Education
University of South Alabama

Dr. Fred Finley
Assistant Professor of Science Education
University of Wisconsin

Subject Area Consultants

Astronomy
Robert Burnham
Associate Editor
Astronomy Magazine and *Odyssey* Magazine

Geology
Dr. Norman P. Lasca
Professor of Geology
University of Wisconsin — Milwaukee

Oceanography
William MacLeish
Editor
Oceanus Magazine

Paleontology
Linda West
Dinosaur National Monument
Jensen, Utah

Physiology
Kirk Hogan, M.D.
Madison, Wisconsin

Sociology/Anthropology
Dr. Arnold Willems
Associate Professor of Curriculum and Instruction
College of Education
University of Wyoming

Technology
Dr. Robert T. Balmer
Professor of Mechanical Engineering
University of Wisconsin — Milwaukee

Transportation
James A. Knowles
Division of Transportation
Smithsonian Institution

Irving Birnbaum
Air and Space Museum
Smithsonian Institution

Donald Berkebile
Division of Transportation
Smithsonian Institution

Zoology
Dr. Carroll R. Norden
Professor of Zoology
University of Wisconsin —
 Milwaukee

Managing editor
Patricia Daniels

Editors
Herta Breiter
Darlene Shinozaki Kuhnke

Patricia Laughlin
Norman Mysliwiec

Designers
Faulkner/Marks

Jane Palecek

Artists
Jim Bamber
Dick Eastland
Claire Eastman
Phillip Emms
Dan Escott
Elizabeth Graham-Yool

Colin Hawkins
Eric Jewell
Barry Salter
John Sibbick
Raymond Turvey

First published by Macmillan Publishers Limited, 1979
Illustrations copyright © Macmillan Publishers Limited
 and Raintree Publishers Inc.
Text copyright © 1981 Raintree Publishers Inc.

Library of Congress Number: 80-22974
1 2 3 4 5 6 7 8 9 84 83 82 81
Printed and bound in the United States of America.

Library of Congress Cataloging in Publication Data
Main entry under title:

Let's discover outer space.
  (Let's discover; 15)
  Bibliography: p. 68
  Includes index.
  SUMMARY: A reference book dealing with the
solar system, the universe, astronomy, and space
travel.
  1. Outer space — Juvenile literature.
[1. Outer space] I. Title: Outer space.
II. Series.
AG6.L43 vol. 15 [QB501.3] 031s [520]
ISBN 0-8172-1762-2   80-22974

LET'S DISCOVER
OUTER SPACE

RAINTREE PUBLISHERS
Milwaukee • Toronto • Melbourne • London

Contents

THE SOLAR SYSTEM

The earth we live on is a large ball of rock. It is floating in space. It is called a planet. It spins as it moves around the sun with eight other planets. The sun and its planets make up the solar system.

6

sun

Mercury

Venus

moon

Earth

Mars

Jupiter

Saturn

Uranus

Neptune

Pluto

eclipse of the sun

sun

moon

Earth

The earth goes around the sun. The moon goes around the earth. Sometimes the moon comes between the sun and the earth. Then we cannot see the sun. This is called an eclipse. It is an eclipse of the sun.

The sun

Our sun is really a star. It looks big and bright to us. That is because it is nearer to the earth than the other stars are. It is a large ball of burning gas.

Never look straight at the sun. Its light will burn your eyes. It can even make you blind.

The sun seems to rise in the morning and move across the sky. It seems to sink at night. The sun is not really doing all this. It seems to move because the earth keeps spinning. As it turns away from the sun, night comes on. But the sun is still shining on the other side of the earth.

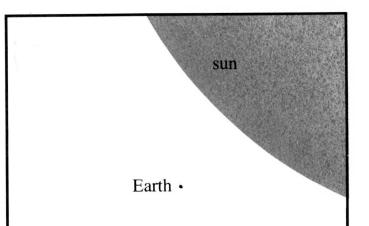

sun

Earth ·

The sun is over 100 times larger than the earth. If the sun was the size of a soccer ball, the earth would be a pinhead.

This picture of the sun was taken from a space station called Skylab. You can see a big loop of burning gas coming out of the sun. This is a solar flare. Cooler dark places are called sunspots.

Mercury

Mercury is the planet nearest to the sun. It is very hot because it is so close to the sun. Nothing can live on it.

This Mariner spacecraft flew past Mercury. It took pictures of this planet. They show that it looks like the moon. It has many holes called craters and no air.

Mercury

Earth

Mercury is the smallest planet.
The diameter of the earth is
about three times Mercury's.

Venus

We do not know much about Venus. It is hidden by thick clouds. Spacecraft such as this Russian Venera have landed on Venus. They have sent back pictures. They show many rocks and craters. Venus is very hot.

You can see Venus in the sky just before sunrise or just after sunset. It is called the morning star or evening star.

Venera spacecraft

DAN ESCOTT

Venus   Earth

Venus is the planet nearest to earth. It is about as big. It is our sister planet.

The earth

The earth is the third planet from the sun. It is a ball of rock covered with a layer of air. The earth travels around the sun. This journey takes one year. The earth spins around all the time. Each spin takes a day and a night.

Astronauts standing on the moon took this picture. It shows the earth rising from behind the moon's surface.

Many years ago, people thought the earth was flat. In India, they thought an elephant carried the earth on its back.

This is what our planet looks like
from a spacecraft. The oceans
and seas are blue. Snow and ice
and clouds are white. The brown
land you see in the picture is
parts of Africa and Arabia.

The moon

The moon is our nearest neighbor in space. But it is still very far away. It moves around the earth. But it always keeps the same side toward us. So we can see only this one side of the moon. It has no air or water. Rocks falling from space made many craters all over it.

moon

American astronauts made six explorations of the moon. They collected moon rocks and brought them to earth.

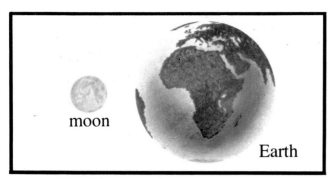

moon

Earth

The moon takes one month to go around the earth. Its diameter is one fourth the earth's diameter.

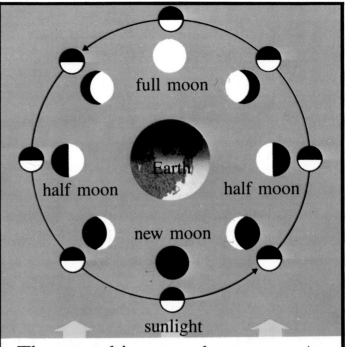

full moon

half moon

Earth

half moon

new moon

sunlight

The sun shines on the moon. As time passes, we see different amounts of its bright side. We always see the same side.

This footprint was left on the moon by one of the astronauts. It probably will stay there forever. There is no wind or water to disturb it.

Mars

Mars looks like a red star. A Viking spacecraft landed on Mars. It found that the rocky surface really is red. Mars is covered with red dust. Strong winds sometimes cause dust storms on Mars. It has larger volcanoes and deeper valleys than those found on earth.

This is a picture of sunset on Mars. Red dust blown by winds makes the sky look pink.

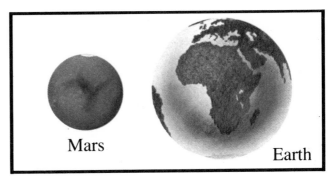

Mars   Earth

Mars is a small planet. It has two moons but little air. It has half the diameter of the earth.

This picture of Mars was taken by a spacecraft. It is really many small pictures joined together. Can you see them? The white part at the top is ice. It is like the Arctic ice cap on earth. You can see a few clouds in the thin air around Mars.

Jupiter

Jupiter does not have a rocky surface. It is just a giant ball of liquid and gas. The colored bands are clouds. They cover the whole planet. Jupiter has a red spot. It could be a storm. It has lasted hundreds of years.

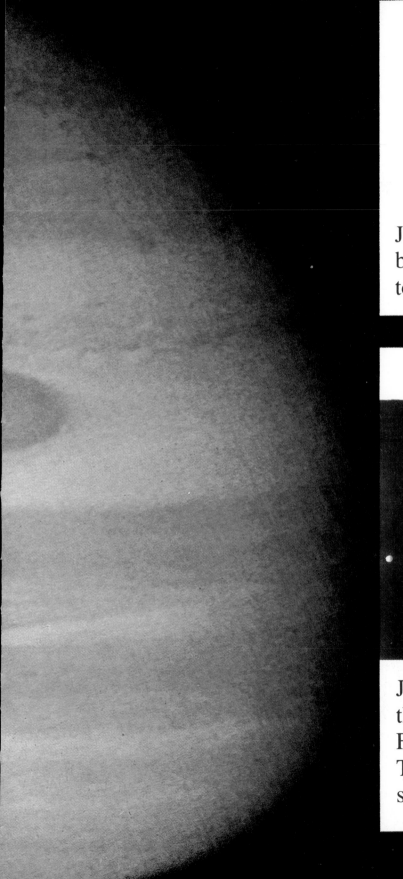

Jupiter   Earth

Jupiter is the biggest planet. It is
bigger than all the others put
together. It has a ring system.

moons

Jupiter has 16 moons. Most of
them are small pieces of rock.
Four of the moons are larger.
They are about the size of the
small planets.

Saturn

The sixth planet from the sun is Saturn. It is the farthest planet we can see without using a telescope. Saturn is much like Jupiter. It is a big ball of liquid and gas. It has colored bands of clouds. Like Jupiter, Saturn spins about twice as fast as the earth.

Thin, flat rings surround Saturn. It also has 15 moons.

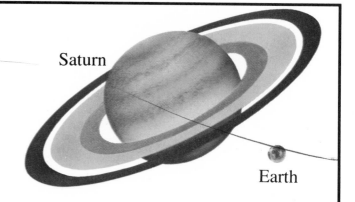

Saturn

Earth

Saturn is much bigger than the earth. Its rings reflect sunlight. That is what makes Saturn look very bright in the sky.

The beautiful rings around Saturn are not a solid mass. They are made up of icy pieces of rock.

Uranus, Neptune, and Pluto

We know little about these planets. They are very far away. Uranus and Neptune are liquid. Each is surrounded by a thick, cloudy atmosphere. Pluto may be a solid ball with an icy surface. All these planets are very cold.

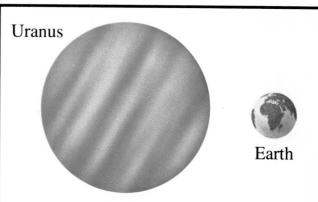

Uranus

Earth

Uranus is much larger than the earth. It has five moons.

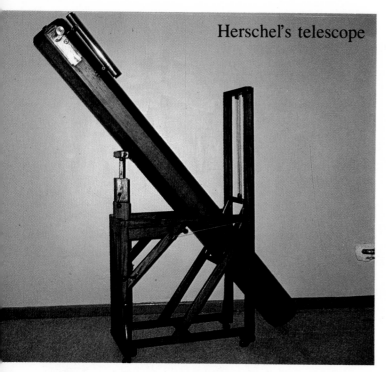

Herschel's telescope

When astronomers began to use telescopes, they soon found Uranus and Neptune. William Herschel discovered Uranus about 200 years ago. He used a telescope like this one. Pluto was discovered in 1930. Recently astronomers found Uranus' rings.

Most planets are named after ancient gods. Uranus was the god of heaven.

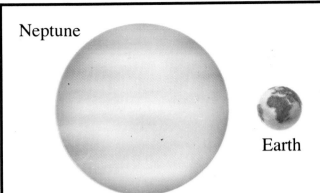

Neptune

Earth

Neptune is almost the same size as Uranus. It has two moons.

The planet Neptune looks blue-green. It was named after the god of the sea.

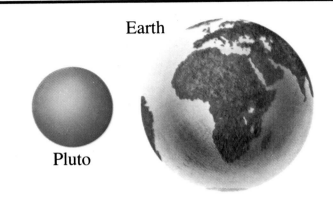

Earth

Pluto

Pluto is about the same size as Mercury. It has one moon.

Pluto was named after the god of the underworld. This was thought to be the land of the dead.

Asteroids and meteors

meteorite

Asteroids and meteoroids are pieces of rock that move around the sun. Meteors are rocks that enter the earth's air. They burn up and can be seen. Some big ones land on earth. They are called meteorites. A large meteorite made this crater in Arizona.

meteorite crater

Bayeaux Tapestry

Comets

Comets are made of dust and ice. They come from far out in the solar system. When a comet is near the sun, we can see its long, bright tail. The people below are watching a comet. The Bayeux Tapestry shown here was made 900 years ago. Can you see the comet in it?

THE UNIVERSE

The universe is the name we give to everything in space. The earth, sun, planets, and stars are part of the universe. With telescopes, astronomers see many more stars in the universe than we can ever see.

There are very thin clouds of dust and gas between the stars. The stars look blue because starlight shines on this dust.

A nebula is a cloud of dust and gas far out in the universe. It can be seen through a telescope. It looks like a dark patch in the sky. This is a picture of the Horsehead Nebula.

Horsehead Nebula

Stars

There are billions of stars in the universe. The stars we see in the sky are only a small part of them. Stars are different sizes and colors. They can be red, white, yellow, or blue. They are all very far away. Some occur in pairs. Others stay in large groups called clusters.

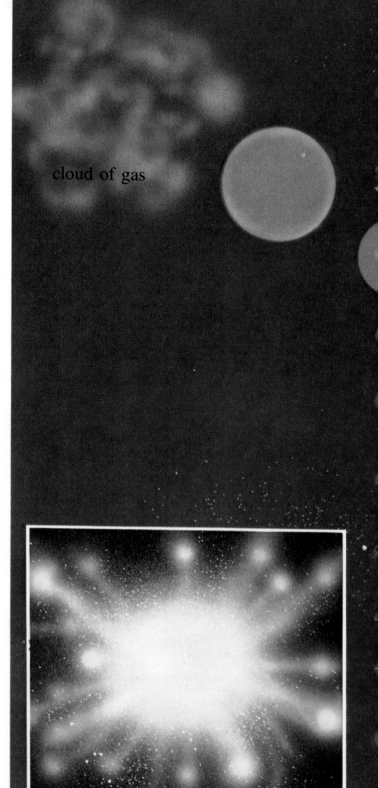

cloud of gas

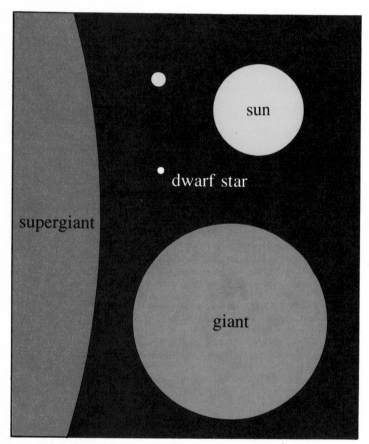

sun

dwarf star

supergiant

giant

The sun is a medium-sized star. It is in the middle of its life. Larger stars are called giants and supergiants. Smaller stars are called dwarf stars.

Some giant stars explode to end their lives. They suddenly shine very brightly. They are called supernovas. Then they go out.

Stars start as a cloud of gas. This cloud draws together to make a ball of hot gas. It starts to burn and give out light and heat as our own sun does. After millions of years, the gas is used up. The star then grows bigger and redder. Finally, it shrinks to a tiny white dwarf.

white dwarf star

Families of stars

The stars cling together in groups. Each large group is called a galaxy. All the stars we see are in our galaxy. On a clear night, you can see a faint band of light in the sky. This light is called the Milky Way. Millions of faint stars make this light in our galaxy.

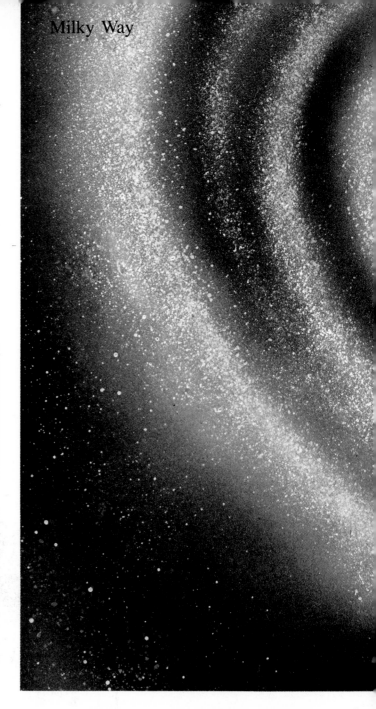

Milky Way

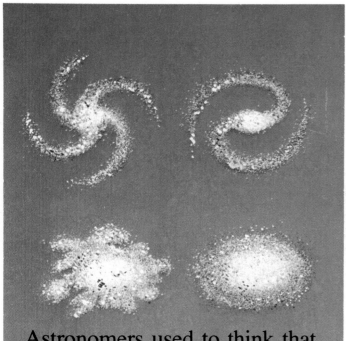

Astronomers used to think that our galaxy was the only one in the universe. We know now that there are many other galaxies. Not all are the same shape. Many, such as the top ones above, are spiral-shaped. Some are egg-shaped. Others have no special shape.

Our galaxy is a flat spiral shape. You can see a drawing of it above. The sun is a tiny dot in one of the spiral arms.

The bottom picture shows our galaxy from the side. The arrow shows where we are.

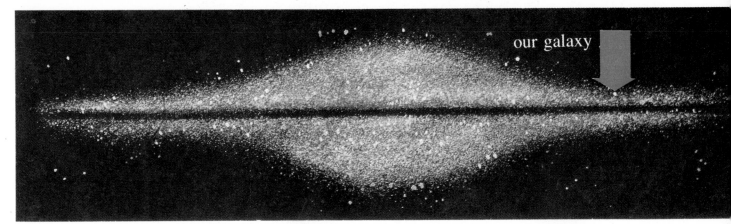

our galaxy

How it all began

Nobody knows how the universe began. Scientists have tried to find out. Some think it started with a big bang. This was caused by a great explosion in space. It sent galaxies spreading in all directions. They think the galaxies are still moving away from each other.

sun

cloud of dust

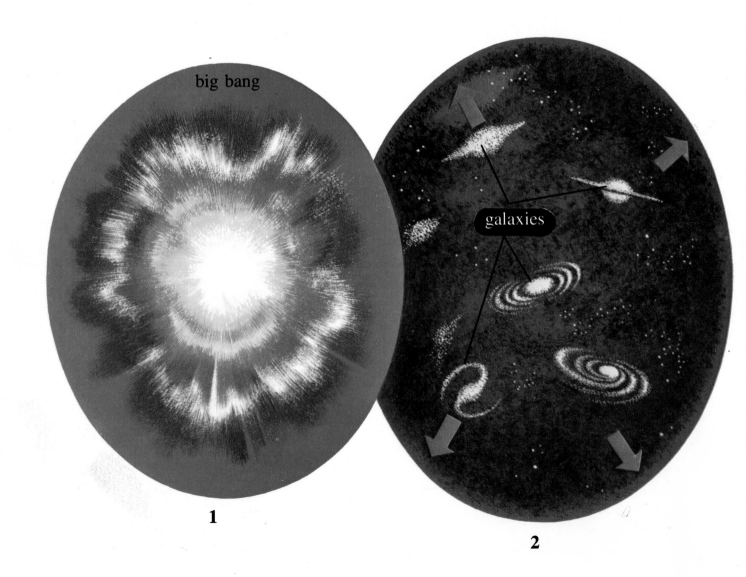

big bang

galaxies

1

2

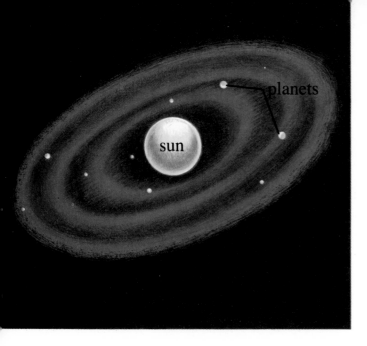

Scientists have tried to find out how the sun and its planets were made. Many think the sun began as a spinning cloud of dust and gas. The gas formed the center of the sun. The rest of the cloud kept moving around the sun. The planets were made from this cloud, they believe.

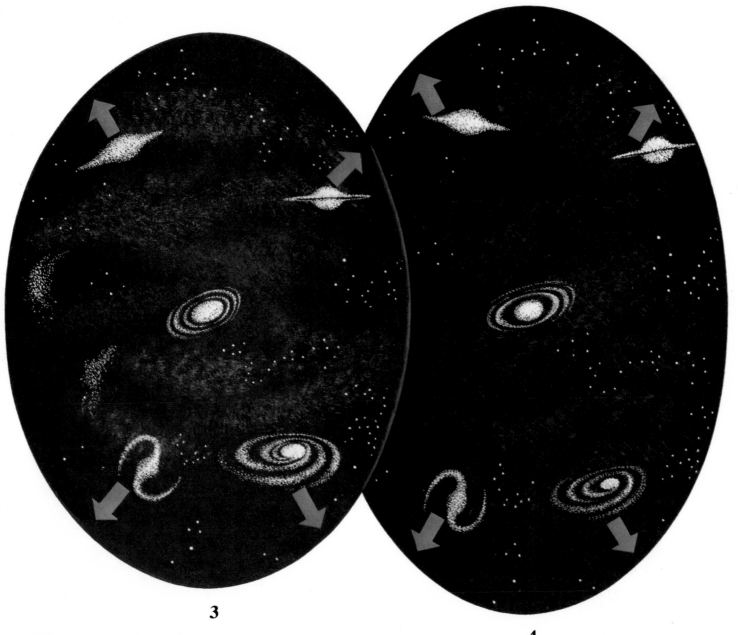

3

4

Life in the universe

There are many kinds of plants and animals on earth. Living things cannot live anywhere else in our solar system. Some people think there may be life in other parts of the universe. Stars are too hot to have our kind of life. But there might be life on some planets.

ameba

There are many kinds of life. The ameba is a tiny and very simple form of life. Animals and people are much more complicated. There is life even in difficult places. Cactus plants live in hot, dry deserts. Bacteria can live even in the Arctic.

cactus

Life on other planets may be as strange as these floating creatures.

simple plants on a rocky planet

ASTRONOMY

Astronomy is the study of the universe. Scientists who study astronomy are called astronomers. They have watched the sun, moon, and stars for hundreds of years. Galileo was the first one to look at the planets through a telescope.

There is an ancient circle of stones at Stonehenge in England. Astronomers probably built it.

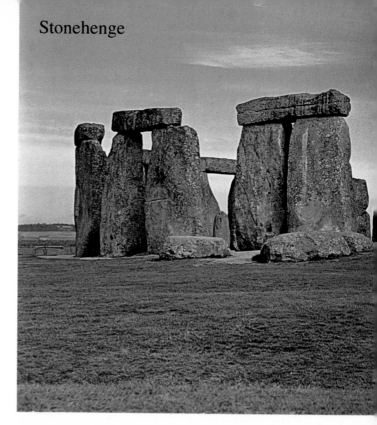

Stonehenge

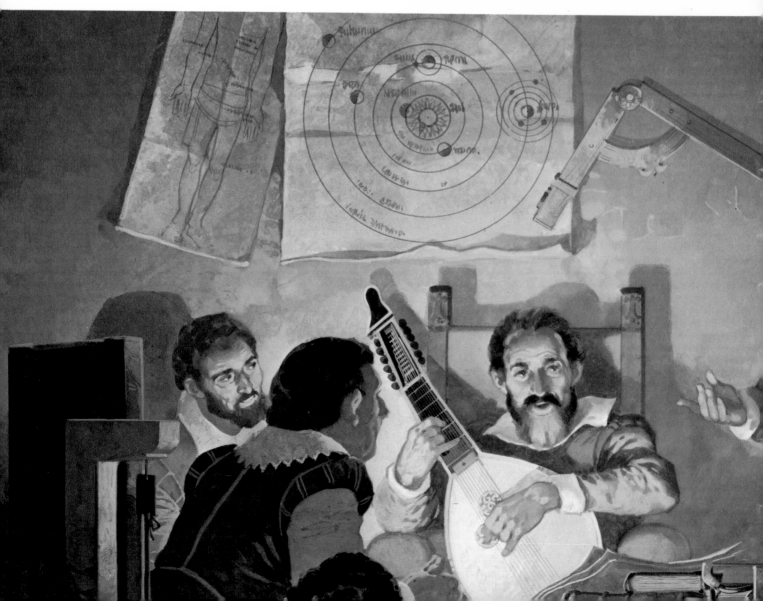

Early telescopes were very small. This one was made by Isaac Newton, a famous scientist. It is a bit shorter than this book.

early astronomers

Telescopes

Telescopes help astronomers study the universe. These instruments make planets look closer. This helps astronomers study the surface of planets. Telescopes also make stars look brighter. They also help us to see farther in space. With their help, we can see many distant stars.

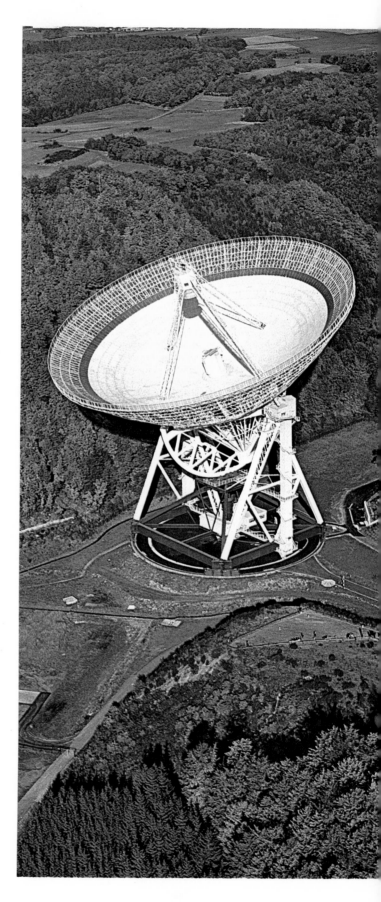

Big telescopes are needed to see distant stars. This one is much bigger than the man using it.

The radio telescope at the right picks up radio waves from stars in outer space.

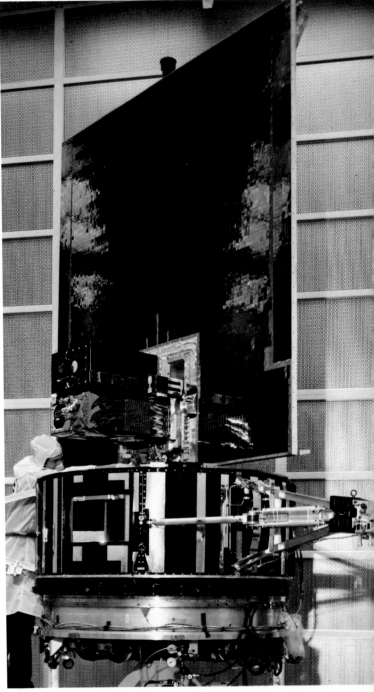

The air around the earth keeps us from seeing stars and planets clearly. Scientists use satellites like this one to study the sun. It travels around the earth above its layer of air.

Spacecraft need powerful rockets to push them away from the pull of the earth's gravity. This large Saturn 5 American rocket sent astronauts to the moon.

SPACE TRAVEL

Gravity is a strong force that keeps us on earth. Spacecraft must travel very fast to get free of the pull of gravity. They must fly much faster than large jet planes.

People cannot live in space without the protection of spacecraft and spacesuits.

When a spacecraft comes back to earth, it passes through the atmosphere. The spacecraft gets very hot. A thick skin called a heat shield protects it. This American spacecraft has just landed in the sea.

spacecraft

Rockets

Spacecraft and satellites are sent into space by powerful rockets. Most of a rocket's weight is fuel. The spacecraft is only a small part near the rocket's nose. When the fuel is used up, the rocket can no longer be used.

The V-2 rocket was the first large rocket ever made. It was built in Germany. Space rockets were later developed from it.

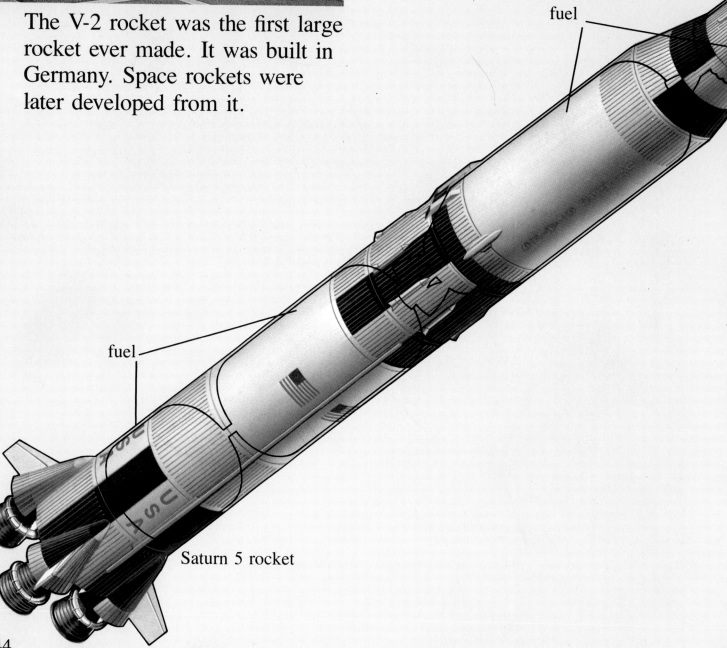

fuel

fuel

Saturn 5 rocket

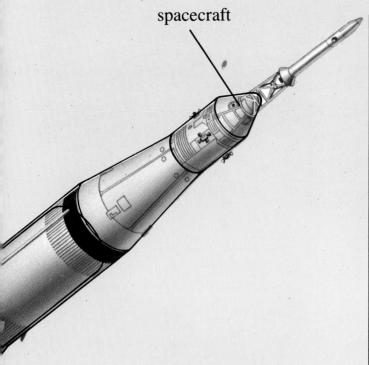
spacecraft

Blow up a balloon and let it go. It will fly away as the air rushes out. This is how a rocket works.

liquid fuel rocket

solid fuel rocket

Robert Goddard built this strange early rocket. It was the first one to use liquid fuel. At that time, most people thought humans would never fly to the moon.

When rocket fuel burns, it makes hot gas. The gas shoots out. The rocket moves forward.

Satellites

Many satellites circle above the earth. Some study weather to help weather forecasters. Other satellites carry telephone messages to distant places. Some satellites send television pictures across the world. People in many places can watch sports events as they are happening. Television cameras photograph the athletes. Satellites carry their pictures across the world.

satellite picture in America

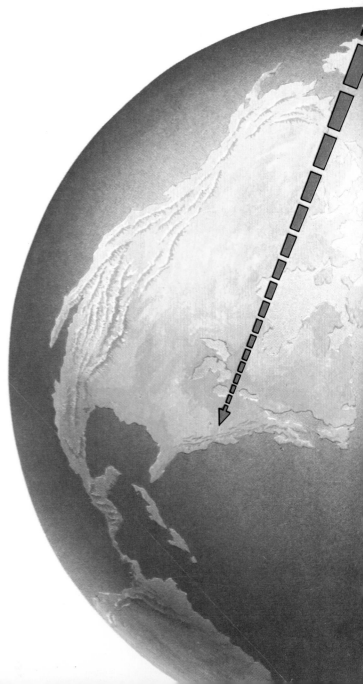

satellite

Invisible waves carry television pictures through the air. These waves travel in straight lines. They cannot bend around the earth's surface. A satellite is used to send pictures to distant places.

The television pictures are sent up to a satellite. It sends them back to earth. People in America can watch sports events being held in Europe.

sports event in Europe

People in space

There are many problems for people in space. There is no food, water, or air in space. The spacecraft must carry all these things. There is little room inside the spacecraft. When American astronauts went to the moon, they were squashed together, as the top picture shows.

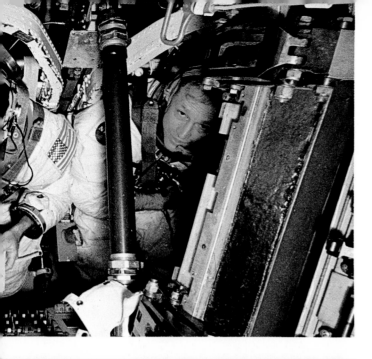

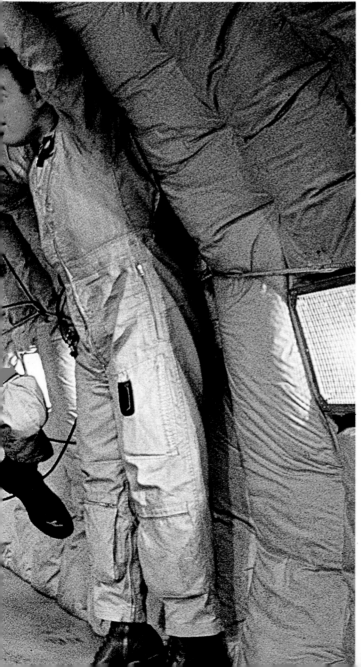

Astronauts must wear spacesuits when outside their spacecraft.

There is no gravity in space. Everything floats. These astronauts are floating during training.

Journey to the moon

A giant rocket sent three astronauts to the moon. They traveled in a small cabin in the nose of the Apollo spacecraft. This was called the Command Module. Near the moon, two astronauts got into a part called the Lunar Module. It took them to the moon's surface.

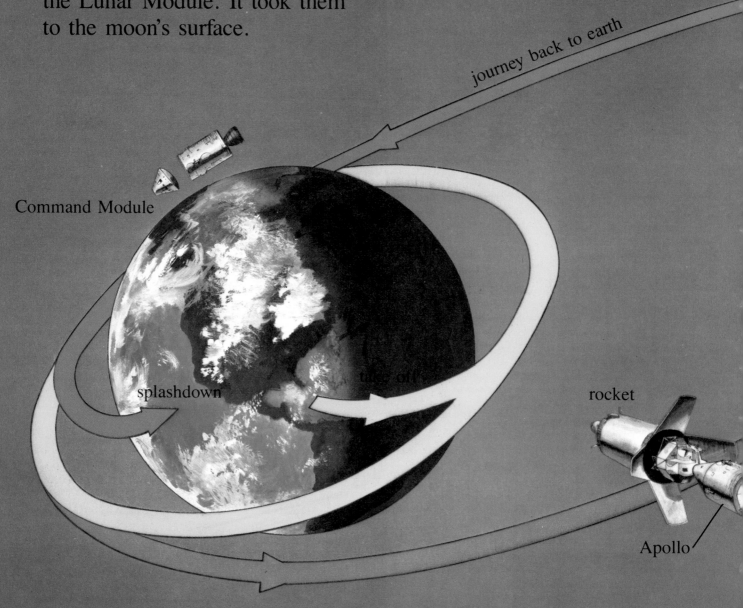

journey back to earth

Command Module

splashdown

take off

rocket

Apollo

moon

moon

Lunar Module

journey to the moon

At the end of the visit, the Lunar Module took the two astronauts back to the Command Module. It later separated from the spacecraft and then splashed into the sea. You can see the moon twice in this picture. First, you see the journey to the moon. Then you see the trip back to earth.

Men on the moon

In all, 12 Americans have walked on the moon. Neil Armstrong was the first to do this. People weigh very little on the moon. So it is not easy to walk on it. These men set up scientific instruments that send information to earth. Below, the Apollo spacecraft is shown above the earth.

Edwin Aldrin was the second man on the moon. He wore a spacesuit and carried air to breathe.

moon car

Lunar Module

Some astronauts took along a moon car to help them travel.

The astronauts on the moon lived in the Lunar Module. It looked like a large metal spider.

Astronauts

In America, space travelers are called astronauts. In Russia, they are called cosmonauts. In 1957, the Russians put Sputnik, the first satellite, in orbit around the earth. Four years later, they sent Yuri Gagarin into orbit. He was the first man in space.

Yuri Gagarin

On the right is the American astronaut Ed White. He is walking in space. The cord joins him to the spacecraft. He is using a space gun to push himself around.

So far, only one woman has flown in space. She is a Russian called Valentina Tereshkova. She circled the earth 48 times. Her flight lasted three days. Some American women are now training to become astronauts.

Valentina Tereshkova

Astronauts must stay healthy. They must train for many months. It is very expensive to send people into space. Luckily, robot spacecraft can do much of the work of astronauts. Robot explorers can go farther than people. They have visited five planets.

Viking spacecraft

Robot explorers

Luna 16 is a Russian robot explorer. It scooped up moon soil and brought it back to earth.

Luna 16

The Russian moon car above is called Lunokhod. Two such cars were sent to the moon. They were controlled by scientists on earth. They crawled over the moon's surface. They carried cameras. They sent pictures of the moon back to scientists on earth.

Robot explorers have also landed on Venus and Mars. An American Viking spacecraft sent back many pictures after landing on Mars. It did not find any life on Mars. This robot explorer is separating from its spacecraft. It is landing on Mars.

Mars

robot explorer

57

Space stations

Space stations are large spacecraft. People can live and work in them for several months. They sleep in bunks and keep food from earth in the kitchen. Astronauts can live in comfort and wear ordinary clothes. Skylab was an American space station.

Spacecraft can carry people to and from space stations. This Russian spacecraft is landing men on the Salyut space station.

The American Skylab was the first space station. It was damaged when it was sent up. Its first crew had to fix it.

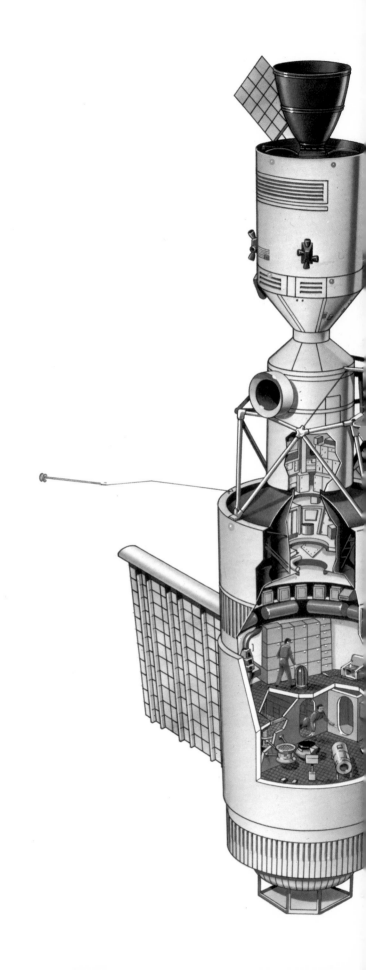

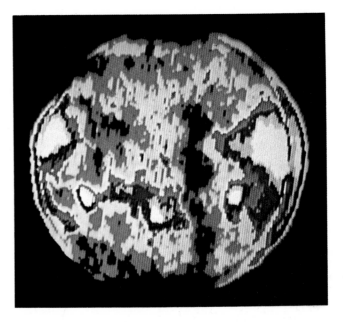

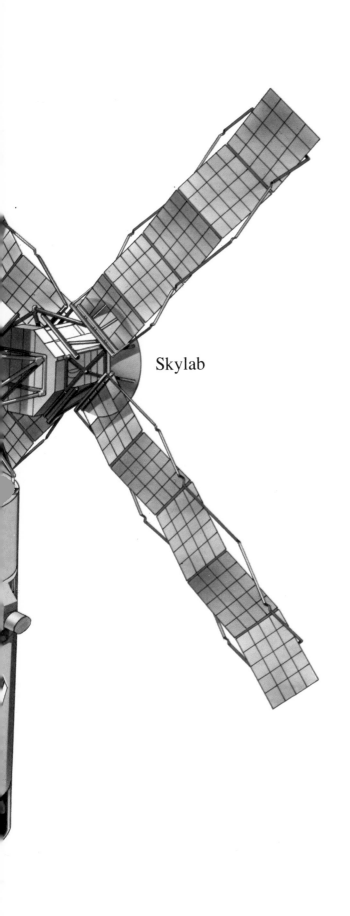

Skylab

In all, nine astronauts lived in Skylab. They took pictures of the sun. Their special camera took this picture of the sun. No camera on earth can do this.

This is Skylab circling the earth. Skylab astronauts took many pictures of the earth. They also studied the clouds.

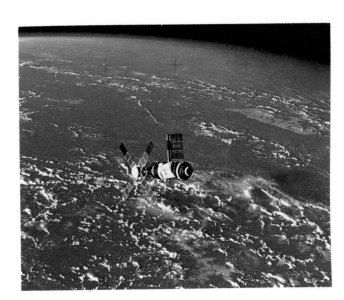

Space Shuttle

The Space Shuttle is a new kind of spacecraft. It is a rocket plane that can be used many times. Booster rockets help it take off from earth. It then circles the earth while people inside do their scientific work. Then it glides back to earth. It lands on an airplane runway.

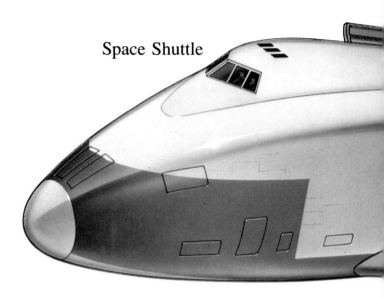

Space Shuttle

booster rocket fires

rockets fall away

Shuttle takes off

rockets land in sea

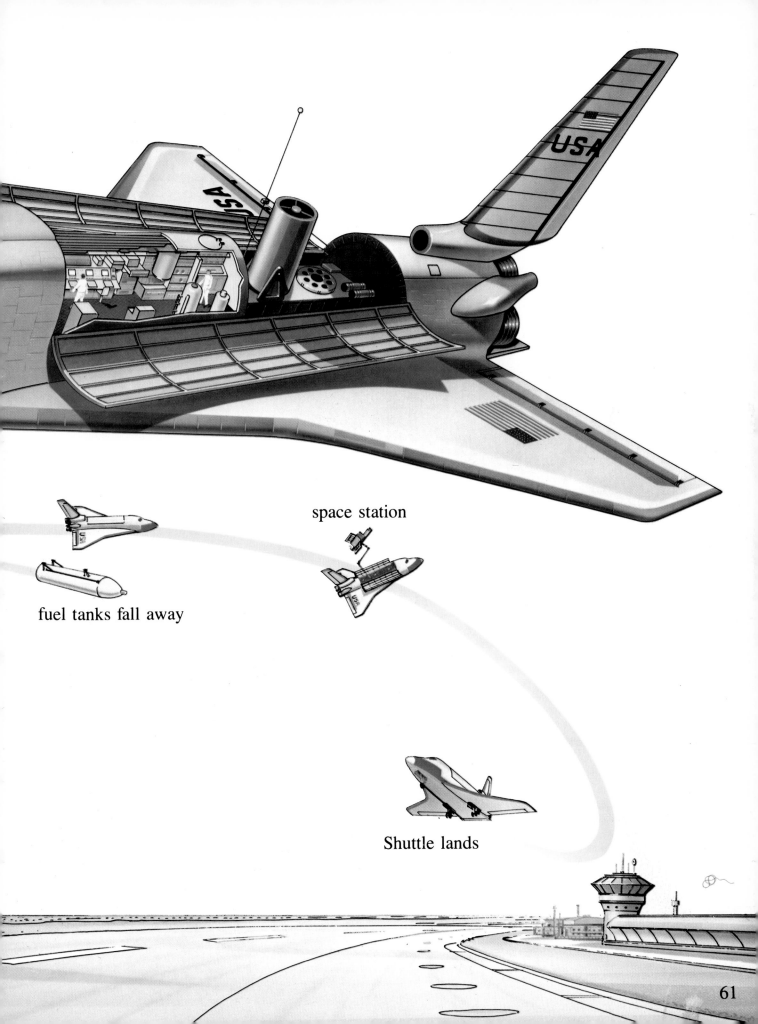

space station

fuel tanks fall away

Shuttle lands

The future

People will continue to explore space. They may even visit other planets. They may build places to live in on the moon. But they may never visit the stars. The nearest star to our sun is very far away. It would take many hundreds of years for a starship from earth to reach it.

Space Shuttle

If the earth gets too crowded, we may need to build homes in space. Perhaps one day some people will live on giant space stations that circle the earth.

The Space Shuttle could take workers to space stations. These workers could collect energy from the sun. They could beam it back to earth for people to use.

space station

GLOSSARY

These words are defined the way they are used in the book.

ameba (uh MEE buh) a tiny one-celled animal

Apollo spacecraft (uh PAHL oh *SPAYS* KRAFT) any of the space planes that flew to the moon

Arctic ice cap (ARK tik *EYES* KAP) a large area of ice and snow that covers the top part of the earth

asteroids (AS tuh roydz) very small planets that go around the sun; they are found mostly between Mars and Jupiter

astronaut (AS treh nawt) name given to American space travelers

astronomer (eh STRAHN uh mur) a scientist who studies the universe

astronomy (eh STRAH nuh mee) the science that studies the universe

atmosphere (AT muh sfihr) the air around the earth

bacteria (bak TIHR ee ah) very tiny one-celled plants that are all around us but which are too small for us to see

big bang (big bang) the name given by some scientists to the start of the universe; they believe a great explosion of matter started it all

booster rocket (BOOS tur ROK iht) a rocket used during space travel to push a spacecraft faster or to change its direction

camera (KAM ur uh) a machine for taking pictures; moving pictures are made with a camera

comet (KAHM iht) a bright long-tailed object that is seen in the sky at certain times

Command Module (kuh MAND MAHDJ ool) the cabin of Apollo spacecraft; this is the part that brought astronauts back to earth

constellation (KON steh *LAY* shun) a group of stars

cosmonaut (KAHZ meh nawt) Russian name for a person who travels in space

crater (KRAY tur) a round, raised ring on the moon; it is believed that rocks from outer space made the moon's craters

diameter (dy AM ih tur) the distance along a straight line through the center of a round object; the size of a planet is given as its diameter

dwarf stars (dworf stahrz) small stars that are not very bright; they are often called white dwarfs

earth (urth) the planet we live on

eclipse (ih KLIPS) darkening of the sun as the moon passes between it and the earth; darkening of the moon as the earth passes between the sun and the moon

equator (ee KWAY tur) an imaginary circle around the middle of the earth

exploration (eks pluh RAY shun) traveling in unknown places to learn about them; astronauts carry on exploration of space

fuel (FEW ihl) a material that is burned; fuels give heat and light and make engines run

future (FEW chur) a time to come; tomorrow and next year are the future

galaxy (GAL ihk see) a group of billions of stars; many galaxies make up the universe

giant star (JY ihnt stahr) a very bright star of great size

gravity (GRAV ih tee) the force that pulls objects to the center of the earth or sun; the gravity of the sun keeps its planets from flying off into outer space

Great Bear (GRAYT bair) a seven-star constellation in the northern sky; it is also called the Big Dipper

heat shield (HEET sheeld) outer covering of a spacecraft that keeps it from burning up as it passes through the earth's atmosphere

Horsehead Nebula (HAWRS hehd NEHB yuh luh) a large nebula that is shaped like a horse's head

Jupiter (JOO pih tur) the largest planet of our sun

Luna 16 (LOO nuh 16) the name of an unmanned Russian spacecraft

Lunar Module (LOO nur MAHDJ ool) the part of Apollo spacecraft that landed on the moon

Lunokhod (LOO nuhk hod) the name of a special Russian robot car that traveled on the moon

Mariner spacecraft (MAIR ih nur SPAYS kraft) the name of several American spacecraft that were sent to different planets, including Venus, Mars, Jupiter, and Saturn

Mars (mawrz) the red planet; it is the fourth one from the sun

Mercury (MUH kur ee) the smallest planet and the one nearest the sun

meteor (MEE tee ur) a piece of rock or metal that falls from outer space and burns up in the atmosphere

meteorite (MEE tee uh RYT) a piece of rock or metal from outer space that lands on earth

meteoroids (MEE tee ur oydz) small rocky pieces that go around the sun; some of them may fall into the earth's atmosphere as meteors

Milky Way (MIL kee way) a wide band of light in the sky; it is made up of millions of stars

moon (moon) a rocky object that moves around a planet as a natural satellite; Jupiter has 16 moons

nebula (NEHB yuh luh) a cloud-like dark spot in the sky

Neptune (NEP toon) the fourth largest planet in our solar system

outer space (OW tur spays) the space beyond the earth's atmosphere

planet (PLAN iht) any of the large objects, such as the earth, that travel around the sun

Pluto (PLOO toh) the sun's farthest planet

radio telescope (RAY dee oh TEL eh skohp) a large dish-shaped machine that picks up radio signals from space

radio waves (RAY dee oh WAVZ) energy that travels through space; these waves carry radio programs to your radio set

ring system (ring SIHS tihm) bands of light around a planet; Saturn's rings are easily seen with a telescope

robot spacecraft (ROH buht SPAYS kraft) a spacecraft that is run by machines only

runway (RUN way) a pathway on which airplanes take off and land

satellites (SAT eh lyts) objects that travel through space around the earth; many kinds of satellites are now circling the earth

Saturn (SAT urn) the second largest planet in our solar system

Saturn 5 (SAT urn fyv) the large rocket that sent Apollo spacecraft to the moon

scientist (SY ihn tist) a person who is trained in one of the sciences such as astronomy and biology

Skylab (SKY lab) the name of the first American space laboratory; astronauts worked in it while it was moving around the earth in space

solar flare (SOH lur flair) a large loop of burning gas that shoots out from the edge of the sun

solar system (SOH lur SIHS tihm) the sun and its nine planets

Space Shuttle (SPAYS SHUT ehl) a special spacecraft that can carry people and supplies from earth to a space station and back again

space station (SPAYS STAY shun) a special satellite that serves as a stopping place for spacecraft; work can be done in a space station

spacesuit (SPAYS soot) clothing worn by astronauts in space

Sputnik (SPUT nik) the name of the first satellite sent into space around the earth; it was put there by Russian scientists

Stonehenge (STOHN henj) a circle of large stones in England; they are very old

sunspot (SUN spaht) a dark area on the sun

supergiants (*SOO* pur JY ihntz) giant stars that have suddenly become much brighter and larger than other stars

supernova (*SOO* pur NOH vah) a star that suddenly becomes very bright and then fades

telescope (TEL eh skohp) a long object through which astronomers look to find out more about stars and planets

television (TEL eh VIZH uhn) a machine that receives pictures sent by radio waves

universe (YOO nih vurs) everything that is; the earth, stars, comets, and space are all part of the universe

Uranus (YUR uh nuhs) the planet that moves around the sun between Saturn and Neptune

V-2 rocket (VEE too ROK iht) a rocket first built by Germany for use in war

valley (VAL ee) a low place between hills or mountains

Venera (vehn IHR uh) the name of a Russian spacecraft that landed on the planet Venus

Venus (VEE nuhs) the planet that is nearest to the earth; Venus moves around the sun between the earth and Mercury

Viking spacecraft (VY king SPAYS kraft) a spacecraft sent into space to learn about Mars, Jupiter, and Saturn

volcano (vol KAY noh) a mountain made by hot gases and melted rock blown out of the earth.

weather forecaster (WETH ur *FAWR* KAS tur) a person who studies the weather and tells us what it will be

FURTHER READING

Asimov, Isaac. *Environments Out There*. New York: Abelard-Schuman, Ltd., 1967. 128pp.

Asimov, Isaac. *Galaxies*. Chicago: Follett Publishing Company, 1968.

Asimov, Isaac. *The Heavenly Host.* New York: Walker and Company, 1975.

Branley, Franklyn M. *The Beginning of the Earth*. New York: Crowell, 1972. 33pp.

Branley, Franklyn M. *Black Holes, White Dwarfs, and Superstars*. New York: Crowell, 1976. 113pp.

Branley, Franklyn M. *A Book of Outer Space For You*. New York: Crowell, 1970. 56pp.

Branley, Franklyn M. *Book of Stars for You*. New York: Crowell, 1967. Unpaged.

Branley, Franklyn M. *Comets, Meteoroids, and Asteroids*. New York: Crowell, 1974. 115pp.

Branley, Franklyn M. *Eclipse: Darkness in Daytime*. New York: Crowell, 1973. 33pp.

Branley, Franklyn M. *Mystery of Stonehenge*. New York: Crowell, 1969. 51pp.

Ciupik, Larry A. and James Seevers. *Space Machines*. Milwaukee: Raintree Publishers, 1979. 31pp.

Collins, Michael. *Flying to the Moon and Other Strange Places*. New York: Farrar, Straus and Giroux, Inc., 1976. 159pp.

Coombs, Charles. *Skylab*. New York: William Morrow and Company, Inc., 1972. 128pp.

Gallant, Roy A. *The Constellations: How They Came to Be*. Bristol, Florida: Four Winds Press, 1979.

Goodwin, Harold L. *All About Rockets and Space Flight*. New York: Random House, 1970. 145pp.

Ivins, Ann. *Beginning Knowledge Book of Stars and Constellations*. New York: Macmillan Publishing Company, Inc., 1969.

Joseph, Joseph M.; Lippincott, Sarah L. 2nd ed. *Point to the Stars*. New York: McGraw-Hill, 1977. 96pp.

Knight, David. *Colonies in Orbit: The Coming Age of Human Settlements in Space*. New York: William Morrow and Company, Inc., 1977. 94pp.

Lambert, David. *The Earth and Space*. New York: F. Watts, Inc., 1979.

McGowen, Thomas E. *Album of Astronomy*. New York: Rand McNally and Company, 1979. 60pp.

Moche, Diane L. *What's Up There?* New York: Scholastic Book Service, 1976.

Nourse, Alan E. *Asteroids*. New York: F. Watts, Inc., 1975.

Rey, H. A. *Find the Constellations*. rev. ed. Boston: Houghton Mifflin Company, 1976. 72pp.

Rutland, Jonathan. *Exploring the World of Robots*. New York: F. Watts, Inc., 1979.

Simak, Clifford D. *Wonder and Glory: The Story of the Universe*. New York: St. Martin's Press, Inc., 1970.

Stilley, Frank. *The Search: Our Quest for Intelligent Life in Outer Space*. New York: G. P. Putnam's and Sons, 1977.

Zim, Herbert. *The Universe*. rev. ed. New York: William Morrow and Company, Inc., 1973. 63pp.

QUESTIONS TO THINK ABOUT

The Solar System (1)

Do you remember?

What is the solar system made up of?

How many planets are in the solar system?

What is the sun made of?

What causes an eclipse of the sun?

How many times larger than the earth is the sun?

How big is Mercury compared to all the other planets?

What is another name for the evening star?

Name two ways that the earth moves.

What caused the craters on the moons?

Find out about . . .

The moon's gravity. How does it compare to the earth's gravity? How did it affect the astronauts who walked on the moon?

Sunspots. What are they? Why are they important to people on earth? How do they affect communications?

The Solar System (2)

Do you remember?

What makes Mars look like a red star?

What is the surface of Mars like?

What causes the great red spot on Jupiter?

How many moons does Jupiter have?

What are the rings of Saturn made of?

When was the planet Pluto discovered?

What are asteroids?

What are meteorites?

What is a comet made of?

Where do comets come from?

Find out about . . .

Halley's Comet. When was it last seen? When will it be seen again? How did people react to it? Was it dangerous? How far away was it?

Mariner spacecraft. What were these spacecraft supposed to do? How did they do it? What did they find out about Mars? How did they prepare the way for the Viking spacecraft?

The Universe

Do you remember?

What makes up the universe?

Why do stars look blue?

What is a nebula?

How many stars are in the universe?

How big a star is our sun?

How does a star form?

What is a white dwarf?

What is a galaxy?

Could there be life in other parts of the universe than just in our solar system?

Find out about . . .

The Viking program. Viking spacecraft were designed to fly by Jupiter and the other outer planets. What have they learned about Jupiter? What kinds of pictures have their cameras sent back to earth? Will the Vikings tell us more about even more distant parts of the universe?

The life of a star. How is a star born? How does it develop? How does it die? Does it leave anything behind?

Astronomy

Do you remember?

What is an astronomer?

Who was Galileo?

What does a telescope do?

How do telescopes today compare with the one used by Isaac Newton?

What does a radio telescope do?

How do satellites help scientists?

Find out about . . .

Telescopes. How many different kinds are there?

Where are the big ones located? What have astronomers discovered with them? Have important discoveries been made with small telescopes? How are radio telescopes different from other kinds? Can they take pictures? What do they tell astronomers?

Constellations. What are their names? Where in the sky can they be seen? Why were they given names of animals and other objects?

Space Travel (1)

Do you remember?

What is gravity?

Why must spacecraft travel very fast?

What happens to spacecraft as they come back to earth?

What are rockets used for?

Who was Robert Goddard?

What do our space satellites do?

Why do objects float in space?

Who was the first person to walk on the moon?

Find out about . . .

Training of astronauts. What did they have to learn about weightlessness? How was this done? What did they learn about eating while weightless? What kind of exercise did they get?

The history of rocketry. Did it really start long

ago in China? What did Germany use V-2 rockets for? How did the United States build on what German scientists did? What part did different fuels play?

Space Travel (2)

Do you remember?

What was the name of the first satellite sent into space?

What is a space gun used for?

What can a robot explorer do that our astronauts cannot do?

On what planet did Viking spacecraft land?

What are space stations used for?

What is the Space Shuttle?

Will people ever visit distant stars?

When might we build homes in space?

Find out about . . .

Mining the moon. What have some scientists suggested about mining the minerals on the moon? Could a kind of space shuttle be used to haul tools and workers to the moon? Could it bring back minerals? Would space stations have to be built along the way?

Future space programs. What is the United States planning? Will weather and climate research be done? What about television, radio, and telephone improvements?

PROJECTS

Project — Our Solar System

Collect 10 round objects of very different sizes. Arrange them on a large piece of wrapping paper on the floor to show what our solar system is like. Put the largest ball in the middle of the sheet. Perhaps it could be a beach ball. This would be the sun. Nearby, place the very smallest object. Perhaps this could be a pebble or a pea. This would be Mercury.

Next, put down a larger object, about the size of a ping-pong ball. This is Venus. Then comes the earth. It could be a golf ball. Next is Mars. It could be a marble. Jupiter could be a basketball. Saturn could be a volley ball. Uranus and Neptune could be two baseballs. And Pluto could be a large marble.

After you have arranged your "planets" properly, draw their orbits around the "sun." Use different colored crayons to do this. Finally, draw a straight line from the sun to Pluto. Along this line write "3,671,000,000 miles." This number means that Pluto is more than three billion miles from the sun. Mercury is only 36 million (36,000,000) miles from the sun. Our earth is 93 million (93,000,000) miles from the sun. Jupiter is 483,000,000 miles from the sun.

Project — My Trip to the Moon

Pretend that you are the winner of a writing contest about space travel. First prize was a trip to the moon. The first stage of your trip is to a space station called Skylab 7. There you will join several astronauts on board a spacecraft headed for the moon. You are supposed to keep a diary about your trip. You are expected to tell what happens each day. You also must tell how you feel about what is happening.

You are now sitting in a Space Shuttle waiting for its big rocket to blast off. Start your diary right now. How do you feel as you wait? What are you thinking about? Then, right after lift-off, tell how it happened and how you felt. There is a small window that you can look out of. What did you see? Or did you keep your eyes closed the whole time?

Tell what happened at the space station. How did the shuttle dock with it? Whom did you see there? How was your first meeting with the astronauts? Did you have trouble getting on board with your big spacesuit? Did you get to fly the spacecraft? How did the earth look as you sped toward the moon? Tell about your first sight of the moon close up. What was the landing like? Were you able to walk easily when you first put your feet on the moon?

Tell what you found on the moon. Where did you stay? What did you eat? What kind of adventures did you have? Write all this in your diary. Then write about your trip back to earth.

Project — Charting Apollo Spacecraft

Originally, the United States planned to have 20 separate missions to the moon. Some would fly around the moon. Others would also land on it. All were called Apollo flights, but each was given a different number. Some missions were not carried out. Make a chart showing when each mission was to take place. Tell also what each was to do and what happened to it.

Make three columns on your chart. In the first column, give the name and number of the mission. In the middle column, give the date of the mission. In the third column, write what it did or did not do.

You can find this information in articles about space travel. Look in encyclopedias. Ask your librarian to help you get started.

INDEX

Photo Credits:
I. M. Ball; Biofotos; California Institute of
Technology; Douglas Dickins; Michael Holford; Matt
Irvine; NASA; Novosti Press Agency; Photri; Space
Frontiers; U.S. Naval Observatory; Zefa.
Cover photo: © Association of Universities for
Research in Astronomy, Inc., the Kitt Peak National
Observatory.

Fuck Nurtras

Fuck Slabs

6 popn   13 popn

2 dapn   14 dapn

South Side

17

G+un

EL

SUR

13

DC 12/3/10

www.harcourt-international.com

Bringing you products from all Harcourt Health Sciences companies including Baillière Tindall, Churchill Livingstone, Mosby and W.B. Saunders

▶ **Browse** for latest information on new books, journals and electronic products

▶ **Search** for information on over 20 000 published titles with full product information including tables of contents and sample chapters

▶ **Keep up to date** with our extensive publishing programme in your field by registering with eAlert or requesting postal updates

▶ **Secure online ordering** with prompt delivery, as well as full contact details to order by phone, fax or post

▶ **News** of special features and promotions

If you are based in the following countries, please visit the country-specific site to receive full details of product availability and local ordering information

USA: www.harcourthealth.com

Canada: www.harcourtcanada.com

Australia: www.harcourt.com.au

Baillière Tindall CHURCHILL LIVINGSTONE Mosby W.B. SAUNDERS

Radiotherapy Physics and Equipment

For Churchill Livingstone:

Senior Commissioning Editor: Sarena Wolfaard
Project Development Manager: Dinah Thom
Project Manager: Derek Robertson
Design Direction: George Ajayi

Radiotherapy Physics and Equipment

Samantha Morris MSc DCR(T)
Formerly Lecturer in Therapeutic Radiography,
Department of Materials and Medical Sciences, Cranfield University, Swindon

Contribution by

Andy Williams DCR(T) HDCR(T)
Deputy Superintendent Radiographer, Northamptonshire Centre for Oncology,
Northampton General Hospital Trust, Northampton

Foreword by

Angela Newing
Professor and Director of Research Students, Gloucester Royal NHS Trust and
Cranfield University Institute of Medical Sciences, Gloucester

CHURCHILL
LIVINGSTONE

EDINBURGH LONDON NEW YORK PHILADELPHIA ST LOUIS SYDNEY TORONTO 2001

CHURCHILL LIVINGSTONE
An imprint of Harcourt Publishers Limited

First published 2001

ISBN 0 443 06211 0

British Library Cataloguing in Publication Data
A catalogue record for this book is available from the British
Library

Library of Congress Cataloging in Publication Data
A catalogue record for this book is available from the Library
of Congress

Note
Medical knowledge is constantly changing. As new
information becomes available, changes in treatment,
procedures, equipment and the use of drugs become
necessary. The authors and the publishers have taken care to
ensure that the information given in this text is accurate and
up-to-date. However, readers are strongly advised to
confirm that the information, especially with regard to drug
usage, complies with the latest legislation and standards of
practice.

The
publisher's
policy is to use
**paper manufactured
from sustainable forests**

Printed in China

Contents

Foreword

The clinical results of radiotherapy have improved constantly and consistently throughout my own long career in medical physics. In recent years the improvement has been dramatic. There have been many reasons for this: there is now a vast range of radiation energies available; advances in engineering incorporated into external beam machines have provided extremely accurate delivery of the treatment prescription; and the geometry and collimation of treatment beams is far superior to that of earlier machines. The degree of sophistication now given to us allows treatments to be tailored more satisfactorily to fit each patient, with multi-leaf collimators and intensity modulation becoming commonplace. Treatment planning is fully computerised and allows for three-dimensional structuring with anatomical details added from CT or MRI scans. Brachytherapy has also experienced major advances, both in the construction and planning of implants and in the range of energies using different isotopes.

Treatment is prepared and delivered by radiographers, whose patient determination to get things exactly right has always been of paramount importance and has made a large contribution to the increased success of radiotherapy and to the well-being of patients undergoing treatment.

The initial education and continuing training of therapy radiographers requires teachers and textbooks of high calibre. Samantha Morris is recognised as a first-class teacher with the gift of being able to put over theory in an interesting and understandable manner. Her former students now deliver radiotherapy all over the world and Samantha should be proud of their achievements. Radiographers and students are fortunate that she has decided to provide this teaching text that all will find eminently readable. The book gives all the information needed for modern radiotherapy, and I am delighted to commend it to the reader.

AN, Gloucester 2001

Preface

It is not intended that this text cover in comprehensive detail each and every aspect of equipment important to the radiotherapy radiographer. Instead, emphasis is placed on those equipment aspects that the author considers are not addressed in current texts at an appropriate level and/or depth for the undergraduate radiotherapy radiographer. In addition, other members of the cancer care team who have not had the opportunity to study the academic principles behind recent technological advances in standard radiotherapy equipment may also find this text of use.

Learning Points feature throughout each chapter, and should be used not only as a form of learning assessment, but also as a springboard linking fundamental physics concepts to the clinical setting. Answers have not been provided, as the author recognises the naïvety of attempting to reflect the range of diversity of clinical practice.

The roles of unsealed radionuclides, CT, MRI and ultrasound, and accelerators producing charged particles have deliberately not been included in this book. These are important and evolving areas in the management of patients with malignant disease, and it is felt that these concepts should be presented in a future text.

Acknowledgements must be made to a number of people. Without their assistance and encouragement this project would not have been successfully completed. I therefore extend my gratitude to:

- Professor Angela Newing for graciously agreeing to write the foreword; Andrew Williams for significant contribution to Chapter 4; and Paul Cloke and Louise Smith for constructive advice on a number of chapters
- James Spencer for much invaluable advice
- numerous cancer patients, in both the UK and abroad, who have allowed me the privilege of observing the effects of malignant disease
- the cancer care team members listed below, and many thousands of others like them, who have taught me how to put the welfare of the patient first: Dr Patricia Golding and Dr Charles Catton; Jill Ward, Tony Summersgill and Charlotte Jackson; Margery Moffatt and Matilda Bruni; and Valerie Alsop.
- my family: Geoff, Jean, Lizzie, Richard, Susan and Baloo for the past, present and future support that has allowed me to re-establish a clarity of vision regarding my own future.

SM, Fareham 2001

1

The simulator suite

Chapter objectives

On completion of this chapter you should be able to:

▓ Explain how X-rays can interact with matter

▓ Describe the design and construction of the whole and relevant components of a conventional radiotherapy simulator so that you may safely utilise the machine during its routine operation

▓ Evaluate the role of the CT (computed tomography) simulator and simulator CT in the modern radiotherapy department

▓ Describe the routine quality assurance tests designed to reduce machine down time to a minimum

▓ Implement relevant legislation for the protection of yourself, the patient and the general public.

INTRODUCTION

The radiotherapy simulator is an X-ray unit designed to replicate the treatment beam in terms of size and direction, but not energy. It has the mobility and accuracy of a treatment unit, but is capable of producing diagnostic quality radiographs and tomographic projections of the desired area. In the early days of megavoltage radiotherapy, traditional X-ray or kilovoltage treatment units were used to produce verification radiographs of the planned treatment area. The former had the advantage over the latter in terms of image quality, owing to the reliance of the photoelectric absorption process (see p. 4) on atomic number. However, neither truly produced an image representative of the actual treatment set-up, primarily because both units are non isocentrically mounted.

The requirement for a simulator in a radiotherapy department developed primarily alongside the evolution of the linear accelerator. Prior to this point, when ^{60}Co units were the main providers of megavoltage external beam radiotherapy, treatment fields were mainly delineated through the skilled application of a knowledge relating anatomical organ positions to surface landmarks. Once field borders had been established, time was then required on the treatment unit to establish if the desired set-up was practically achievable. Megavoltage radiographs were then taken for verification purposes.

A greater need for localisation accuracy arose with the advent of the linear accelerator; its ability to deliver X-ray beams with significantly higher percentage depth doses resulted in a more widely applied awareness of the need to avoid radiosensitive structures, and the long-term costs of poorly planned radiotherapy. Additionally,

the availability of higher dose rates and the subsequent ability to deliver larger and more effective daily and total tumour doses has led to the routine use of increasingly smaller radical field sizes. Conventional simulators soon became widely used in the radiotherapy department, and a more efficacious use of departmental equipment resources was demonstrated, as many of the procedures routinely conducted on the accelerator were transferred to the simulator.

Today, the frequent application of the principles of conformal external beam radiotherapy to many disease sites has led to increasingly more stringent demands for accuracy being placed upon the processes of localisation, verification, patient immobilisation and reproducibility of set-up. To this end the CT simulator and simulator CT have provided the cancer care team with a currently unsurpassed ability in terms of accuracy, in the localisation of anatomical sites of local and remote malignant disease and in the verification of treatment set-ups. Much work is still needed, however, regarding the ability of currently available immobilisation devices to support the positioning requirements of conformal radiotherapy treatment techniques, and

KEY POINTS

The simulator became widely used for the following:

- The provision of excellent quality radiographic images in projections mimicking the range of geometrical and mechanical movements of megavoltage equipment

- Localisation of the clinical target volume (i.e. defining the position of the treatment field in relation to the tumour by the use of fluoroscopy)

- The production of transverse, sagittal and coronal contours of the treatment volume, and for the marking of reference points on the skin surface of the patient

- Confirmation that the selected immobilisation device holds the patient in the desired position

- Localisation of sealed sources for brachytherapy patients

- The determination of mobile volumes by the use of the fluoroscopic facility

- Quantitative visualisation of a change in patient contour, separation or set-up

- Verification of planning target volume

- Confirmation of the accuracy of beam divergent alloy blocks, and lead shielding where used

- Design of new treatment techniques without the need to use valuable treatment machine time

- Initial and continuing education of the health care team.

extensive research must be conducted in order to resolve the implications on such techniques of moving internal organs.

X-RAY INTERACTIONS IN THE PATIENT

Ionising radiation interactions with matter have not been afforded a chapter of their own in this book, primarily because students often struggle with the clinical significance of such processes when they are presented in the abstract. Instead, an attempt has been made to present the information at points where it is of significant clinical importance. X-ray interaction processes are therefore introduced in this chapter, since it is in the simulator that the patient is first subject to radiation for therapeutic intent.

The principles underlying the interaction of X-rays with matter are fundamental to the fields of radiobiology, radiation protection and radiation detection. A comprehensive understanding of the nature of such interactions is also fundamental to the work of the radiotherapy radiographer. Only X-ray and gamma-ray interactions are reviewed in this chapter, with the aim of providing the reader with an understanding of the types of interaction that occur in the patient who is irradiated by a simulator, kilovoltage treatment unit, ^{60}Co unit, or linear accelerator. The explanations which follow assume a basic understanding of the nature of electromagnetic radiation and the theory of wave particle duality (see Ball & Moore 1997, Wilks 1987). The process which results in the production of X-rays, and other electron interactions, are discussed in a similar manner in the accelerator and kilovoltage chapters (Chs 5 and 7). Whilst an understanding of X-ray production is clearly an important concept in explaining simulator operation, the decision was taken to present this information in the kilovoltage chapter (Ch. 7) to prevent the student from initially grouping together the processes leading to the production of X-rays in a target, and the subsequent interaction of those X-rays in the patient.

With respect to the working environment of the simulator, it is essential to understand how X-rays interact with the patient in order to produce a radiograph using the least amount of radiation consistent with an image of optimum quality.

Processes of attenuation

Owing to their lack of charge, X-rays and gamma rays are not subject to the forces (known as coulomb forces) exerted by electrons present in the matter being irradiated. These radiations have no particular affinity with any atomic particle, and so a direct collision is required before a radiation interaction is initiated. During each interaction process, an X- or gamma ray will transfer a significant amount of energy to the resultant product(s) of that particular interaction process.

When X-rays interact in matter they are attenuated solely in intensity rather than in energy, due to the removal of X-rays from the beam as a result of absorption (photoelectric absorption or pair production) and scattering (Compton scatter) processes. Such attenuation occurs in an exponential manner, and is described by the following equation (Wilks 1987, p. 439).

$$I_x = I_0 e^{-\mu x}$$

where I_x = intensity through a medium of thickness, x

I_0 = incident X-ray intensity

μ = linear attenuation coefficient

One important quantity, used when considering the beam attenuation caused by atoms of an absorbing medium, is known as the interaction cross-section – in simpler terminology it can be thought of as the size of the area presented to the X-ray by a potential interaction partner. The scattering cross-section, σ, is measured in units of cm^2 or barns (where 1 barn = 10^{-28} m^2). The larger the scattering cross-section, and the greater their total number, the higher the probability that an X-ray will interact at that particular point.

The amount of attenuation occurring is quantified in terms of the linear attenuation coefficient (LAC), μ m^{-1}, which is defined as the fraction of X-rays removed from a beam per unit thickness of medium (Wilks 1987, p. 439). Terms used to describe the destination of the energy removed from the beam are as follows:

- The linear energy transfer coefficient, μ_{tr}, is the amount of energy transferred from the X-ray to any charged particle(s) produced as a result of an interaction process.
- Of the total energy transferred to the charged particle, some will be absorbed in collision type interactions, and the remainder will be lost through radiative (Ch. 7) interactions. The energy then lost to the surrounding medium is known as the linear energy absorption coefficient, μ_{ab} (often annotated as μ_{en}).

For further details of these concepts, the reader is referred to Chapter 2 of the text by Metcalfe et al (1997).

Linear descriptions of energy transfer and deposition are not particularly useful quantities in the clinical situation as values will vary depending upon the density of the attenuating tissue in question. Consequently it is common to see the use of the concept mass attenuation coefficient (MAC); this is the value of the LAC divided by density, ρ, and is given the symbol $\frac{\mu}{\rho}$ m^2 kg^{-1}. The MAC is formally defined as the fraction of X-rays removed from an X-ray beam of unit cross-sectional area, in a medium of unit mass (Wilks 1987, p. 440). It is used to describe the probability of one or more interaction processes occurring, whilst the parallel concepts of mass energy transfer coefficient and mass absorption coefficient describe the fraction of energy transferred and then absorbed per unit mass of medium.

Coherent scattering

This is also known as an elastic, classical, or Rayleigh interaction process, and occurs only when the energy of the incident X-ray is much less than the binding energy of the orbiting electron. The X-ray passes very close by the electron, setting it vibrating within its orbital position, at the same frequency as the incident X-ray. There is no energy transfer, but the path of the X-ray is diverted by its interaction with the orbital electron. Consequently this process causes a very small amount of beam attenuation. It is of minimal importance in the field of radiotherapy, owing to the dependence of the interaction

process on the atomic number of the absorbing medium, and a very small demonstrable interaction cross-section at radiotherapy energies. It is, however, a significant interaction in the field of X-ray crystallography.

Mass attenuation coefficient for classical scattering, $\left(\frac{\mu}{\rho}\right)_{coh} \propto \frac{Z^2}{E}$ where Z is the atomic number of the absorber, and E is the energy of the incident X-ray.

Photoelectric absorption process

This is the predominant interaction at diagnostic radiography and simulator energies. Figure 1.1 uses the Bohr model of the atom to illustrate a direct collision occurring between the incident X-ray and a bound atomic K, L, M or N shell electron of the absorbing material, resulting in the total absorption of the X-ray and the production of a free electron. If the energy of the incident X-ray is equal to, or greater than, the binding energy of the orbital electron, the electron will be ejected from its orbit leaving the atom ionised. The probability of this interaction occurring is greatest when the X-ray energy is just equal to the binding energy of the orbital electron in question, and this is demonstrated

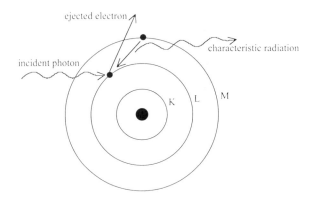

Figure 1.1   The photoelectric absorption process, illustrating an X-ray being totally absorbed, the result of which is the ejection of an electron from the L shell. An outer shell electron fills the orbital vacancy, following which a characteristic X-ray is emitted (from Metcalfe et al 1997, with permission).

in graphs of the photoelectric contribution to the total mass attenuation coefficient. As shown in Figure 1.4a, sharp absorption peaks are evident within the photoelectric component. These correspond to the energy of the orbital K, L, M and N electrons. The ejected particle is called the photoelectron, and has an energy equal to the energy of the incident X-ray minus the binding energy of its original orbit. In soft tissue, the photoelectron has a considerable energy as the binding energy of a K shell electron is in the region of 0.5 kV. It can undergo several charged particle interactions before its total energy is lost.

The ionised atom fills its orbital vacancy with one of its own outer orbital electrons. As the electron drops down to an inner orbit, the potential energy it loses manifests as a characteristic X-ray. Depending on the atomic number of the material, this characteristic radiation may not be absorbed in the medium, but may escape from it. Calculated values for the mass absorption coefficient will therefore be less than that of the mass attenuation coefficient, particularly for high atomic number materials:

$$\text{MAC for photoelectric absorption } \left(\frac{\mu}{\rho}\right)_{pe} \propto \frac{Z^3}{E^3}$$

Compton scatter

When an X-ray undergoes a compton scattering process (Fig. 1.2), it is subject to both scattering and partial absorption. It is also the most significant X-ray interaction process for radiotherapy energies.

The incident X-ray, with an energy very much greater than the binding energy of the electron, collides with a 'free' electron in an outer electron orbit. Although technically bound within an orbital shell, the energy loss from the X-ray as a result of ejecting the electron is negligible. The electron recoils under the force of the interaction and, having gained some of the energy of the X-ray, leaves the atom; it is thereafter known as a recoil electron. The X-ray is left with reduced energy and is subsequently referred to as the scattered X-ray.

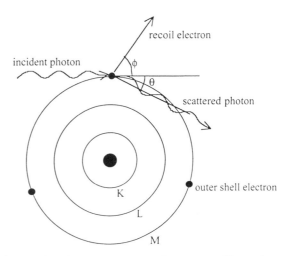

Figure 1.2 The compton scattering process, illustrating the production of a recoil electron and scattered photon (X-ray) (from Metcalfe et al 1997, with permission).

By applying the basic law of physics relating to the conservation of momentum and by knowing the energy of the incident X-ray, it is possible to predict the energy division and direction of the scattered X-ray and recoil electron. The Klein Nishina formula (Leo 1994) describes how the amount of total energy is distributed between the scattered X-ray and the recoil electron. The loss of energy from the X-ray depends upon the angle through which it is scattered after interaction. Energy loss is greatest when the scattered X-ray is deflected through 180° back along the path of the incident X-ray. The maximum deflection occurs more frequently with lower energy X-rays. The higher the energy of the incident X-ray, the greater the probability of forward deflection of the scattered X-ray. Such knowledge is essential when considering the design and placement of primary and secondary radiation barriers (Ch. 3).

The interaction coefficient for compton scatter is expressed in terms of the probability of interaction per electron. All electrons have the same probability of interacting with an incident X-ray of a specific energy, and almost all atoms contain the same number of electrons per gram of material. Consequently, within a specified energy range, most materials demonstrate equal incidence of compton scatter. However, hydrogen is unique – owing to its lack of neutrons, the atomic electrons have twice the chance (Leo 1994, Wilks 1987) of interacting with an incoming X-ray. As hydrogen is found in water and 70% of the human body is made up of water compton scatter is demonstrated more readily in soft tissue.

MAC for compton scatter $\left(\dfrac{\mu}{\rho}\right)_{cs} \propto \dfrac{E_d}{E}$ where E_d is the electron density per kilogram.

The compton scatter MAC is a measure of the total removal of energy from the primary X-ray beam, and values of mass energy transfer coefficient and mass energy absorption coefficient will obviously be of significance for this interaction process.

Pair production

If an incident X-ray has an energy greater than twice the rest mass of an electron (1.02 MeV), the X-ray may be absorbed within the electromagnetic field surrounding the nucleus of an atom. As shown in Figure 1.3, the product of this pair production interaction process is an electron positron pair each with an energy of 0.511 MeV. These two particles are identical in every way apart from charge polarity. All energy in excess of the threshold value becomes apparent as the kinetic energy of the electron positron

pair. The term 'rest mass' is derived from Einstein's equation $E = mc^2$ which suggests that a dynamic relationship exists between mass and energy – essentially, mass can be created from energy and vice versa. When an object such as an electron gains energy in the form of velocity, it will change its mass in response. Rest mass simply refers to the mass of a stationary electron.

The positron is an unstable particle and tends to recombine fairly rapidly with an electron from the irradiated medium. This process results in the disappearance of the electron positron pair. This is followed by the subsequent production of two X-rays, each with an energy of 0.511 MeV, which emerge at 180° to each other.

This process can also happen when an X-ray passes very close to an atomic electron, resulting in the same positron electron pair plus a third particle – the original electron – which recoils away from the point of interaction.

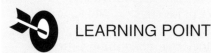

LEARNING POINT

As indicated above, a knowledge of X-ray interaction processes is fundamental to the work of the radiotherapy radiographer. During the simulation and treatment process, radiographic images of the patient are acquired, for a variety of purposes, across a range of beam energies.

Question
Primarily by reference to X-ray interaction processes, evaluate radiographic image quality produced whilst the patient is undergoing the following procedures:

- Localisation of the target volume (incorporating the use of contrast media) on a conventional simulator
- Verification of field placement using a megavoltage source of X-rays.

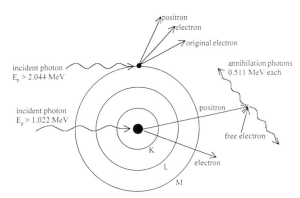

Figure 1.3 The pair production process – illustrating pair production resulting from both a nuclear and an electron interaction (from Metcalfe et al 1997, with permission).

MAC for pair production $\left(\dfrac{\mu}{\rho}\right)_{pp} \propto (E - 1.02)Z$

The importance of total mass attenuation coefficient graphs

From the study of X-ray interaction processes, it can be seen that the attenuation of an X-ray beam as it passes through the patient is closely dependent upon:

- Energy spectrum of the X-ray beam
- Density and atomic number of the tissues that the X-ray beam passes through
- The separation of the patient.

The total mass attenuation coefficient (shown in Fig. 1.4b) is the sum of the individual mass attenuation processes described above, plotted as a graph of energy against incidence. A study of this

type of graph allows the user to see the percentage of each interaction occurring at the energy range of interest, which is clearly of interest in the fields of radiation protection, radiobiology and the detection of radiation.

THE SIMULATION PROCESS

The pathway a patient is directed along as he or she passes from diagnosis to the first follow-up appointment post delivery of treatment assumes that the same patient has been directly referred to a multidisciplinary cancer care team on the diagnosis of a malignant disease.

At this time such an assumption is a topical and very relevant issue to the cancer patients of the UK; however, it will not be raised here simply because it encompasses fields of cancer care beyond the aims and objectives of this

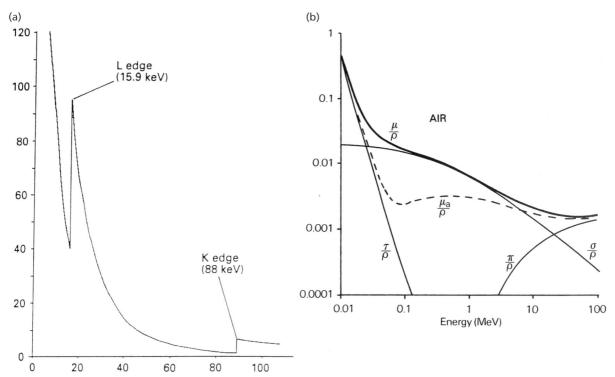

Figure 1.4 **(a)** The variation in photoelectric absorption mass attenuation coefficient (in lead) (from Ball & Moore 1997, with permission from Blackwell Science Ltd). **(b)** Total mass attenuation coefficient (solid line) of air as a function of energy (MeV). The dotted line represents the total mass absorption coefficient.
$\frac{\tau}{\rho}$ = mass attenuation coefficient for photoelectric absorption ρ
$\frac{\sigma}{\rho}$ = mass attenuation coefficient for compton scatter ρ
$\frac{\pi}{\rho}$ = mass attenuation coefficient for pair production ρ (from Wilks 1987, with permission).

KEY POINTS

Every patient has individual requirements, but all should proceed at least through the following phases:

- *Diagnosis*. It is rare for this not to involve at least some form of incisional or excisional biopsy.
- *Referral to cancer care specialist*. This takes the form of an appointment at an outpatient clinic run by the multidisciplinary cancer care team. Here a range of investigations will be ordered, aimed at confirming the

initial diagnosis and establishing the stage and grade of the patient's disease. The patient is then provided with an appointment for planning the radiotherapy treatment.

- *Simulation and treatment planning*. Here the immobilisation, localisation, isodose distribution production and verification procedures are explained and carried out.
- *Treatment*.
- *Patient follow-up*.

particular text. While it has been easy to draw that line in this book, regrettably the cancer care team is not afforded the same luxury in the clinical setting and has to deal on a daily basis with the ramifications of post code related general practitioner referral patterns. Several steps are involved in treating a patient with radiotherapy. The whole process is reviewed briefly above, and the immobilisation, localisation, isodose plan production and verification procedures are discussed in detail later in this chapter.

SIMULATOR SPECIFICATIONS

When first selecting a new piece of equipment, specifications relating to mechanical performance, image detection mechanism and X-ray source must be formulated. The process to follow when selecting new equipment is reviewed in Chapter 6, and a guide to functional performance values for these units may be found by consultation of the appropriate range of International Electrotechnical Commission (IEC) documentation (BSI 1994, 1993a, 1993b). However, for a simulator this can be a particularly onerous process owing to the two main conflicting roles of the simulator: it must emulate the range of megavoltage equipment likely to be found in a radiotherapy department, as well as being able to produce optimal quality radiographic and fluoroscopic images.

Furthermore, it should meet the following general criteria.

- It should be mechanically and geometrically as compatible with as many of the departmental treatment units as possible. Obviously the more apparent mechanical movements are self-explanatory, but major problems can stem from apparently less significant mechanisms if a comprehensive review of all mechanical and geometrical unit characteristics are not initially documented. For example, uniformity in the format and presentation of positional data is a simple concept, but if variability exists within a department confusion and errors may ensue.
- It should be well constructed, so that tolerances set by the manufacturer are maintained to the same standard during routine use.
- It should be of a suitable size to fit into the designated room.
- It should be of variable film to focus distance (FFD) to match the focus to skin distance (FSD) of the range of treatment techniques and equipment available. Additionally X-ray cassettes of larger than average size are required for irregular field sizes relating to mantle and extended FSD techniques. The image intensifier assembly should readily support such cassettes.
- It should be DICOM (Digital Imaging and Communications in Medicine) compatible to facilitate digital communication between other areas of the department.

COMPONENTS OF A SIMULATOR

A conventional simulator is described here, rather than the latest technological developments which occupy this particular position in the following chapters of this text. Although the CT simulator and simulator CT have firm advantages over the standard alternative, the latter still very much has its foot in the door of the radiotherapy department of the present and the future. The basic features of a simulator are illustrated in Figure 1.5. The figure shows the simulator X-ray head and image intensifier mounted at either end of the isocentric gantry.

X-ray head

The components of the X-ray head (see Fig. 1.6) are as follows:

- Rotating anode X-ray tube
- Field defining wires
- Primary and secondary collimator systems
- Field defining light
- Optical distance indicator
- Collimator rotation scale
- Attachments for lead tray and electron applicator
- Crash guard
- Filtration and ionisation chamber (not shown).

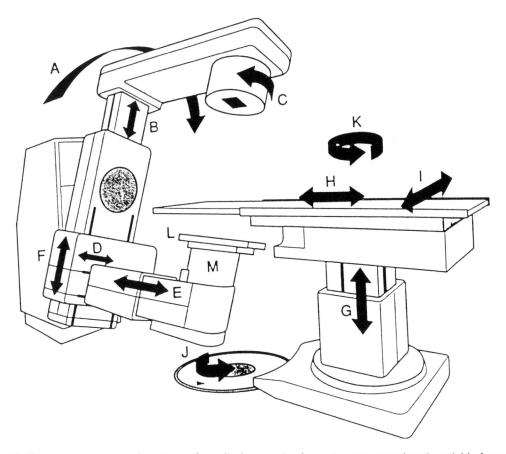

Figure 1.5   The basic components and motions of a radiotherapy simulator. A, gantry rotation; B, variable focus to axis distance (FAD); C, collimator rotation; D, lateral movement of image intensifier; E, longitudinal movement of image intensifier; F, radial movement of image intensifier; G, vertical couch movement; H, longitudinal couch movement; I, lateral couch movement; J, floor rotation; K, couch rotation about isocentre; L, X-ray cassette holder; M, image intensifier (from Williams & Thwaites 1993, by permission of Oxford University Press).

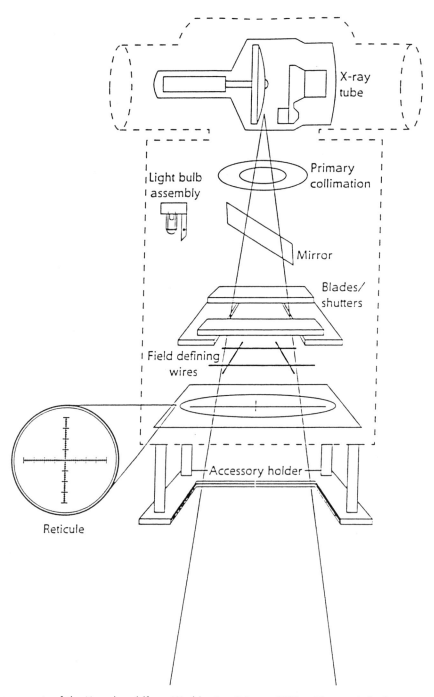

Figure 1.6 Components of the X-ray head (from Washington & Lever 1996, with permission).

The basic principles of X-ray tube design, operation and X-ray production (bremsstrahlung) are discussed in detail in Chapter 7. The information presented below is restricted to areas where the rotating anode and stationary anode tube differ.

The cathode is a dual tungsten filament structure containing a broad and fine focus where the filaments are of approximately 1.2 mm and 0.8 mm in length respectively. Focus selection is determined by the purpose of the exposure: use of a broad focus means that a greater area of the target will be bombarded by the electron beam, resulting in a larger beam output; the fine focus is used to image areas where detail is paramount and a sharp image with minimal penumbra (see p. 126) is required. This latter requirement is aided by the 13° target angle, which is significantly smaller than that used in the X-ray tube of the kilovoltage treatment unit. Once the electrons have been produced by thermionic emission at the filament, they are focused towards the target by the considerable positive potential difference existing between the cathode and the anode, as well as the negative charge existing on the focusing cup. The anode structure is formed from a target which sits on an anode disc, plus the stem, rotor and stator. The rotating anode is used instead of a stationary anode because of its ability to produce higher X-ray beam intensities as a result of bremsstrahlung production (see Ch. 7) happening over a larger area and its superior cooling characteristics. The tungsten and rhenium target is supported on the bevelled edge of a molybdenum disc which has a high specific heat capacity. Heat is prevented from travelling along the beryllium anode stem and into the rotor and stator assembly by the poor thermal conductivity of the molybdenum and the narrow diameter of the anode stem. This stem supports the anode disc and connects it to the rotor and stator mechanism, the latter producing movement of the anode.

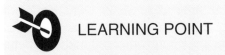

LEARNING POINT

Question
How many mechanisms of heat dispersal are employed within the X-ray tube?

The anode and cathode are supported within an evacuated glass insert which contains a radiolucent area directly beneath the target so that the X-rays can pass through with minimum attenuation. Mineral oil surrounds the majority of the insert, facilitating the transfer of heat by conduction from the target to the outer casing and air and acting as electrical and mechanical insulation. A safety mechanism exists so that if the oil is required to remove excessive amounts of heat, its thermal expansion beyond a certain point will activate a microswitch that terminates radiation exposure.

The concepts of inherent and external filtration are explained in Chapter 7. In the rotating anode X-ray tube the inherent filtration is formed by the glass insert, the cooling oil and the radiolucent window in the outer casing. Additional external filtration, in the form of thin aluminium (Al) sheets, is required to remove the low energy X-rays remaining in the beam once the X-rays have left the tube itself. For beam energies up to 70 kV an additional 1.5 mm Al is required; 2 mm for 70–100 kV, with 0.1 mm Al for every 1 kV above 100 kV.

The ionisation chamber (see p. 33) records the output of the X-ray tube and is positioned between the external filtration and the collimation system.

The field defining light system consists of a light bulb and a radiolucent mirror. It is important that the field defining light carefully represents the exact position of the X-ray beams for the radiographic and fluoroscopic modes. A simple test to establish its accuracy routinely forms part of the simulator quality assurance (QA) programme. The diaphragm system is slightly more complex than that which would be found in a treatment machine. The lead primary collimator, along with the target angle and focal spot size, defines the maximum beam size available. The multiplane lead blades or shutters move independently, acting as secondary collimators to reduce the maximum available beam solely to the area of interest. The radiopaque field defining wires are then moved to represent the borders of the clinical target volume or planning target volume, depending on whether the patient is undergoing a localisation or verification procedure. It is good working practice to ensure that the blades always track 3–5 cm behind the position of the field defining wires. Newer simulators automatically implement this practice, but in older models it is a role that falls to the radiographer.

The reticule is a thin plastic tray into which are embedded lead markers. These markers are positioned to delineate the centre beam axis of the field defining light as it shines onto the patient. If the simulator is operated at more than one focus to skin distance (FSD), it will be necessary to use a separate plastic tray for each distance as the lead markers are spaced to represent the geometry of the field at a specific treatment distance. The optical distance indicator (ODI), also known as the rangefinder, is used to project a scale onto the skin of the patient which indicates the X-ray tube FSD in centimetres. The scale must be carefully aligned with the central axis point of the X-ray beam; usually the scale is only in focus at this one particular point. The device is normally mounted at some point on the outside of the gantry head, and, unfortunately, this means it can be easily knocked out of alignment.

Gantry mounting and movement

The gantry arm is a rigid C-shaped structure which provides support for the gantry head and the image intensifier systems. It moves in a manner such that its alignment with the central axis of the beam, and therefore the isocentre, is maintained over the life of the unit. It has a variable speed of rotation, and additionally the head of the gantry can move vertically along the gantry to reflect variable FSD positions which may be required for treatment. A scale is centred at the middle of the gantry and is used to indicate the position of the gantry as it rotates around the treatment couch.

The treatment couch is isocentrically mounted, and is designed to provide support identical to that found on the treatment units. This is often not the case, even with units produced from the same manufacturer, so care must be taken to assess reproducibility of patient position when

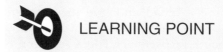

LEARNING POINT

Radiolucency of the couch can be produced in a number of ways. One method is to remove specific couch panels and replace them with a support similar in appearance to a tennis-racket. Over time, this type of replacement panel is renowned for not demonstrating the same level of support.

Question
What are the implications of this in terms of reproducibility of patient position?

new units are installed in a department. The couch should preferably be radiolucent, or have panels that can be removed and replaced with a material that minimally attenuates the X-ray beam, in order to produce radiographic or fluoroscopic images. The couch should be able to reproduce all the movements of a couch on a treatment unit, and should allow immobilisation devices and other accessories to be attached in an identical manner.

Image intensifier

The image intensifier produces a real time visible image, its mode of operation requiring the use of relatively little radiation considering the intensity of image produced. It converts the X-ray pattern received from the patient into a light image by a process known as fluorescence (see Ch. 2), which is then converted to an electrical signal by the TV camera system.

As shown in Figure 1.7, the intensifier is an evacuated glass envelope [1]; it is encased almost entirely in a light tight metal container (not shown). The metal casing also protects against X-rays from anywhere other than the patient, and from external magnetic fields. To one side is an input screen, which is formed from two layers. The outermost layer is a caesium iodide phosphor [2] which coats the inside of the glass envelope. This absorbs in the region of 60% (Farr

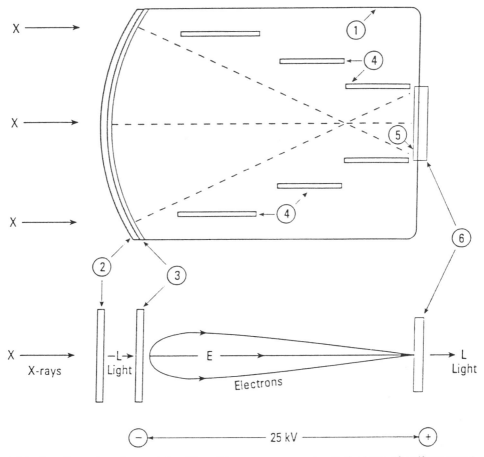

Figure 1.7 **(a)** Section through an image intensifier; **(b)** processes occurring in the intensifier (from Farr & Allisy-Roberts 1997, with permission).

& Allisy-Roberts 1997) of the X-rays emitted from the patient, converting them into light – the amount of light emitted being proportional to the energy absorbed by the phosphor. Directly beneath the phosphor is a zinc cadmium photocathode [3]. These two layers must fit closely together: gaps between them may compromise the final image quality. The purpose of the photocathode is to produce electrons in proportion to the amount of light absorbed within its structure. To protect these two layers, a titanium foil cover is placed on the outermost surface of the input phosphor (not shown).

As these electrons leave the inner surface of the photocathode they accelerate towards the output phosphor screen [6] under the influence of a potential difference in the region of 25–35 kV.

Additional focusing onto the output phosphor screen occurs from negatively charged electrodes [4] which are positioned across the long axis of the intensifier structure. These electrodes force the accelerating electrons towards the aspect of the output phosphor screen furthest from their point of inception, thereby minimising and inverting the intensified electron pattern reaching the output phosphor.

This final phosphor screen acts to convert the electron pattern back into light. To prevent any of this light pattern from reflecting back into the intensifier, a thin layer of aluminium [5] is placed across its inner face. The resultant light signal is directly coupled to a TV camera, having been inverted by a lens or mirror array, and displayed on a monitor.

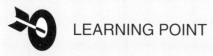

LEARNING POINT

Question
When might it be advantageous not to invert the image prior to reaching the monitor?

Last image hold, or 'freeze frame' facility, allows the operator to grab the static fluoroscopic image – thereby being able to study a particular view of the patient without having to deliver additional radiation to the patient. Regrettably this is an option that must still be asked for with some manufacturers, as it is considered as an 'extra' performance specification, and is provided at additional cost to the purchaser.

The edges of the resultant image may demonstrate less intensity than its centre. This is due to an inability to exert the same degree of control over the electrons produced at the very edges of the photocathode compared to those produced at its centre. The magnitude of this problem is reduced by curving the front face of the input phosphor screen.

When using the image intensifier, it is important to remember that it should be brought as near to the patient as the anti-collision device will allow in order to reduce the magnification of the image produced. When activated, an automatic centring device ensures that the image intensifier will remain aligned with the central axis of the X-ray beam. This is a useful safety device as it reduces patient dose, particularly during radiographic mode when the cassette has been positioned in the holder but the holder is not totally aligned with the X-ray beam.

A further useful feature is the automatic exposure control facility for use when operating in radiographic mode. It consists of an ionisation chamber positioned on the face of the image intensifier. It usually occupies a space just below the X-ray cassette holder, which is placed on the patient side of the titanium foil cover. The ionisation chamber terminates the exposure when a predetermined exposure value

has been reached. Its use allows the inexperienced user accurately to compensate for the varying degrees of beam attenuation caused by patients of varying physical size.

Control panel

There are two sets of controls for the simulator. Local controls are situated inside the simulator room and allow the operator to move the couch, gantry, collimator and image intensifier, as well as being able to adjust field, laser and room lights. Outside the simulator room are found a remote set of controls. For safety reasons these must be positioned so that the operator can see the patient inside the room while making adjustments to the couch, gantry, collimator or image intensifier settings from outside. They also contain separate controls for radiographic and fluoroscopic procedures, emergency stop, patient communication, mains on and off and a control transfer button. The purpose of the last is to ensure that only one set of controls may be used at any one time.

RADIOGRAPHIC RECORDING MEDIUM

Radiographic film is frequently used as a recording device. For simulator work it is used contained within a light tight and physically robust holder known as a cassette (Fig. 1.8). Sitting either side of the film, and fixed into the cassette, are two fluorescent intensifying screens.

On irradiation, the film and screens act together to produce an invisible representation of the X-ray field emitted from the patient. This image is stored within the emulsion of the radiographic film and is known as the latent image. It is converted to a visible image by chemical processing, a procedure carried out in an automatic processor.

Radiographic film structure and function

A diagrammatic representation of a double sided (duplitised) film is illustrated in Figure 1.9. At its

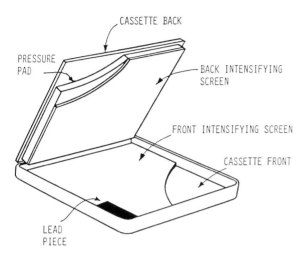

Figure 1.8 The components of an X-ray cassette (from Jenkins 1980, with permission).

SUPERCOAT
EMULSION
SUBBING LAYER
BASE
SUBBING LAYER
EMULSION
SUPERCOAT

Figure 1.9 A schematic diagram of the structure of a double sided X-ray film (from Taylor 1988, with permission).

centre is a thick polyester base which supports all the other layers of the film; the purpose of this is to be strong, flexible, transmit light to the emulsion and be chemically inert. The base is generally tinted to reduce the glare presented to the viewer when placed on a light box, the colour of the tint being manufacturer dependent. The photosensitive emulsion layers are attached to

the base by an adhesive known as a subbing layer, and a protective layer of gelatin known as the supercoat covers both sides of the film.

There are a number of theories which attempt to explain the formation of the latent image and its subsequent development into a visible image. Referral to current diagnostic radiography equipment textbooks (e.g. Ball & Price 1995) is advised, as these address these two issues in appropriate depth and breadth. The following is merely a superficial review of latent image formation and its development.

The emulsion consists of silver halide crystals suspended in a gelatin binder. The gelatin contains carefully controlled amounts of sulphur. This acts as an impurity, causing defects in the structure of the silver halide crystal. The size, shape and distribution of the halide crystals, plus the presence of sensitising dyes to increase the amount of light each crystal can absorb, will determine how quickly the halide (usually silver bromide) responds to radiation. On irradiation, X-rays interact with the fluorescent screens to produce light in proportion to the amount of radiation absorbed within them. As this light reaches the emulsion it releases electrons within the emulsion. These electrons interact with the silver halide crystals, converting them to silver ions; the result of this is the formation of a latent, or hidden, image. This process happens on both emulsions, but as they are superimposed they are considered as one image. The advantage of a duplitised film is that for a required radiographic image density less radiation is required because two copies of the image are produced.

The emulsion on a film may be double or single sided. Single sided emulsion tends to be used for radiographic images produced during mammography, CT and magnetic resonance imaging (MRI) as well as for producing copies of radiographs for a range of other purposes. It is important to place the emulsion side of the film towards the source of irradiation, and single sided film tends to be produced so that the emulsion side looks and feels different. Double sided emulsion films are used for general radiography and radiotherapy work. Several different types of film may be found within a radiotherapy department:

• Direct exposure or non screen film relies on radiation alone for the production of density on the film. It is used mainly for the production of images at radiotherapy energies. In order to produce verification images across an energy range of anywhere from 200 kV to 25 MV, such film must demonstrate a wide latitude and slow speed (see below). The speed of direct exposure film varies, so that film can be left in a treatment room throughout an entire fraction or for merely part of a fraction.

• Screen type films are used with intensifying screens. These will be used in the simulator suite, and may be sensitive to different wavelengths of light; the specific wavelength tends to vary with manufacture. A monochromatic film is sensitive to light in the blue and ultraviolet range, and should be matched with fluorescent screens that produce light in this range. Matching of film and screen in this manner is known as an appropriate film screen combination. When processing monochromatic film, the darkroom safe light should emit orange light as this type of film is least sensitive to light in this range. An orthochromatic film is sensitive to light in the blue, green and yellow regions of the spectrum – such film requires a red darkroom safe light. In certain circumstances it is desirable to slow down the response of the radiographic film, and one way of achieving this is to mismatch the film screen combination.

Fluorescent screen structure and function

The purpose of the fluorescent intensifying screen is to produce and amplify light in response to ionising radiation. In this manner, dose to the patient is reduced whilst image density is maintained. Each screen absorbs radiation and, as a result of fluorescence (Ch. 2), produces light in proportion to the amount of radiation absorbed.

The screen is composed of the following layers: a curl control backing, a structural support, an undercoat, a phosphor layer and an overcoat.

The curl control backing prevents the screen from curling up within the cassette, and reducing the homogeneity of contact between the film and intensifying screen. This can be a significant problem as it can result in divergence of light photons, and the quality assurance programme for the simulator suite should incorporate a test to regularly evaluate film screen contact. The support acts in a similar manner to the film base and is strong, flexible and chemically inert. Made from a range of materials, it is typically produced in polyester. The undercoat acts as a bonding layer and contains a white pigment which reflects light produced from the underlying phosphor layer back towards the film emulsion. This latter feature can be a problem as it will not necessarily reflect the light directly back along its incident path; instead it bounces back at an angle which tends to cause blurring of the resultant radiographic image. The overcoat is a simple protective lacquer to reduce screen damage during routine use. The phosphor layer contains a uniform distribution of phosphor crystals suspended in a base. Modern fluorescent intensifying screens contain phosphors of the rare earth elements such as gadolinium. These substances are by far the most efficient at converting X-rays to light, thereby minimising further the amount of radiation to which the patient needs to be exposed. Light is produced by fluorescence in an isotropic manner; again this is a problem because

 LEARNING POINT

Justification and optimisation are two important concepts relating to the delivery of ionisation radiation for medical purposes.

Question
How, and why, is this achieved in the simulator suite?

it produces image blurring so it is reduced in a similar manner to that described in the undercoat layer by the inclusion of a coloured dye in the phosphor layer.

Development of the latent image

Automatic processing of radiographic film occurs via a roller feed system which transports the radiograph through a series of temperature controlled solutions, for varying lengths of time. In order to convert the latent image into a visible one, a three stage process is necessary:

- Development
- Fixation
- Washing and drying.

By immersing the film into an alkaline reducing agent known as a developer, silver ions are reduced to silver atoms. Silver halide crystals unaffected by irradiation are also unaffected by this short period of immersion within the developer solution. During the subsequent fixing stage, further development of the latent image is suppressed by immersion in an acidic thiosulphate solution. This also dissolves the unexposed silver halide crystals out of the emulsion. Finally the film is washed to remove all excess chemicals, and dried to improve handling.

Radiographic film density

The density produced on a radiograph is a result of the amount of film blackening caused by metallic silver deposits remaining in the emulsion of the film after development. The degree of blackening is dependent on the level of radiation exposure received by the film. It is quantified in the following manner:

$$\text{Optical density} = \log_{10} \left(\frac{I_0}{I_t} \right)$$

where I_0 = incident light intensity and I_t = transmitted light intensity.

This quantity is measured using a densitometer; this shines a light onto the area in question and records the intensity of transmitted light, producing a point value of optical density.

Typically, for radiographic film, optical density values range from 0.2 in areas of high transparency to approximately 4 in the blackest region. When such a radiograph is viewed on a light box, density differences are apparent. This is termed the radiographic contrast.

Radiographic contrast is formed from the following:

1. Subject contrast
2. Film contrast.

Subject contrast is produced as a result of the beam of X-rays being differentially attenuated (by photoelectric absorption and compton scatter) as they pass through the patient. The degree of this attenuation will vary depending upon:

- The atomic number and density of the irradiated area
- The presence of any contrast media
- The kilovoltage (kV) selected (as a result of the dependence of photoelectric absorption on energy, the higher the chosen kV, the poorer the subject contrast – and vice versa)
- The patient separation
- Total beam filtration (increasing the amount of filtration removes more of the lower energy components of the bremsstrahlung spectra, thereby increasing beam energy and consequently reducing subject contrast).

Subject contrast may also be considerably degraded by the presence of scattered radiation should it reach the radiograph. Collimation of the primary X-ray beam, reducing the patient separation by displacing tissue from the path of the beam, minimising sources of scatter and reducing the amount of forward scatter from the patient by selection of the lowest kV consistent with the desired image quality all reduce the amount of scattered radiation produced at source. The use of secondary radiation grids and an air gap between the patient and the radiograph to reduce the intensity of scattered radiation both minimise the amount of scatter reaching the radiograph.

Film contrast is inherent in the film itself, but is considerably influenced by exposure factors, processing, viewing, storage and handling

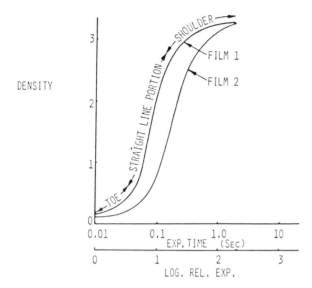

Figure 1.10   An example of the characteristic curve; density plotted as a function of X-ray exposure (from Jenkins 1980, with permission).

conditions. The study and measurement of the relationships between exposure factors, processing conditions and individual film response is known as sensitometry. These relationships are usually graphically illustrated by the characteristic curve (Fig. 1.10), which is a plot of optical density against the log of the relative exposure. It is also commonly referred to as the H & D curve, after the two main pioneers of the field of sensitometry, Hurter and Driffield. For a particular film speed, the shape of this curve will vary depending upon the exposure and storage conditions of the radiographic film. Once a baseline characteristic curve has been produced for each new batch of film – under optimum exposure, storage and processing conditions – changes in the shape of the curve can be used to monitor fluctuations in subsequent processing and storage conditions. This procedure therefore permits daily monitoring of the operating performance of an automatic processor, an integral part of the simulator suite quality assurance programme.

The production of a characteristic curve is straightforward. The film is subject to a series of known radiographic exposures – usually achieved by placing a stepped wedge on top of the radiograph prior to exposure. The metallic wedge contains a series of steps that increase by a constant amount, very much like a staircase. The thickest part of the wedge should be of significant separation to ensure that the beam is totally attenuated so that no measurable effect is produced on the radiograph from the exposure. This allows the user to determine the minimum film density. The thinnest part of the wedge should result in all silver halide grains in the emulsion being activated, thereby allowing measurement of the maximum film density obtainable.

A similar optical density range can be produced by a commercially available device known as a sensitometer. This uses light to produce exactly the same effect as radiation – and as a result removes the need for the radiotherapy radiographer to be exposed to radiation, and also decreases the time taken to produce a characteristic curve. The resultant sensitometric strip features a series of numbered densities.

As shown in Figure 1.10, the characteristic curve has several distinct features:

• The toe
• The shoulder
• The straight line portion.

The toe region provides information on basic fog levels. In this region the film does not demonstrate a response in the form of activated silver halide crystals, as it has not received sufficient light. It is therefore possible to measure the inherent base density of the film, which may include density as a result of unintentional exposure to light or radiation. Collectively this density is termed basic fog, and all readings taken further along the characteristic curve must have this value subtracted from them. The shoulder region and the area to its right demonstrate the maximum obtainable density. All silver halide has been reduced to silver, and further increases in exposure will not result in any further film blackening. If film irradiation continues past this point of maximum obtainable density, the total amount of deposited silver begins to diminish by a process known as reversal. The area of the curve between the toe and the shoulder is known as the straight line portion. Within this region, increases in film exposure result in increasing film density. Several film features can be calculated from a knowledge of the shape of this particular area of the curve:

- *Contrast*. This is calculated from the slope of the gradient, and represents the upper and lower points of the useful density range for this particular film. Rarely is this naturally a straight line, and values of average gradient are usually calculated by drawing a straight line between two points, one just above the toe and the second just below the shoulder.
- *Film and exposure latitude*. Film latitude reflects the range of exposures that a particular film screen combination can demonstrate, in other words the difference between the upper and lower limits of the log relative exposure that produce densities in the useful range. Exposure latitude is a measure of the range of exposure factor combinations this particular film type may be subject to that will still produce a correctly exposed image of a given subject.
- *Speed* – the exposure required to produce a given image density. A fast film will produce a specific density using less radiation than a slower film. Typically, a density of 1 is used to assess comparative film speed.

Assessment of changes to these film features on a daily basis forms the basis of processor quality assurance (QA). The speed, contrast and basic fog levels are read from the sensitometric strip. The speed will be the step that produces an optical density of 1, basic fog can usually be assessed from the first step, and contrast will be calculated by subtracting the step that matches the density produced at the lowest point of the straight line portion from that which matches the density at the highest point of the straight line portion. These values can then be plotted in a QA log, with clearly stated tolerance to each value along with the action to be taken in the event of the tolerance being exceeded.

THE TREATMENT PLANNING PROCESS

The following planning process is consistent with the use of a conventional radiotherapy simulator:

Principles of immobilisation

The immobilisation of the patient in a manner that allows the accurate reproduction of the treatment position on a daily basis is one of the most important steps in the planning process. The selection and production of an immobilisation device to provide a comfortable, stable and accurate position for the patient is a skill that relies heavily on the ability of the radiographer to communicate effectively with the patient and the clinical oncologist. The importance of taking time to clearly and simply explain the procedure to the patient cannot be overstressed, especially prior to the production of a head and neck immobilisation device. This time will reap rewards in that the patient will understand the expected outcome of the forthcoming procedure and will maintain a relaxed and reproducible position.

KEY POINTS

A wide range of immobilisation devices is available to the radiographer, but all should comply with the following general requirements of any fixation system:

- The device should be patient and user friendly, well-fitting, comfortable, safe and quick to make.
- The device should be of a high quality to ensure low 'spread' throughout the simulation and treatment stages.
- The device will integrate well with existing systems.
- The device will be cost-effective.
- The device will retain positioning marks and will allow the user to modify these as required.
- The presence of the device should not limit the range of field and beam parameters available.
- The device will enable the slun sparing effect to be maintained where required.

Localisation

This process consists of a series of steps which are taken in order to delineate the required clinical target volume. Prior to reviewing this process, terms defined by ICRU Report 50 (International Commission on Radiation Units and Measurements 1993) and which are used to describe the desired treatment area are explained below:

Gross tumour volume (GTV)

Gross tumour volume 'is the gross palpable or visible/demonstrable extent and location of malignant growth' (p. 6). Clearly, if surgical intervention has removed the primary tumour, then the GTV cannot be defined. It is a volume that may be entirely different depending on the investigation used to delineate it, and therefore the method(s) used must be indicated when describing it.

Clinical target volume (CTV)

Clinical target volume 'is a tissue volume that contains a demonstrable GTV and/or subclinical microscopic malignant disease, which has to be eliminated. This volume thus has to be treated adequately in order to achieve the aim of therapy, cure or palliation' (p. 6). This is gross tumour plus subclinical disease, and it is recommended that this volume be described solely by anatomic-topographic terms. More than one CTV can be defined (i.e. a primary tumour plus lymphatic disease, or high dose and low dose volumes typically found with shrinking field techniques). Additional CTVs are designated as CTV II, CTV III, etc. Both the GTV and CTV are terms based on general oncologic principles and are used within the fields of clinical, medical and surgical oncology. The following term is a concept limited solely to the delivery of external beam radiotherapy.

Planning target volume (PTV)

Planning target volume 'is a geometrical concept, and is defined to select appropriate beam sizes and beam arrangements, taking into consideration the net effect of all the possible geometrical variations, in order to ensure that the prescribed dose is actually absorbed in the CTV' (p. 7). Departments rarely have totally comparable criteria for the definition of an acceptable isodose distribution. In order to meet these criteria, the radiographer who produces this graphical dose record may need to make minor adjustments to the beam parameters determined during localisation. In this manner, the dose prescribed to the CTV can only be achieved by encompassing it within a PTV that very closely mimics the size, shape and position of the CTV.

During localisation, the patient is placed on the simulator couch using any required immobilisation devices necessary to ensure that the position is comfortable, reproducible and allows unhindered access to the required areas.

Production of an isodose distribution

This part of treatment planning is discussed in Chapter 2. However, in order to present a comprehensive picture, the concepts are summarised below:

1. Patient data should be checked in terms of patient identity.

2. Data are then programmed into the 3D planning computer. This may involve scanning in radiographs or CT images, or digitising in contours, clinical target volume and critical structures by hand. Correction for varying magnification and the allocation of electron density data to individual structures is necessary.

3. An isodose distribution is subsequently produced. This must conform to the criteria for an acceptable treatment plan for the department in question. Consideration therefore must be given to the optimal technique for this particular patient, homogeneity of dose across the planning target volume, ICRU reference point for dose prescription, dose limits of nearby critical structures, position of hot spots, etc.

4. All patient data are then approved by the referring clinical oncologist, and forwarded back to the simulator for verification.

KEY POINTS

Localisation then consists of the following steps:
- Visual alignment of the patient using anatomical bony landmarks
- Fluoroscopic placement of the superior, inferior, lateral, anterior and posterior margins of the clinical target volume, and permanent records of this position – usually in the form of appropriately labelled orthogonal radiographs, digital images or laser print-out
- Production of transverse and/or coronal and sagittal contours through the centre of the clinical target volume, and documentation of patient separation(s) and its variation throughout the defined volume

- The production of permanent marks indicating the exact position of the clinical target volume. These may be in the form of tattoos on the skin of the patient, or marks placed on the immobilisation device. If tattoos are used, it is essential to take measurements indicating their position in relation to permanent anatomical landmarks, and document this on the treatment sheet
- Approval of the radiographic representation of the delineated clinical target volume by an approved person, indication on the radiographs of any areas requiring shielding and a comprehensively completed and signed treatment sheet.

 LEARNING POINT

Question
Why do we not take orthogonal radiographs for patients likely to have external beam treatment delivered by the following techniques:

- A parallel opposed pair
- A single field?

 LEARNING POINT

Question
Evaluate the methods currently available for producing the contours listed in point 3 above with respect to:

- Accuracy
- Cost
- Patient comfort
- User friendliness.

Verification

This process confirms that the information documented on the treatment sheet and the isodose distribution produces a PTV consistent with that delineated in the orthogonal localisation radiographs. The patient is set up in the decreed position using any documented immobilisation devices, and beam parameters are set as illustrated on the isodose distribution. Radiographs are taken at each and every beam entry point; the result is compared against the initial orthogonal radiographs by an approved person, taking into consideration any minor adjustments made during the planning process to ensure that

the individual patient plan complies with the department's acceptable planning criteria.

CT SIMULATOR AND SIMULATOR CT

As reviewed earlier in this chapter, the conventional simulator has a more diverse role than simply that of a localisation and verification tool. However, diagnostic CT images are superior for the localisation of many disease sites because:

- Superior qualitative information can be obtained regarding irregular anatomical structures

LEARNING POINT

Reproducibility of patient set-up is fundamental to the concepts of localisation, verification and treatment.

Question
Identify the potential sources of error that may result in inaccurate patient positioning, and consider ways in which their magnitude can be eliminated or minimised.

- Quantitative tissue density data are available
- The exact location of the tumour is apparent (with a conventional simulator such data may have to be inferred from a knowledge of anatomical landmarks)
- Planar radiographs superimpose overlying anatomy, whereas the CT image is produced in an orientation to surmount this problem.

The CT simulator

This is a system consisting of a CT scanner (perhaps even a spiral CT scanner), laser posi-tioning aids and a 'virtual' simulation treatment planning computer. Virtual simulation is a term that refers to the process of storing all patient localisation, verification and portal image data in a computer and completing by computer alone many of the procedures that would usually be conducted during a scheduled simulator appointment.

Images are obtained from the scanner with the patient lying on a flat CT couch in the required treatment position. These data are then exported to the virtual simulation software, which has the capability of the 3D volumetric and multiplanar reconstructions usually required for treatment planning.

Once the CTV has been defined and organs and volumes of interest have been contoured, digitally reconstructed radiographs (DRRs) can be generated, and onto these are superimposed the PTV. DRRs are computer reconstructions from CT slices which are made to imitate the divergent X-ray images that would be created with a conventional simulator (Stephenson & Wiley 1995). In other words, the computer recon-structs the stored CT data and produces a 'pseudo radiograph' – for example, in a projec-tion along the path of the intended treatment angle, also known as the beam's eye view (BEV). DRRs along other projections can also be produced. The DRR can be produced in virtually any desired orientation, making it superior to the conventional radiograph for the simulation of noncoplanar treatment techniques. Digitally composite radiographs (DCRs) are also available in certain virtual simulation packages, and these are defined in a similar manner to DRRs. By the use of a sophisti-cated image compositing algo-rithm (Picker 1997), more detailed soft tissue definition, and therefore better image quality, is available with the DCR.

Finally, isocentric reference marks are placed on the patient. All data are then transferred to the treatment planning software and an isodose distribution is produced, using conven-tional, independent or multileaf planning tools. Additionally, dose volume histograms, which display the dose received according to the percent volume of tissues, of the PTV and critical organs can be used to enhance the quantitative precision of dose homogeneity across the tumour volume and other regions of interest.

Once complete, the isodose distribution is digitally exported back to the virtual simulation software, where a second set of DRRs of the planned fields is produced. These are then compared against the original DRRs. Alternatively, portal image data from a linear accelerator can be compared against the localisation DRRs, or the isodose distribution can be sent on line to a conventional simulator where, by the use of an automated set-up facility, swift verification of the isodose distribution may occur.

Whilst almost any external beam radiotherapy technique may be simulated in this manner, Hunt (1998) points out that considerable forethought should be given to the construction of a working protocol in the following situations:

1. Abutting fields
2. The dynamic range of the DRR can be limited, particularly in the thorax, where it may be desirable to visualise vertebral bodies, heart and bronchus simultaneously

3. Materials used as skin markers, and the use of wire for denoting regions of interest on the skin surface.

Summarising, CT simulation can be seen to have considerable advantages over conventional methods. Superior localisation ability, the generation of DRRs and DCRs in transverse and noncoplanar orientations, image manipulation technology and swifter simulation procedures make it an attractive complement to the portfolio of radiotherapy equipment. However, it is an expensive alternative to the conventional simulator, DRRs and DCRs demonstrate poorer quality of image in comparison to the humble radiograph, it cannot produce an image of a moving structure, the virtual software requires a large number of CT slices, and it can be difficult to attach routine immobilisation devices to the CT couch.

The simulator CT (or simulated CT)

The simulator CT offers the ability to produce cross-sectional anatomical images that may be used to supplement its standard radiographic modes. Tomographic images can be produced from a simulator by the addition of relatively inexpensive hardware and software, namely:

- A pre collimator attached to the head of the unit at the lead tray position, and a post collimator attached in front of the image intensifier (usually in the cassette holder). Both are constructed as a lead plate containing a narrow aperture; their function is to limit the X-ray field to a narrow fan beam of radiation which then rotates around the patient, and to limit the radiation reaching the detector to primary beam X-rays only.
- A radiation detector. This may be the image intensifier and TV camera system, or an additional solid state (see Ch. 2) or scintillation detector array.
- A software package to collate the patient data and convert them to CT images.

By performing one or more 360° rotations around the patient, X-ray beam data are sampled and collected as a series of linear attenuation coefficient data sets. This is then converted into Hounsfield units, and the image reconstructed by the convolution and back projection method (Farr & Allisy-Roberts 1997, Webb 1996).

Prior to rotating, the detector and central axis of the X-ray beam are positioned so that the detector is laterally offset from the centre of the beam. One edge of the detector is positioned along the superior inferior central beam axis so that a larger diameter rotation around the patient, also known as the field of view (FOV), is permissible.

The benefits of such a unit are clear; a larger FOV allows CT images to be produced when the patient is supported in a positioning device that will not fit through the aperture of a diagnostic CT unit, capital and maintenance costs are much lower, the image reconstruction method requires less data than the CT simulator, and the simulator CT has mechanical and geometric movements which are more comparable to megavoltage treatment units.

Disadvantages include poorer CT image quality than that produced by a diagnostic or CT simulator, the number of available CT slices is limited by the cooling capacity of the rotating

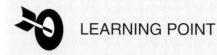

LEARNING POINT

Question

Evaluate the role of the CT simulator and the simulator CT in the following scenarios:

- A patient to be treated with palliative intent
- A patient to be treated with radical intent
- Paediatric patients
- For those patients prescribed conformal megavoltage radiotherapy.

anode, and image quality is compromised even further in the thorax and abdomen as a result of breathing during a typical scan time of 1 minute per slice.

ROOM DESIGN AND RADIATION PROTECTION

See Chapter 3 for a review of the principles of room design and radiation protection.

QUALITY ASSURANCE

The principles of quality assurance (QA) are reviewed in Chapter 4. However, the simulator consists of three main systems, and it is important to ensure that any QA programme encompasses the entire simulator suite, which is as follows:

1. The mechanical system
2. The image forming system
3. The image detection system.

RECOMMENDED READING

Bentel G C 1999 Patient positioning and immobilization in radiation oncology. McGraw-Hill, New York
Butler E K, Helton D J, Keller J, Hughes L L, Crenshaw T, Davis L W 1996 A totally integrated simulation technique

for three-field breast treatment using a CT simulator. Medical Physics 23(10): 1809–1814

BSI 1993a Medical electrical equipment. Part 2. Particular requirements for safety BS 5724, Section 2.129, specification for radiotherapy simulators. BSI, Milton Keynes

BSI 1993b Medical electrical equipment. Part 3. Particular requirements for performance BS 5724, Section 3.129, methods of declaring functional performance characteristics of radiotherapy simulators. Supplement 1. Guide to functional performance values. BSI, Milton Keynes

BSI 1994 Medical electrical equipment. Part 3. Particular requirements for performance BS 5724, Section 3.129, methods of declaring functional performance characteristics of radiotherapy simulators. BSI, Milton Keynes

Dakin J 1991 In search of a simulator. Radiography Today 57(647): 11–19

Stephenson J A, Wiley A L 1995 Current techniques in three-dimensional CT simulation and radiation treatment planning. Oncology 9(11): 1125–1132, 1135–1140

REFERENCES

Ball J, Moore A 1997 Essential physics for radiographers, 3rd edn. Blackwell Scientific, Oxford

Ball J, Price T 1995 Chesneys' radiographic imaging, 6th edn. Blackwell Scientific, Oxford

BSI 1993a Medical electrical equipment. Part 2. Particular requirements for safety BS 5724, Section 2.129, specification for radiotherapy simulators. BSI, Milton Keynes

BSI 1993b Medical electrical equipment. Part 3. Particular requirements for performance BS 5724, Section 3.129, methods of declaring functional performance characteristics of radiotherapy simulators. Supplement 1. Guide to functional performance values. BSI, Milton Keynes

BSI 1994 Medical electrical equipment. Part 3. Particular requirements for performance BS 5724, Section 3.129, methods of declaring functional performance characteristics of radiotherapy simulators. BSI, Milton Keynes

Farr R F, Allisy-Roberts P J 1997 Physics for medical imaging. W B Saunders, London

Hunt M 1998 Clinical implementation of CT simulation. AAPM refresher course, August 8–10. San Antonio, Texas

International Commission on Radiation Units and Measurements (ICRU) 1993 Prescribing, recording and reporting photon beam therapy. Report 50. ICRU, Maryland

Jenkins D 1980 Radiographic photography and imaging processes. MTP Press, Lancaster

Leo W R 1994 Techniques for nuclear and particle physics experiments: a how-to approach, 2nd revised edn. Springer-Verlag, Berlin

Metcalfe P, Kron T, Hoban P 1997 The physics of radiotherapy X-rays from linear accelerators. Medical Physics, Madison

Picker International 1997 Digitally composited radiographs (DCRs) AcQsimTM CT simulation package product data. Picker, USA

Stephenson J A, Wiley A L 1995 Current techniques in three-dimensional CT simulation and radiation treatment planning. Oncology (Nov)

Taylor J 1988 Imaging in radiotherapy. Croom Helm, Kent

Washington C M, Lever D T (eds) 1996 Principles and practice of radiation therapy: physics, simulation and treatment planning. Mosby Year Book, Missouri, vol. 2

Webb S (ed) 1996 The physics of medical imaging. Medical Science Series. Institute of Physics, London

Wilks R 1987 Principles of radiological physics, 2nd edn. Churchill Livingstone, Edinburgh

Williams J R, Thwaites D I (eds) 1993 Radiotherapy physics in practice. Oxford University Press, Oxford

Measurement of ionising radiation, and calculation of absorbed dose

Chapter objectives

By the end of this chapter, you should be able to:

- Evaluate how the different effects of ionising radiation are used as a basis of measurement in the radiotherapy department

- Describe the structure, function and typical application(s) of the following radiation dosimeters: thimble and parallel plate ionisation chambers, thermoluminescent dosimeter, silicon diode, radiographic film, scintillation counter and Geiger counter

- Discuss the issues surrounding the development and implementation of a protocol relating to the introduction of the use of an in vivo dosimeter – such as a semiconductor – for the routine measurement of entrance and/or exit dose measurements for all new patients on a megavoltage linear accelerator

- Evaluate the use of tissue equivalent materials in your own department

- Explain how readings of exposure in air are converted to absorbed dose to water, and describe the mechanisms which provide a national (UK) consistency in the manner to which absorbed dose to water is measured and calculated

- With respect to the treatment unit calculations carried out in your own department, identify and explain the function of each of the calculation components used

▓ With respect to the dose and fractionation schedules used in your own department, compare the relative biological effectiveness of two fractionation schedules commonly employed for the treatment of one particular disease site.

INTRODUCTION

This chapter reviews a number of seemingly unrelated concepts; however, the uniting theme is that they may all influence the dose that the patient receives. So, this chapter looks at:

• How ionising radiation may be measured
• Units of dose
• Conversion of one dose unit to another
• The principles of monitor unit calculations
• The production of an isodose distribution
• The potential manipulation of dose and fractionation schedules.

MEASUREMENT OF RADIATION

Effects of ionising radiation used as a measure of absorbed dose

In the radiotherapy department, radiation detectors are employed to measure absorbed dose; this is defined below as the energy absorbed within the irradiated tissue per unit mass of that same tissue. The calorimeter is the only method that directly measures this energy, the very nature of its design making it an impractical meter to use clinically. Consequently other effects of ionising radiation (indicated below) are more commonly used to assess how body tissues respond during irradiation. This tissue response is then converted into absorbed dose by a series of correction factors (see p. 47).

Characteristics of an 'ideal' ionising radiation detector

When attempting to evaluate the use and performance of any radiation detector, it is important to have a series of ideal performance characteristics against which each detector may be compared. In practice, it is rare for any one detector to match all of the features listed on page 29.

Developing a protocol for the implementation of a radiation detector as part of the verification of patient set-ups

Many departments routinely use some form of radiation detector to confirm the dose being delivered to a patient during radiotherapy

KEY POINTS–MEASUREMENT OF RADIATION

Effects of ionising radiation employed as methods of measuring absorbed dose are listed below (those routinely used in the radiotherapy department are discussed in further detail later in the text):

▓ *Biological methods.* The threshold erythema dose (TED) was commonly used in the past as a measure of radiation dose, and relied on the fact that ionising radiation produces skin erythema. This method is highly unreliable; it is subjective in terms of observer interpretation of the degree of erythema, and patient response will vary considerably with skin type, volume irradiated, dose and fractionation schedule used, dose rate and the selected radiation energy and modality.

▓ *Chemical methods.* Certain chemicals change colour on irradiation. Chemicals commonly used in the past include ferrous sulphate and barium palatinocyanide. Again, both rely on the subjective interpretation of the observer; the atomic numbers of the two chemicals are not representative of that of tissue; toxicity can be an issue in the case of accidental release into or onto tissue; and the sensitivity of both chemicals to radiation dose is low.

KEY POINTS (continued)

- *Calorimetry*. This is the precise quantification of minute temperature changes in irradiated materials, thereby directly measuring the energy absorbed as a result of the irradiation process. It is the only direct method of measuring dose, but a complex monitor is required in order to measure the very small temperature increases produced. Clinical monitors that can be used on a daily basis have yet to be designed at an affordable cost, and so this detector is not discussed in any further detail.

- *Ionisation*. This is a measure of the charge liberated in air by ionising radiation. This method is highly effective, simple and commonly employed.

- *Fluorescence*. This principle forms the basis of the scintillation detector, the interaction of ionising radiation within a fluorescent material resulting in the production of light from that material. This light is then collected by a photomultiplier tube which converts it into an amplified electrical signal.

- *Thermoluminescence*. Thermoluminescent material has the capability to absorb energy from ionising radiation and to store that energy within its crystalline structure. At some point later in time the energy can be released in the form of light. However, considerable heat energy must be provided to the material in order to release this light.

- *Current flow in semiconductors*. This detector is often considered in terms of being a solid ionisation chamber. Irradiation releases free charge carriers, and if it is connected to an appropriate meter a measurable current is produced.

- *Optical density produced in radiographic film.* Ionising radiation is well known to produce blackening of radiographic film, and this blackening can be quantified by the use of a device known as a densitometer. The degree of blackening is expressed in terms of optical density (see Ch. 1), and will be proportional to the amount of energy absorbed by the film. The high atomic number of silver in comparison to soft tissue makes this detector unsuitable for quantitative measurement at kilovoltage energies. The amount of blackening produced on a radiograph for a set dose of radiation will also vary tremendously upon automatic processing, storage and handling conditions.

KEY POINTS–CHARACTERISTICS OF AN 'IDEAL' IONISING RADIATION DETECTOR

A range of performance features is indicated below. The list is not exhaustive, and the reader is referred to Metcalfe et al (1997), Leo (1994) and Knoll (1989) for a more comprehensive review.

- *Accuracy*. This is the ability of the detector to correctly indicate dose; it is defined by Graham (1996, p. 85) as 'a measure of the correspondence of the result obtained and the exact value'. Statements of accuracy must take into consideration the incidence of errors in detector performance and measurement technique. Such errors are split into two categories: random (or stochastic) and systematic errors. Random errors are unpredicted events whose magnitude is reduced by taking the average of a number of measurements. Systematic errors are predictable, have consistent magnitude, and are the result of subjective displays of detector output and subsequent observer interpretation, as well as from variations in detector and radiation machine performance. Repeating measurements will not improve accuracy with respect to the incidence of systematic errors.

- *Specificity*. In other words, is the detector capable of producing a useable signal for the given type and energy of radiation?

KEY POINTS (continued)

■ *Sensitivity.* Can the detector produce a signal of sufficient magnitude for very small amounts of radiation intensity as well as for the larger intensity values?

■ *Energy resolution.* This is the ability to distinguish between two or more closely lying energies.

■ *Response time.* How long does it take to form a signal after the arrival of the radiation?

■ *Signal duration.* Is the detector capable of registering a second radiation event whilst in the process of producing a signal as a result of the first radiation event?

■ *Precision.* This can be defined as the reproducibility of the detector response under equivalent irradiation conditions. It is important that the same reading is produced

following the receipt of the same amount of radiation.

■ *Dose response.* Over a defined energy range, it is helpful if the detector produces a signal that is proportional to the amount of incident radiation.

■ *Objectivity of the method of data display.* Can the data be displayed in a method that produces minimal subjective interpretation by the observer?

■ *Detector efficiency.* This is split into two categories: absolute and intrinsic. Absolute detector efficiency is a measure of its ability to measure the total events emitted by the source of ionising radiation. Intrinsic efficiency reflects the ability of the detector to produce a signal for each quanta of radiation incident upon it.

treatment. This may be on day one of treatment, once a week throughout a course of treatment, or more frequently. Whatever the practice, it is useful to have some sort of explicit written protocol on how this process should be conducted. In this manner, ambiguity in the interpretation of dosimeter readings is reduced.

The protocol should address, at the very least, the following areas:

• Which patients should measurements be taken on – radical, palliative, specific sites or all sites?
• At what point should the measurements be taken, and how frequently?
• For what purpose is the dosimeter being used – to demonstrate calculation errors, highlight errors in machine output, etc.?
• What is considered an acceptable reading?
• Who should view the results?
• What action should be taken with respect to an unacceptable result – repeat dosimeter measurement, stop treatment, etc.?
• What should the readings be compared against?

 LEARNING POINT

For a megavoltage machine in your department where dose measurements are taken as part of the treatment verification, try to answer the questions in the preceding checklist.

Questions
Is there a written protocol for the collection and documentation of such measurements?
Who was involved in the production of this protocol?
Does your protocol work? If the answer is no, why not?

• How and where will the readings be documented?
• Who will perform trend analysis on the readings?

Calibration chain for external beam radiotherapy

The purpose of a UK wide X-ray dosimeter calibration protocol is to achieve a specified degree of accuracy and consistency in the measurement of X-rays. The precise delivery of a prescribed amount of radiation to a planning target volume depends upon many factors, one of these being the need for accurate dosimetry. Dosimetry measurements are themselves classified into two different types: relative and absolute.

Relative dosimetry measurements are those where dose is measured under specific irradiation conditions (such as those machine parameters used during the delivery of treatment), and which are then compared to the dose given at a specific depth for reference machine parameters (i.e. those used for monitor unit calibration during accelerator commissioning). Absolute dosimetry measurements are those made at this specific depth for those reference machine parameters.

Because all other clinically useful beam data are produced by comparison with these absolute dosimetry reference parameters, it is imperative that the latter are precise and specific. In the UK, all radiotherapy departments follow a specific protocol originating from the National Physical Laboratory (NPL) when calibrating dose monitors used during the calibration and routine clinical operation of radiotherapy equipment producing X-rays, gamma rays and electron beams. Achieving such national standardisation in this particular dosimetry aspect allows valid intercomparison of clinical external beam radiotherapy trials and machine performance to be made – ultimately leading to continual monitoring and ongoing improvement of baseline quality (Thwaites 1998).

All dose monitors involved with the calculation of absorbed dose to water from X-rays are traceable back to a primary standard calorimeter at the National Physical Laboratory. This standard sits at the very top of a hierarchy of measurement standards. Other instruments (secondary standards) are brought to the primary and are calibrated by a comparison of their performance, under controlled irradiation conditions, against this primary (Duane & McEwan 1996). These secondary standards are not clinically employed instruments, but are kept at a radiotherapy department and are often shared between a number of such departments. In this manner, those instruments used on a daily basis (tertiary or field instruments) can then be calibrated, under controlled irradiation conditions at the parent hospital, against the secondary standard on a regular basis.

Instrument calibration for clinically used devices should be carried out:

- At the purchase of the instrument
- Against the secondary standard at least every 3 years
- After any repair
- When it is suspected that the response of the instrument has changed, usually for an unidentified reason.

Megavoltage electron dosimetry follows an alternate route, and is based upon instruments calibrated in terms of air kerma.

DETECTORS OF IONISING RADIATION

Free air ionisation chamber

This instrument resided at the NPL, and was the primary national standard for the measurement of exposure. It has now been superseded by the primary standard calorimeter referred to for the measurement of absorbed dose to water.

Illustrated in Figure 2.1, this is a device designed to measure the ionisation as a result of irradiation within a defined mass of air. A beam of X-rays is produced from a source of radiation (S), and this is focused towards the ionisation chamber by passing through a collimator (K). The X-rays then enter the free air ionisation chamber and pass between an upper and lower electrode, producing photo and recoil electrons that ionise the air contained within the chamber. This results in the production of ion pairs, and these are collected by the electrodes, which are separated by a set distance (d). The lower electrode is connected to a meter (M) which

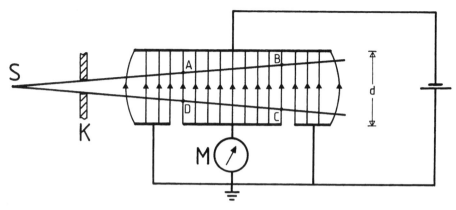

Figure 2.1 A diagrammatic section through the free air ionisation chamber (from Graham 1996, with permission).

measures the total negative charge produced within the chamber. This particular electrode is separated into three sections of which only the middle section feeds collected negative charge to meter M. This design feature is necessary because the solid black arrowed vertical lines between the two electrodes (indicating the lines of electric field strength) bow out at the lateral extent of the chamber. As this device aims to measure the ionisation produced in area ABCD, it is important that the electric field strength is homogeneous throughout this particular region.

The distance (d) must be such that it is greater than the range of highest energy electron likely to be produced. This ensures that all energy is then lost from this particle into the air before it reaches the electrode.

It is also crucial to have a carefully controlled potential difference existing between the two electrodes. This must be of a value sufficient to prevent the ion pairs recombining once they have been produced, and high enough to collect every ion pair produced – this latter value is known as the saturation voltage. Once this saturation voltage has been reached, and is maintained, any charge collected by the meter results from irradiation conditions. If the voltage continues to rise past the level of saturation, it is possible that the ion pairs themselves will ionise other air atoms prior to reaching the electrodes.

The collected signal will then be proportional to the radiation entering the ionisation chamber, rather than being an absolute quantitative representation of the energy deposited in the chamber by the incident radiation.

Photo or recoil electrons may have enough energy to travel out of area ABCD. Similarly, electrons produced from air outside ABCD may travel into this region. In order to use this device to measure exposure (see below), the electrons generated within ABCD that are lost to the periphery of the ionisation chamber must be balanced by those produced in the periphery that enter the defined air volume. This chamber status is referred to as electronic equilibrium. When a chamber is operated under these conditions it is then appropriate to implement the definition of exposure.

Above 300 kV incident X-ray beams, it becomes very difficult to use the free air ionisation chamber. With increasing energy the nature of its design makes it unwieldy and impractical for clinical use. Additionally, the potential difference required between the charge collecting electrodes becomes prohibitively high. Consequently, smaller and more practical versions of the ionisation chamber are employed in clinical practice. These are known as the thimble and parallel plate ionisation chambers – and both work on the principle of an air wall equivalent (see below).

For measuring any reading for absolute dosimetry purposes, it is important to consider whether any correction factors should be applied to the chamber readings. A comprehensive discussion of the range of such factors can be found in Metcalfe et al (1997) and Williams & Thwaites (1993).

The main correction to be considered relates to temperature and pressure. For chambers which are open to the air, the number of air molecules contained within ABCD will vary depending on changes in ambient temperature and atmospheric pressure. As the calibration of each ionisation detector is compared against a national standard, it is necessary to compare the atmospheric conditions existing during this measurement against those present during primary standard calibration. Any chamber readings must then be corrected appropriately; i.e.:

$$\text{Corrected reading } R_c = R \times \left[\frac{T_1}{T_0}\right] \times \left[\frac{P_0}{P_1}\right]$$

where T_0 = temperature during primary calibration; $0°C = 273$ K
T_1 = temperature during new irradiation procedure: 273 + ambient room temperature (K)
P_0 = atmospheric pressure during primary calibration; 760 mmHg (may be in kPa)
P_1 = atmospheric pressure during new irradiation procedure; 760 + atmospheric pressure (mmHg or kPa).

It should be emphasised at this point that such correction factors need to be applied to ionisation chambers which are routinely used under constantly changing environmental conditions. Since the free air chamber was designed as a primary standard this sort of correction factor should only need to be applied to the meter reading of thimble and parallel plate ionisation chambers used clinically.

Thimble (cylindrical) and parallel plate (pancake) ionisation chambers

These are clinically employed ionisation chambers favoured for their versatility, ease of use and portability. They operate in a very similar

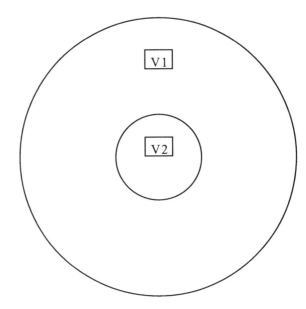

Figure 2.2 A schematic diagram relating to the maintenance of electronic equilibrium in the thimble ionisation chamber.

manner to the free air ionisation cham-ber, but are based upon the principle of air wall equivalence. They are commonly used as follows:

- For measurement of machine output during acceptance and commissioning tests
- As part of the programmed quality assurance tests for beam flatness, output and dose rate
- With a tissue equivalent material in order to verify the accuracy of in vivo set-ups
- Secondary standard chambers are used to calibrate field instruments
- Transmission parallel plate ionisation chambers are found in the head of linear accelerators and other equipment producing ionising radiation.

With respect to Figure 2.2, V2 and V1 are air volumes, where V1 is very large in comparison to the range of secondary electrons produced in V2, and V2 is very small in comparison to the range of those same secondary electrons.

V1 is large to ensure that all the electrons produced in V2 dissipate their energy within V1.

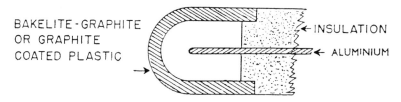

BAKELITE-GRAPHITE
OR GRAPHITE
COATED PLASTIC

←INSULATION
← ALUMINIUM

Figure 2.3   The thimble chamber (from Meredith & Massey 1977, with permission of Butterworth-Heinemann, a division of Reed Educational and Professional Publishing Ltd).

Some electrons released within V1 – by the same source of X-rays – will produce ion pairs in V2. Electronic equilibrium exists as long as the number of electrons leaving V2 equal the number of electrons entering it from V1. This is the same as the situation in the free air chamber.

In order to be used clinically, V1 is replaced by a material of equivalent atomic number to tissue, but with increased density. In this manner, the diameter of the structure is reduced so that it may be used in clinical situations without diminishing the status of electronic equilibrium.

In addition to this wall material having an equivalent atomic number, it also needs to function as an electrical conductor because, as in the image of the thimble chamber shown in Figure 2.3, it also acts as one of the collecting electrodes. Typical materials used include bakelite and carbon, or plastics internally coated with a thin layer of graphite, the latter acting as the collecting electrode. The second aluminium electrode is positioned along the centre of the thimble chamber, with a potential difference existing between the two in order to facilitate the collection of any ion pairs produced within the air volume. Chamber output is then transferred to a meter (known as an electrometer), where it is commonly presented as a value of dose or dose rate. Whilst carbon (6) and aluminium (13) have lower and higher atomic numbers respectively than air (7.4), the total system is considered to act exactly as an air volume.

Air filled chambers are favoured because of air's comparative atomic number and therefore, over a wide range of energies, its ability to absorb ionising radiation in a manner similar to that of soft tissue and water. The composition of air is similar across the world, and the material is cheap and readily available.

The thickness of the air wall must be equal to the range of any electrons produced within it, and if this is so, no electrons produced outside of the detector will reach the air volume within. This maintenance of electronic equilibrium within the detector becomes a problem with increasing incident X-ray energy, so much so that O'Boyle & Maloney (cited in Cherry & Duxbury 1998) and Metcalfe et al (1997) recommend that dosimeter measurements based upon this principle should not be conducted in X-ray beams of an effective energy greater than 2–3 MeV. However, van Gasteren et al (cited in Metcalfe et al 1997) have indicated that this problem may not be insurmountable.

A build-up cap is used when it is impractical to make the air wall equivalent thickness of the thimble chamber equal to the maximum range of electrons produced. These are caps of similar air equivalent material which are placed around the outside of the thimble chamber. At increasing energies the build-up cap becomes so thick that it begins to attenuate the incident X-ray beam, thereby making a true in air reading no longer possible.

A range of chamber sizes is on the market: the larger volumes (e.g. 35 cm^3) are used in areas of low beam intensity, and the smaller volumes (e.g. 0.6 cm^3) for main beam readings of dose and dose rate.

A schematic diagram of a parallel plate ionisation chamber is shown in Figure 2.4. It is used for dose measurements in areas of steep dose gradients, and is favoured over the thimble chamber for this sort of application because the typical diameter of the latter is significant in comparison. The parallel plate chamber is therefore frequently used for kilovoltage and electron beam dosimetry, as well as being excellent for

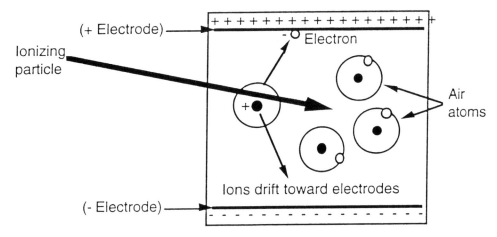

Figure 2.4 A simple parallel plate ionisation chamber (from Stanton & Stinson 1996, with permission).

measurements required in the skin sparing region of the megavoltage X-ray beam. Apart from its significantly reduced size, it is very similar in structure and function to the free air ionisation chamber. In this instance, however, radiation enters the chamber through one of the electrodes, and so they tend to be made of aluminium which does not significantly attenuate the incident radiation beam.

Ionisation of semiconductor materials

These measurement devices are referred to by a multitude of names: silicon diodes, solid state diodes, and direct patient dosimeters (DPDs). The fundamental mechanism by which they operate relates to the electrical conducting properties of the chosen material. Semiconductors exhibit electrical conducting properties midway between that of a conductor – where electrical charge moves easily throughout the material – and that of an insulator – where such charges are unable to flow.

The band theory of atomic structure is often used to facilitate an understanding of how such materials work. As seen in the Bohr model of the atom, the orbiting electrons of a single atom occupy a series of discrete energy levels. When many atoms exist in close proximity, and form bonds with those neighbours, the nature of these discrete energy levels changes to broad energy bands. The outermost filled electron band is known as the valence band (see Fig. 2.6), and this is separated from the conduction band by an area known as the forbidden gap. This latter region does not contain any energy levels, and so electrons do not reside within it. Electrons in the conduction band are free to move around the material, where they may interact with neighbouring atoms.

Semiconductors – silicon in particular – exhibit a very small forbidden gap, such that at room temperature, electrons may gain sufficient energy to transfer from the valence band into the conduction band, allowing the material to act as a conductor.

The conduction properties of semiconductor materials are enhanced by the introduction of small amounts of carefully chosen impurities. These create discrete energy levels within the forbidden gap region, increasing the number of electrons that can reach the conduction band. This process is known as doping of the semiconductor.

Silicon is one of the most commonly employed semiconductor materials in radiotherapy; it has an atomic number of 14. Germanium is also used to some extent, but its higher atomic number of 32 makes silicon the preferred choice for radiotherapy measurements.

Two variants of silicon semiconductors are produced. The first is known as 'n' type silicon. It is produced by adding a group V periodic table element such as phosphorus or arsenic to the group IV silicon. This means that for each silicon and phosphorus atom that bonds, there is one extra electron in the valence band. The second variant is 'p' type silicon. Silicon is combined with group III elements such as aluminium or boron; the result of this is that there is an electron deficit in the valence band. When used as a radiation detector, the 'p' and 'n' type are joined together (see Fig. 2.5a). It is unusual for equal amounts of each material to be used; normally there is a very small amount of one type and a larger amount of the second. However, such detectors are always referred to as 'p' or 'n' type, the label denoting the greatest percentage type of silicon.

When the two types of silicon are fused together, the free electrons in the 'n' type are attracted to the free holes (i.e. an electron deficit) in the 'p' type. As a result of recombination, at the join of the two types of silicon there is an area where there are no free charge carriers. This area is referred to as the depletion zone. Its appearance means that the flow of free charge carriers stops, mainly because the principally positive 'p' type silicon now contains a very small region of negative charge, and similarly the principally negative 'n' type silicon contains a narrow region of positive charge. This acts as a charge barrier (Fig. 2.5b), and at room temperature the remaining free charges have insufficient energy to surmount it.

If a potential difference is applied across the semiconductor and the material is then irradiated, ion pairs are produced and charge once again will flow. This charge is evident as an ionisation current, the magnitude of which is dependent on the amount of ionising radiation absorbed within the detector. The energy required to produce an ion pair in silicon (3 electron volts) is very much less than that required to produce an ion pair in air (33 electron volts), and because of this the detector will produce more ion pairs per gray of absorbed dose. This makes it far more sensitive than an ionisation chamber (Ball & Moore 1997).

This process of ionisation will ultimately destroy the detector, and 'n' type silicon is far

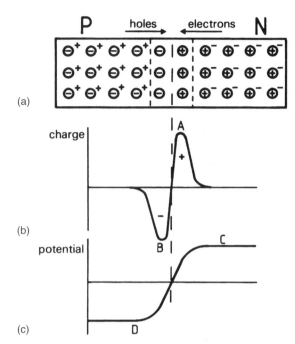

Figure 2.5 The *PN* junction. **(a)** Electrons diffuse across the depletion zone from the 'n' type silicon towards the 'p' type, and free positive 'holes' move from the 'p' type to the 'n' type; **(b)** shows the charge across the depletion zone as a result of this charge flow; **(c)** shows the potential difference across the barrier (from Graham 1996, with permission).

more liable to such damage. When this sort of damage is sustained, detector sensitivity will change. However, Meiler & Podgorsak (1997) indicate that this is easily corrected for by regular calibration of the dosimeter. Doped silicon therefore has a number of advantages.

- Because of its sensitivity, it can be produced as a tiny device. This means that it can be used in a wide range of clinical situations.
- It produces a real time readout of dose. Additionally a number of detectors can be connected up to an electrometer, and all can then be used on the same patient during one fraction of treatment.
- It is independent of air pressure.

There are, however, some considerable disadvantages to balance the very real benefit of having a device that produces real time values of patient dose. These include:

- An atomic number of 14 means that silicon will exhibit preferential absorption of ionising radiation in the photoelectric absorption and pair production energy ranges.
- There is a slight temperature dependence, which increases with the age of the detector. (This can be compensated for by the simple measure of ensuring that the detector reaches body temperature prior to use.)
- Each piece of silicon is covered by a stainless steel build-up cap. This is designed for the user to continue to take advantage of the favourable size of the detector – but in the clinical situation the depth of the cap may be insufficient for the energy of interest.

Thermoluminescent detector and the TLD badge

Thermoluminescence is a characteristic of certain phosphors, a phosphor being a material which emits light when irradiated.

Once again, the band theory of the atom is applicable. The thermoluminescent process commences with an X-ray interacting with the material and undergoing a photoelectric or Compton scattering interaction process. This enables electrons in the valence band to enter the conduction band, where they are able to move around the material. As energy is lost from these electrons, they attempt to return to the valence band. As shown in Figure 2.6, as these electrons fall back towards this band they are caught in

artificially created electron traps existing in the forbidden gap. The number of electrons caught within these traps is a function of the amount of incident radiation absorbed. Such traps are produced by the introduction of specific chemicals (a process known as doping). It is very difficult to accurately control the amount of dopant put into each batch of thermoluminescent dosimeters (TLDs), and consequently it is essential that the user calibrate each and every batch of TLDs so that the response per gray of dose is predictable over a known range of energies and types of ionising radiation.

Electrons caught in this manner are unable to leave this position until they are provided with sufficient energy – heat to the temperature of approximately 300°C. Once released from the trap they return to the conduction band, and then drop back to the valence band, having traversed through something known as a luminescent centre. This latter feature is characteristic of the material in question, and when an electron passes through such a site, the energy lost from the electron as it passes from the upper to the lower aspect of the luminescent centre becomes evident as a continuous spectrum of visible light. This light emission is presented graphically in Figure 2.7 in the format of light

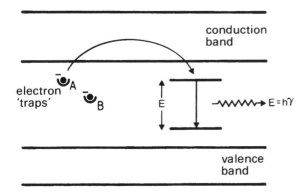

Figure 2.6 The stages of thermoluminescence (from Graham 1996, with permission).

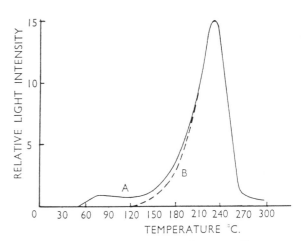

Figure 2.7 A thermoluminescence glow curve (from Meredith & Massey 1977, with permission from Butterworth-Heinemann, a division of Reed Educational and Professional Publishing).

intensity as a function of temperature; it is traditionally referred to as a glow curve. The area under the curve is related to the energy absorbed within the thermoluminescent material, and so is used as a measure of absorbed dose. Lithium fluoride (LiF) is the material preferred for radiotherapy dosimetry purposes, primarily because of its comparable effective atomic number of 8.14. It is available in a variety of forms – powder, rods, discs, and as LiF impregnated onto Teflon® – which enhances its diversity of use. There are two selected dopants for LiF, magnesium and titanium, and conventionally the dosimeter is referred to as LiF; Mg, Ti.

One problem with LiF is that it exhibits supralinearity at certain dose levels. This means that the light output per unit dose increases above a certain dose level. This is clearly something that needs to be corrected for.

The heating cycle necessary to produce the light output is delivered within a specially designed TLD reader. The heating pattern is specific to each type of material, and usually consists of the following phases:

1. *Preheat*. During this stage the phosphor is heated to a low level, the aim being to release electrons from any traps that may have been filled as a result of room temperature rather than irradiation. This is not entirely necessary, since the same effect can be achieved by leaving the TLD 24 hours prior to reading.

2. *Read*. The temperature is increased into the region of 300°C+. This liberates electrons caught in the traps as a result of irradiation. The light is collected by a photomultiplier tube and converted to a quantitative signal which is usually displayed on the control panel of the TLD reader.

3. *Anneal*. It is important to ensure that absolutely every electron trap is emptied prior to reusing the TLD, otherwise the sensitivity of the detector may change between uses. This is done by heating the materials to temperatures in excess of the read phase. New TLDs should be annealed three or four times prior to being used clinically – this stabilises their response to radiation.

4. *Cooling*. Each manufacturer recommends a cooling cycle that produces a slow return back to room temperature.

The advantages of LiF are numerous:

- Its atomic number means it can be used across a wide range of energies, with minimal response variation
- It is small and therefore versatile
- There are no high voltages or trailing cables
- It is reusable
- With the use of filters it is possible to distinguish the type and energy of radiation.

Disadvantages include:

- The inability accurately to control the amount of dopant – this means that the response of one particular batch of TLDs may vary tremendously from that of another
- It produces a retrospective readout
- There is no permanent record for future reference
- The detector exhibits supralinearity at higher dose levels.

The TLD monitor

This is a particular application of thermoluminescent materials, and is specifically designed to be used as a personnel monitor.

Between two and four LiF impregnated Teflon® discs are placed upon a metal template. This template is enclosed in a light tight plastic sheath onto which is placed an identification number. Surrounding the TLD material is the TLD holder (see Fig. 2.8).

The holder is made of plastic, and has three specific design features. The first is an oblong hole which should be aligned to the TLD identification number. The second is a circular hole, under which sits one of the TLD discs. Dose registered here will be representative of the likely skin dose of the wearer. The third area is a thick plastic dome under which sits a second TLD. Dose registered on this monitor will be representative of levels of absorbed dose within the internal organs of the wearer.

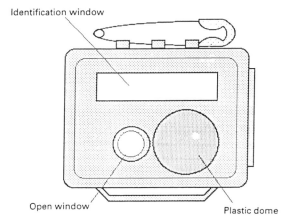

Identification window

Open window

Plastic dome

Figure 2.8   The plastic holder of a thermoluminescent personnel dosimeter used for measuring whole body dose (from Ball & Moore 1997, with permission from Blackwell Science Ltd).

This device tends to be favoured over the traditional film badge (p. 40) because it is sensitive to lower levels of radiation and the reading process is automated, and this has implications on the cost of the service to the employer.

Radiographic film and the film badge

When referring to radiographic film as a dosimeter, the mind invariably leaps to the film badge. Obviously this is an important application, but as a detector radiographic film is also used elsewhere in the radiotherapy department.

Chapter 1 reviewed the structure of radiographic film, the formation of the latent image, and the definition and measurement of optical density, and so none of this material is repeated here. The relatively high atomic number of silver gives radiographic film a significant disadvantage when being used as a dosimeter in the photoelectric absorption and pair production energy ranges. The percentage of interactions happening within the dosimeter at these energies is not representative of what would happen in a patient, and so is not well suited for absolute dosimetry, particularly as optical density is significantly influenced by variations in film batch, storage, handling and automatic processing conditions.

Film is used widely for qualitative measurements – in other words, a comparative review of how specific machine factors may change with the addition of another variable such as energy. Frequently it is employed for the following purposes:

- Taking verification images on the treatment unit
- As part of the treatment machine QA programme – confirming coincidence of the beam defining light and the radiation field, evaluation of electron beam flatness, and wrapping around kilovoltage and electron applicators, or the head of an accelerator to evaluate levels of leakage radiation
- For the production of 2D dose distributions along the central axis of the beam, as well as at right angles to it. If used in conjunction with an appropriate tissue equivalent material and a densitometer, this is a very quick way of producing beam data which may then be used to confirm other readings. Such use clearly requires an understanding of the need for careful quantification of optical density to dose relationship for the particular type of film being used
- In a personnel monitor.

The film badge

This device, illustrated in Figure 2.9, is similar in appearance to the previously mentioned TLD badge.

A strip of dual emulsion film is used, with one side slow emulsion and the other side fast emulsion. In the event of the wearer receiving a large dose of radiation that totally blackens the fast emulsion, it is then possible to strip off this layer and estimate dose from the remaining slow emulsion.

The holder contains an array of filters, all of which are designed to produce an estimate of energy and type of radiation by a comparison of the levels of optical density apparent on the section of film that lies beneath each filter.

The filters can be described as follows:

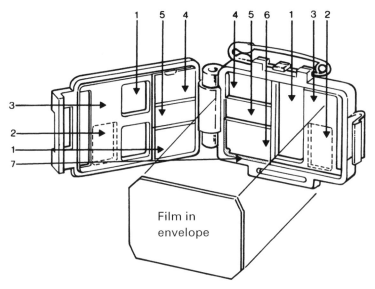

Figure 2.9   The film badge holder and film as used in personnel monitoring (see text for explanation of the filters). (Produced with permission from National Radiological Protection Board, Chilton, Oxfordshire. Copyright remains the property of the NRPB.)

1. An open window designed to allow the wearer identification number to be visible
2. Thin plastic, providing an estimate of skin dose and dose to the lens of the eye
3. Thick plastic, providing an estimate of internal organ dose
4. Aluminium alloy
5. Tin and lead
6. Cadmium and lead
7. Lead strip separating filters 5 and 6 (Graham 1996).

Filters 3–6 absorb beta rays, and X- or gamma radiation will penetrate through filter 5. Cadmium is used as it permits an estimate of thermal neutron dose. Neutrons of this energy will be captured by the cadmium, and will emit a gamma ray which then blackens the film underneath.

Obviously, when reading these monitors, it is important to produce a calibration curve from a series of radiographs that have received known doses. The response evident on the dose monitor is then compared against such a calibration curve.

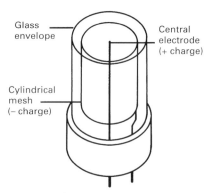

Figure 2.10   A schematic diagram of the Geiger–Müller tube (from Graham 1996, with permission).

Geiger–Müller tube

This is often referred to as the GM tube or Geiger counter, and has routinely been used since 1928 for the detection of ionising radiation. It is a form of ionisation chamber, and operates on the principles of gas multiplication, providing a signal of equal magnitude for each absorption event, irrespective of energy. Its structure is seen in Figure 2.10, which shows a cylindrical outer electrode and an inner central electrode. The chamber is filled with a gas such as argon which is under low pressure.

A potential difference exists between the two electrodes, very like that of the ionisation chamber described previously. However, the potential applied is much higher, and this detector operates by exploiting the ability of an electron to create further ionisations by collision with the gas molecules within.

When ionising radiation interacts within the gas volume, an ion pair is produced. At a critical value of the electric field strength, as they are attracted to the electrodes the ions collide with other gas atoms, creating more ion pairs. This builds to an avalanche of ion pairs which is also termed the gas multiplication effect. A typical pulse results in the formation of 10^9–10^{10} ion pairs, but once the avalanche reaches a certain size this chain reaction is terminated by a natural reduction in the ionisation current. At this point the gas ions recombine. During this period of termination and recombination, the detector cannot register further interactions with ionising radiation – this is termed the dead time. The number of pulses is presented as the count rate on some form of digital or analogue scale which has a useful audible component.

The GM tube has many potential applications, mainly because it is simple in operation, low in cost and easy to operate. It is used primarily as a survey meter, but if reduced in size it is useful as a personnel monitor, and it is also found attached to a wall in radiotherapy treatment rooms. It has a very high detection efficiency at low X-ray energies, but response to gamma rays and higher energy X-rays depends on the ability of the incident radiation to interact within the material of the detector. As this is not substantial, detection efficiency drops at higher energies.

Scintillation detector

This radiation monitor is based upon the principle of fluorescence – the ability of a material to emit low energy light on the absorption of ionising radiation. Suitable materials must be able readily to absorb ionising radiation, exhibit a high efficiency at converting energy to fluorescence and be transparent to the fluorescent light photons produced. High atomic number materials are suitable for X- and gamma rays, but unfortunately they are rarely transparent.

The process of fluorescence is very similar to thermoluminescence, and therefore reference is once again made to the band theory of atomic structure (see Fig. 2.11).

Ionising radiation is absorbed in the phosphor, usually via the photoelectric absorption process. This enables an electron from the

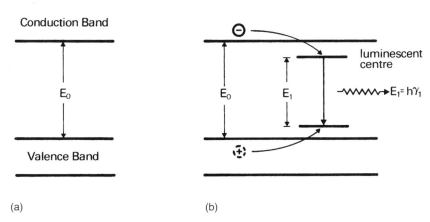

(a)   (b)

Figure 2.11   Mechanism of fluorescence in a crystal: **(a)** shows the outer electron structure of a pure crystal; **(b)** shows an impurity atom creating electron levels within the forbidden gap. Levels such as these are known as luminescent centres (from Graham 1996, with permission).

valence band to be elevated to the conduction band. As this electron loses energy, it falls back towards the valence band and emits a photon of visible light as it drops back through the luminescent centre. The light output of such materials can be enhanced by the addition of substances that mimic luminescent centres – terbium is one such substance.

There is available a wide range of solid and liquid materials that exhibit fluorescence and are therefore suitable for incorporation into a scintillation counter, but choice of such a material is strongly influenced by the energy and type of incident radiation. Gadolinium oxysulphide, doped with terbium, is an example of a fluorescent material commonly employed in X-ray cassette intensifying screens, and caesium iodide, doped with sodium, commonly forms the basis of image intensifiers.

Sodium iodide (NaI) is frequently selected for the detection of gamma photons in nuclear medicine applications. It forms the basis of the gamma camera, but it is also used in a portable detector for this energy range, the structure of which is seen in Figure 2.12.

The crystal of NaI is seen to the left hand side of the image. It is doped with thallium (Tl),

which enhances the number of luminescent centres naturally present. The NaI(Tl) crystal is covered with a light tight reflective coating which also prevents moisture from reaching the crystal and causing opacity within it as a result of the deliquescent nature of NaI(Tl).

Ionising radiation interacts in the crystal, and light is produced by fluorescence. The crystal is optically coupled to a photomultiplier tube (PMT), and all light produced is reflected down into the PMT, which amplifies the signal received. Amplification is achieved by the following process:

1. On leaving the crystal, light hits the photocathode of the PMT. This is coated with a material that produces electrons (by the photoelectric absorption process) when bombarded by light photons.

2. These electrons enter the evacuated PMT, and are accelerated towards the anode by the potential difference existing between the ends of the tube.

3. On the journey to the anode, this potential is arranged in order to divert the electrons towards positively charged plates known as dynodes. Each dynode is coated with a material

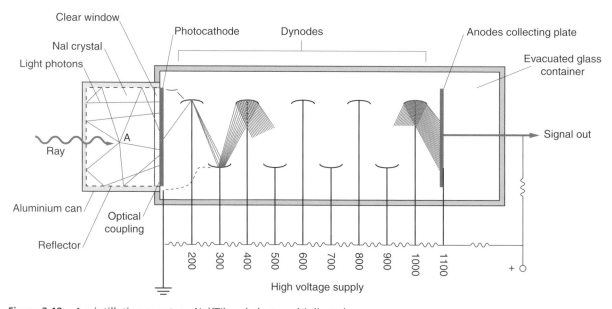

Figure 2.12 A scintillation counter – NaI(Tl) and photomultiplier tube.

LEARNING POINT

List the types of radiation detectors used in your department.

Questions
How effective is each of these at achieving its intended aim of use?
Could a better detector be used?
If so, what might the reasons be for that detector not being used?

that will produce electrons in proportion to the number that hit it, usually in the region of an amplification factor of 1:6.

4. Ultimately an amplified pulse (by a factor in the region of 10^6) is produced at the anode end of the PMT, and this pulse is proportional to the energy absorbed in the NaI(Tl) crystal. This pulse is typically fed to a pulse height analyser which allows a visual display of pulse height as a function of energy.

The scintillation counter is a detector widely used in nuclear medicine, but survey meters are required in many areas within the hospital and therefore it is important to include this detector (and the Geiger–Müller counter) in this chapter. It is suited to its task because it can detect individual ionisation events and is able to provide information regarding the energy of the incident radiation. Signal response is fast and linear, whilst its sensitivity to a wide range of energies makes it suitable as an environmental monitor, particularly as it is available in a variety of sizes.

PRINCIPLES OF TISSUE EQUIVALENT MATERIALS

A tissue equivalent material (TEM) is a substance chosen to ensure that ionising radiation will interact within it in the same manner, and to the same degree, as would occur if the material was replaced by a patient. In other words it closely mimics the scattering and absorption properties

of human tissue, and is usually known as a geometric TEM. Depending upon the intended use of the TEM, it may also be desirable that it closely replicates the external and internal contours of a patient – in this situation it tends to be known as an anthropomorphic TEM. These materials are also referred to as phantoms, solid water, bolus, etc., and they are commonly seen in use within a radiotherapy department.

Clearly, values for these quantities vary for bone, air, muscle, fat, water, etc.; texts such as Bomford et al (1993) and Metcalfe et al (1997) may be consulted for values of the majority of such specific elements.

KEY POINTS

In order for a material accurately to simulate the type and percentage of radiation interactions that would occur in a patient, it is necessary for that material to have characteristics similar to that of human tissue, specifically in terms of:

- Atomic number
- Electron density
- Equivalent density and specific gravity.

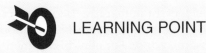

LEARNING POINT

List the types of TEMs used in your own department, and the purpose of each.

TEMs have a variety of functions within the radiotherapy department. These include:

- The production of beam data at the commissioning stage of a new piece of treatment equipment
- Confirmation of in vivo measurements, and therefore confirmation of dosage calculations
- Practising new techniques
- Compensation for irregular contours at kilovoltage and megavoltage energies
- Manipulation of percentage depth doses

- Training purposes
- To enable optimum equipment parameters to be set, e.g. programming of exposure factors for the simulator.

Water is one of the most commonly used TEMs, mainly because it is cheap, readily available and a major constituent of a significant percentage of human tissue types. Water tanks (free standing or attachable to the treatment head) are useful for a number of clinical measurements where it is necessary to move a calibrated detector around within a tissue equivalent environment such as measurements of beam output, dose rate and flatness.

A variety of solid materials (often called solid water) are also used as TEMs for situations where time is a limiting factor, or waterproofing of the dosimeter is unwanted or not feasible. Each solid material TEM is cross-calibrated against a liquid water phantom; this process is evident as an additional correction factor which must be applied to the resultant meter reading. Commonly used materials include polystyrene, Perspex® (PMMA), wax, polymerised rubber in slabs or moulded onto bone, and muscle, tissue and bone analogues.

UNITS OF DOSE

Within the field of radiotherapy, two physical quantities are used as a measure of radiation: kerma and absorbed dose. For clinical dosimetry measurements, kerma is the preferred unit of measurement when taking measurements in air. However, of paramount interest to the radiotherapy specialist is the quantification of how much radiation is absorbed in the patient within the planning target volume and nearby critical structures. Water has long been considered representative of soft tissue, and so the concept of absorbed dose to water is used when dosimetry measurements are made by placing a dosimeter within a TEM such as water.

Exposure

When X- or gamma rays interact in a volume of air, excitation and ionisation of the air molecules occurs. Consequently, the air can conduct electrical current. If the electrical conductivity of this air is measured, a value for the quantity of radiation causing the ionisation is obtained. This value is referred to as a measure of exposure, where

$$\text{Exposure } (X) = \frac{Q}{m} \text{ coulombs per kilogramme (C kg}^{-1})$$

Q is defined as a measure of the total electrical charge of one sign, produced in a small volume air of mass m, when all the electrons liberated by the incident X- or gamma rays are completely stopped within the defined volume of air.

This unit of measurement may only be used for X- and gamma rays, and is defined only in an air medium. It cannot be used for any other types of radiation or materials. Consequently, exposure is not a value commonly used in radiotherapy departments, and something known as the absorbed dose in air (or air kerma) is more frequently employed.

The principle of ionisation of air is the fundamental principle underlying the operation of the ionisation chamber. Strictly speaking, exposure is a measurement which may only be obtained when true electronic equilibrium is achieved. In this manner it is then possible to say that all the energy deposited in the air by the secondary electrons has been measured, and only then is it appropriate to convert the reading of exposure to absorbed dose in the patient.

The old unit of exposure was known as the roentgen, where $1R = 2.58 \times 10^{-4}$ C kg^{-1}.

Absorbed dose

This is the amount of energy absorbed from the incident beam by a medium as a result of ionising radiation passing through that medium.

$$\text{Absorbed dose } (D) = \frac{E}{m} \text{ grays (Gy), or joules per kilogramme (J kg}^{-1})$$

where E is the energy absorbed by a medium of mass m. This unit of dose is applicable to all ionising radiations, can still be used where electronic equilibrium does not exist, and is directly related to the resultant radiation side-effects.

At megavoltage X-ray energies, the primary interaction process in tissue is Compton scatter (Ch. 1). When the incident X-ray interacts with an atom of the absorbing medium, it ejects an electron from the outer electron orbit of that atom. This process causes the incident X-ray to lose energy and be scattered away from the interaction point on a path different to its initial course. The ejected electron is termed the recoil electron, and this particle has significant kinetic energy. It therefore has the capability of travelling away from the point (and volume) of interaction, and maintains the potential to interact with other atoms of the medium in either a radiative or a collisional manner (Ch. 7). Each subsequent interaction will mean that energy is lost from the recoil electron.

The dose absorbed by the medium – in a specific volume of tissue – will equal the energy attenuated from the incident X-ray beam providing that all the recoil electrons produced in this specific volume deposit all of their energy within the same volume (this is assuming that the product(s) of all radiative or collisional interactions are also absorbed within the same volume).

If the recoil electrons have enough energy to travel out of the volume of interest, as happens at megavoltage X-ray beam energies, then the absorbed dose in that particular volume will be less than the total energy attenuated from the incident X-ray beam. A prime example of this is the concept of the 'build up effect' (Ch. 5), which occurs at megavoltage energies. The absorbed dose at the skin surface is relatively small because only a few X-ray interactions happen in the first few layers of the skin. Consequently only a small number of recoil electrons are initially set into motion. At an increasing depth, more and more recoil electrons are produced. This process continues until the recoil electron intensity is balanced by increasing attenuation of the incident X-ray beam by the absorbing medium, and the influence of the inverse square law. This process results in the dose maximum from each individual treatment field being delivered below the skin surface, at a depth characteristic of the energy of the incident radiation beam. This is a positive feature of megavoltage beams, since the resultant skin reaction the patient must endure is significantly less than would occur if the treatment had been delivered at a kilovoltage energy, where the dose maximum is on the skin surface.

The old unit of absorbed dose was the rad (r), where 100 r = 1 gray (Gy).

Kerma

This acronym stands for the kinetic energy released per unit mass. It is the energy that is imparted to a medium, which may then subsequently be deposited at a specific point in tissue, thereby giving rise to a value of absorbed dose at that point (Graham 1996).

$$\text{Kerma} = \frac{E_{tr}}{m} \text{ grays or J kg}^{-1}$$

where E_{tr} is the energy transferred from the uncharged ionising radiation (the X-ray) to the

LEARNING POINT

The difference between measurements of kerma and absorbed dose can be seen in Figure 2.13 as a comparative illustration of absorbed dose and kerma values measured at 100 kVp and 4 MeV X-rays. For a specific depth, at 100 kVp the two dose values are coincident because the energy attenuated from the beam is absorbed within the initial interaction volume. However, in the megavoltage range the recoil electrons have increased energy, and therefore travel away from the point of initial interaction. This is particularly evident in the build-up region.

Question
Outside of the build-up region of the 4 MeV graph, for a specific depth in tissue why is the value of absorbed dose greater than the value of kerma?

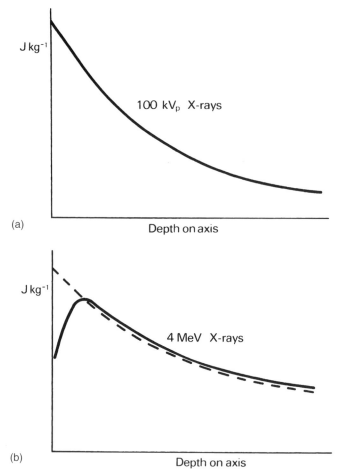

Figure 2.13   Kerma (broken line) and absorbed dose (solid line) for **(a)** 100 kVp diagnostic beam and **(b)** 4 MeV therapy beam (from Graham 1996, with permission).

charged particle (recoil electron), the latter being the result of the ionising radiation interaction process that the X-ray undergoes within the medium of interest. Because kerma gives a measure of dose (Gy) at the point where energy is transferred from the X-ray to the recoil electron – therefore prior to the recoil electron undergoing any subsequent interactions – it is a dose value that includes any energy the recoil electron may later lose owing to processes such as bremsstrahlung, characteristic radiation and fluorescence. Kerma is a concept used only in relation to an X-ray field, and is specific to the medium of interest.

CONVERSION OF EXPOSURE TO ABSORBED DOSE

In order to obtain a value of absorbed dose, it is usually necessary to start with a radiation quantity value that a radiation monitor can detect. This is usually exposure, and as indicated above:

$$\text{Exposure } (X) = \frac{Q}{m} \text{ C kg}^{-1}$$

This is the value of the charge released as ionisations per unit mass of the detector medium – usually air when considering measurements made with an ionisation chamber. In order to calculate the amount of radiation that caused this number of ionisations, it is important to know the amount of energy deposited in the air volume. This is calculated from a knowledge of the charge produced per unit mass of air (X), and the energy required to produce a single unit of charge, the latter being indicated by the following equation:

The energy deposited in air per coulomb of

charge (of one polarity) released $= \left[\dfrac{W}{e} \right]_{air} JC^{-1}$

where W (eV per ion pair) is the mean energy required to produce an ion pair in air, and e is the charge on each electron.

Consequently the absorbed dose in air is then given by the following:

$$D_{air} = X \left[\frac{W}{e} \right]_{air} Gy$$

The final step is to then convert to a value of absorbed dose in tissue. The energy absorption characteristics per $m^2 \, kg^{-1}$ of material, at a specific energy, is unique for each and every absorbing medium. Therefore the ratio of absorbed dose between air and tissue can be represented by the ratio of mass absorption coefficients (see p. 4, and Stanton & Stinson 1996) for each medium; such coefficients describe the probability of energy absorption within a specific medium as a result of various X-ray interaction processes (Cherry & Duxbury 1998, Metcalfe et al 1997, Graham 1996, Stanton & Stinson 1996):

$$\frac{D_{tissue}}{D_{air}} = \left[\frac{(\mu_a / \rho)_{tissue}}{(\mu_a / \rho)_{air}} \right]$$

Therefore,

$$D_{tissue} = D_{air} \left[\frac{(\mu_a / \rho)_{tissue}}{(\mu_a / \rho)_{air}} \right]$$

where (μ_a / ρ) describes the mass energy absorption coefficients of air and tissue.

Exposure can continue to be measured and therefore absorbed dose calculated in this manner up to approximately 2 MeV. At this point it becomes increasingly difficult to maintain electronic equilibrium while still ensuring that the monitor is a practical device for clinical use, and the accurate calculation of absorbed dose from exposure readings becomes no longer feasible (Cherry & Duxbury 1998). From this energy point onwards, the Bragg–Gray cavity theory (see below) must be applied in order to estimate absorbed dose in the patient from clinical measurements.

Bragg–Gray cavity theory

The derivation of absorbed dose from a measurement of exposure, as described above, is based upon the ability to maintain electronic equilibrium within the body of the radiation detector. At megavoltage energies this becomes technically unfeasible owing to the increased energy of the recoil and photoelectrons (also known as secondary electrons) produced within the wall of the detector.

The alternative proposal is based upon measurement of charge resulting from the irradiation of a tissue equivalent medium which contains a radiation detector. The Bragg–Gray theory operates under the assumption that the detector is small enough to ensure that the magnitude and flow of secondary electrons

 LEARNING POINT

Such calculation of absorbed dose is heavily dependent on the type of medium, and the energy of the incident X-ray beam.

Question
With respect to X-ray interaction processes, discuss how absorbed dose at a specific point within a patient may vary across the energy range 100 kV–25 MV (assuming that all set-up parameters – apart from beam energy – remain constant).

produced in the medium, as a result of irradiation, is unchanged from the pattern that would exist if the detector was not present. This is clearly only going to be the case if the detector has the same characteristics as the medium into which it is placed. If this is so, and under conditions of charged particle equilibrium, the energy lost from these secondary electrons in the air of an ionisation chamber compared to the energy they would lose to tissue is the same as the ratio

of the restricted mass stopping powers $\left[\dfrac{L}{\rho}\right]$ of air

to tissue. Restricted mass stopping powers are a derivation of mass stopping powers of electrons (see Ch. 5), and take into consideration the fact that X-ray interactions in tissue produce a spectrum of secondary electron energies.

Consequently:

Absorbed dose to the material $(D_{med}) = D_{air}\left[\dfrac{L}{\rho}\right]$

(Metcalfe et al 1997, Kember 1994).
In order for this theory to hold true, it is also important to assume the following:

- The direct interaction of X-rays with the air in the ionisation chamber is negligible
- All ion pairs produced in the ionisation chamber are the result of secondary electrons arising in the medium into which the ionisation chamber has been placed. Those electrons then enter the ionisation chamber and ionise the air within
- The medium of interest is uniform in nature, and is irradiated by a uniform intensity of X-rays
- Charged particle equilibrium exists in the absence of the ionisation chamber
- The secondary electrons lose energy by transferring a small amount of energy during a large number of interactions.

Corrections to this equation are also needed to account for varying sizes of ionisation chamber that may be used. Additionally, further correction is required because consideration is not given to the fact that a secondary electron may

have enough energy to produce a further electron (known as a delta ray) with the capability of causing further air ionisations. This latter point is significant because the Bragg–Gray equation, as written above, assumes that energy of the secondary electron is dissipated at the point of each of its interactions.

Clinical codes of practice (CoP), produced by the Institute of Physics in Engineering and Medicine (IPEM), exist to ensure consis-tency across the UK in how absorbed dose to water should be calculated from measurements of kerma and exposure. Specific details of each of the recommended codes for super-ficial and orthovoltage therapy, megavoltage X-ray and electrons can be obtained from the documents listed in the recommended reading section. Codes relating to the calculation of absorbed dose at megavoltage X-ray energies are highlighted below to emphasise the coexistence of two separate but equally acceptable methods.

In the megavoltage energy range there are currently two recommended methods for deriving absorbed dose to water. The first is the code of practice based upon the National Physical Laboratory (NPL) 2 MV air kerma calibration service (HPA 1983), and the second is based upon the NPL absorbed dose calibration service (IPEMB 1996).

Code of practice based upon the NPL 2 MV air kerma calibration service

Absorbed dose to water $(D_w) = 1.142 \times R \times N_k \times C_\lambda$

N_k is the calibration factor converting the instrument reading, R, to kerma for a beam of 2 MV X-rays or ^{60}Cobalt, and C_λ is a conversion factor relating to the radiation quality of interest. This latter factor also corrects for the displacement of the tissue equivalent material by the ionisation chamber, the energy deviation from the calibration energy, and the lack of equivalence of the clinical ionisation chamber to that 'perfect' chamber required by the Bragg–Gray theory.

Code of practice based upon the NPL absorbed dose calibration service

$$D_w = R \times N_D$$

R_D is the calibration factor required to convert the instrument reading, R, to absorbed dose in water. Such factors are provided by the NPL for a range of energies, and therefore an energy correction factor is unnecessary when collecting readings within this energy range.

PRINCIPLES OF MONITOR UNIT CALCULATIONS

For a specific set of beam parameters, there are many methods of calculating the required number of monitor units necessary to deliver a prescribed tumour dose to a patient. These are covered comprehensively in Metcalfe et al (1997), Stanton & Stinson (1996) and Washington & Leaver (1996). Many variables must be considered when deriving the required monitor units, and the very best teacher of this subject can be found in every radiotherapy department – the radiotherapy radiographer. Use this resource wisely, and hopefully you will then not only be able to carry out such calculations with accuracy and confidence, but you will also:

- Understand why such calculation data may be presented in a variety of formats
- Appreciate the need for effective methods of checking completed calculations
- Understand how the basic monitor unit calculation will vary for extended SSD (source to skin distance) treatments, or fields with irregular beam shapes.

This section presents the very minimum of factors to be considered when attempting to calculate monitor units (linear accelerator) and treatment times ([60]Cobalt). Kilovoltage calculations will not be addressed here.

Quantities used in treatment calculations

Distance related terminology

Focus to skin distance (FSD) is the distance measured from the focal spot of the machine to

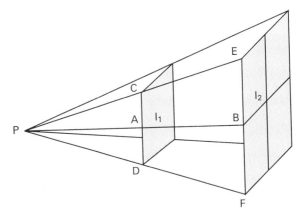

Figure 2.14 The inverse square law. Radiation intensity at I_2 is spread over four times the area of I_1, therefore the intensity at I_2 is one quarter of the intensity at I_1 (from Graham 1996, with permission).

the skin surface of the patient. Source to skin distance (SSD) is a comparable term.

Focus to axis distance (FAD) is the distance from the focal spot of the machine to the isocentre, and is also referred to as the source to axis distance (SAD).

Inverse square law. This is an important concept. With reference to Figure 2.14, and assuming that there is no significant scatter coming from the head of the treatment machine or absorption in air, the intensity of radiation I_2 emitted from a point source, P, will be inversely proportional to the square of the distance, d, from the radiation source:

$$\text{Intensity of the radiation } (I_2) \propto \left(\frac{1}{d^2}\right)$$

It is important to apply this principle when machine output data are being used at a distance other than the one they were collected at (i.e. for FSDs shorter or longer than the traditional 100 cm). For example:

If the output from a 10×10 cm linear accelerator field is 2.5 Gy min^{-1} at 100 cm, what is the output at 150 cm?

$$\text{Output at 150 cm} = 2.5 \times \frac{(100)^2}{(150)^2}$$
$$= 1.1 \text{ Gy min}^{-1}$$

Machine output and output correction factor

This is the dose rate of the machine under reference beam parameters. It is usually measured in air for kilovoltage machines, and in a tissue equivalent material for megavoltage machines – usually being expressed in terms of Gy per monitor unit (linear accelerator), Gy min^{-1} (^{60}Cobalt), or C/kg/min (exposure) at the dose maximum position of the beam.

Clinical treatment set-ups rarely use these reference parameters, and so an output correction factor needs to be applied to the output factor to take into account the changes to machine output for differing collimator settings. This is usually known as the output correction factor.

For ^{60}Cobalt calculations, output will vary as a result of the decay of the source. It is really only appropriate for each individual department to decide a policy for output correction, but decay is approximately 1% per month, and for an extended course of treatment it is not unusual to see the output and therefore time calculation corrected after 30 days.

The equivalent square of a rectangular field. A rectangular field will produce less backscatter (see below) along the central axis of the beam than will a square field of the same area. Most beam data are produced for square fields only, and if the calculation was based on the square field of the same area as the rectangle being used for treatment, the patient would receive the incorrect dose.

Consequently, when looking up the equivalent square of a field, the user is actually looking up the equivalent square of a smaller field – in other words, the square field that will produce the same amount of backscatter on the central axis as the rectangle being used for treatment.

Standard tables of equivalent squares are frequently used. However, backscatter is heavily dependent on the collimator design. If this is not accounted for by other aspects of beam data, it may be appropriate to have equivalent square tables for each accelerator produced by a different manufacturer. A rule of thumb

for calculating the equivalent square is as follows:

$$\text{Equivalent square} = \frac{2(AB)}{(A+B)}$$

where A and B are the length of each side of the rectangle being used for treatment.

Field size. This is defined as the width between the 50% isodose lines at the depth of dose maximum, for an FSD of 100 cm. Occasionally a variable of this may be used that defines the field size as the distance between the 80% isodose lines at the depth of dose maximum for an FSD of 100 cm.

The isodose curve. This is a graphical representation of the distribution of dose within a uniform absorber such as a radiotherapy phantom. Points of equal dose are joined together to present a 2D image, usually along the central axis of the beam. Images of these can be found in the linear accelerator, ^{60}Cobalt and kilovoltage chapters (Chs. 5, 6 and 7).

Patient attenuation factors

Percentage depth dose. Figure 2.15 illustrates the dose at any point within a phantom, P_2, as a percentage of the maximum dose on the central axis of the beam, P_1.

$$\text{Percentage depth dose (\%DD)} = \frac{P_2}{P_1} \times 100\%$$

The central axis depth dose is the %DD as measured along the central axis of the beam. %DD may be measured at a number of sites away from both of the central axes, and in this situation it is usually referred to as an off axis %DD.

Central axis depth dose is a useful concept when wishing to compare different energies or types of ionising radiations, particularly when aiming to select an energy that will deliver a specific percentage depth dose at a point of interest.

Tissue air ratio. As a concept, percentage depth is dependent on FSD. Whilst this can be corrected for fairly simply by the use of an inverse square law correction factor, it becomes tedious when treating three or more fields. Consequently,

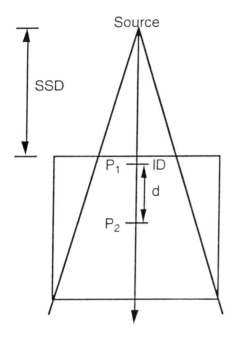

Figure 2.15   Depth dose definition. Dose at point $P_1(d_{max})$ is compared with dose at depth d, point P_2 (from Stanton & Stinson 1996, with permission).

LEARNING POINT

Percentage depth dose (%DD) is a factor commonly employed in FSD calculations, and is dependent upon the following factors:

- Field size
- FSD
- Type and energy of radiation
- Position in the beam
- Depth of the point of interest.

Question
Explain how percentage depth dose varies with each of the parameters listed above.

the tissue air ratio factor (TAR) is used for calculations where the FSD is constantly changing – i.e. the isocentric set-up. This factor accounts for the amount of attenuation caused by the presence of the patient, for each treatment field.

With reference to Figure 2.16, the TAR is a ratio of dose measured at a point, P, in a phantom, against that same point when the patient is not there. The distance from the source of radiation to the measurement point stays constant between both measurements.

$$TAR = \frac{\text{dose at point P in the phantom}}{\text{dose at point P in air}}$$

When the TAR is measured as a ratio of points at the depth of the dose maximum of a beam, it is also known as the backscatter factor, or peak scatter factor.

Tissue maximum ratio.   The most commonly used patient attenuation factor is the tissue maximum ratio TMR. Unfortunately, above approximately 2 MeV it becomes very difficult to obtain an accurate in air reading as required by the TAR concept. This is mainly because the build-up cap begins to attenuate the beam.

The TMR does not require the collection of an in air reading, because it compares two points within the patient (see Fig. 2.17).

For both readings, the FAD remains constant between the source of radiation and the measurement points P_1 and P_2 and the only variable is the amount of tissue equivalent material sitting above the measurement points.

$$TMR = \frac{\text{dose at depth of interest} - P_1}{\text{dose at } d_{max} - P_2}$$

Tissue phantom ratios are also in frequent use, and these are identical in principle to the TMR, apart from the fact that the readings are a comparison to a point other than the dose maximum of the beam. Occasionally the TMR is referred to as the maximum tissue phantom ratio (MTPR).

Percentage backscatter.   When measuring dose at a point in a tissue equivalent material, it must be remembered that values obtained are as a result of primary beam radiation and scattered radiation. This factor is an important concept in dosimetry, and the backscatter correction factor

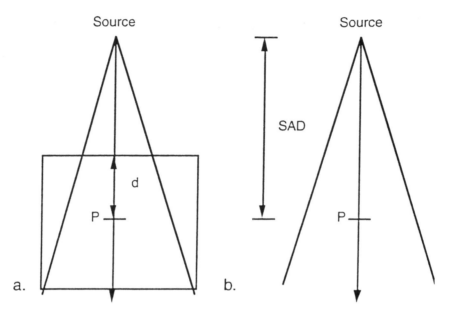

Figure 2.16   Tissue air ratio (from Stanton & Stinson 1996, with permission).

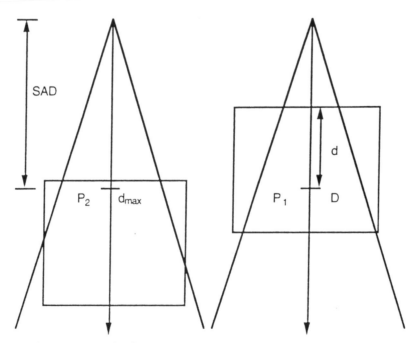

Figure 2.17   Tissue maximum ratio. In this factor, the ratio calculated is between two measurements in a phantom – one at depth and the other at d_{max}. The measurement points P_1 and P_2 are both at the same distance from the source (from Stanton & Stinson 1996, with permission).

accounts for radiation that is scattered back to the central axis of the beam when readings are taken in a tissue equivalent material. Its magnitude is influenced by:

- Area irradiated
- Thickness of underlying tissue
- Energy of radiation
- Field shape.

The backscatter factor is very similar to the concept of TAR in that they are both a ratio of readings. If these readings are taken at the dose maximum of the beam (i.e. one taken at the dose maximum point in a phantom, and the second taken at that same point when the patient is not there), then they are identical. However, this parallel only exists for a TAR measured at this dose maximum; for any other TAR it is important to include a backscatter correction factor in the calculation.

TMRs, being measured at the dose maximum, are readings taking into consideration full backscatter conditions, so when TMRs are used in a calculation, there is no need to use backscatter factors as well.

Accessory equipment attenuation factors

Any device that is placed in the path of the beam will attenuate, to varying degrees, the amount of radiation that reaches the patient. This means that correction factors must be produced for equipment such as wedges, compensators, secondary electron filters and the trays that each of these devices may need to be mounted upon.

The correction factor is simple in that it is obtained as a ratio of measurements of the amount of radiation intensity reaching a particular point when the device is in the path of the beam, and repeating the measurement when the device is not there. Often this factor will change for changing field size, energy and type of radiation.

The calculation process

Only isocentric monitor unit calculations will be presented here.

The method is as follows:

1. Calculate daily tumour dose per field, taking into account weightings where appropriate (see below)
2. Work out the equivalent square for each collimator setting
3. For each field depth, look up factors (using the equivalent square value) for output correction factor and TMR
4. Find factors for beam modifying devices such as wedges, compensators and shielding tray
5. Use the appropriate equation to establish monitor unit or timer settings for each field.

Linear accelerator

Daily monitor units for field of depth $\times$ cm =

$$\frac{TD}{output \times OF \times TMR \times CF}$$

where

TD	=	daily prescribed tumour dose for field of depth = $\times$ cm
Output	=	output in Gy μ^{-1} for reference beam parameters
OF	=	output factor for equivalent field size of interest
TMR	=	TMR for equivalent field size of interest, and depth of $\times$ cm
CF	=	any correction factors for lead shielding trays, wedges, etc., assuming such factors each have a value of less than unity

What if each field is not equally weighted with respect to dose? Assume the following scenario:

A total of 2 Gy is to be delivered, each fraction, from the three fields indicated in Figure 2.18; the contribution of each field to the isocentre may be calculated as follows:

Total weighting = field 1 (0.9) + field 2 (0.7) +
field 3 (0.6)
= 2.2

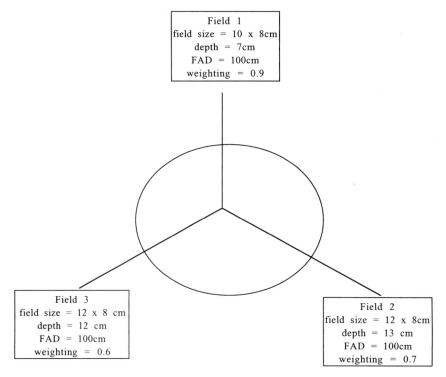

Figure 2.18 An example of potential beam weightings.

Contribution from

Field one $= \dfrac{0.9}{2.2} \times 2\,\text{Gy}$

$= 0.82\,\text{Gy per fraction}$

Field two $= \dfrac{0.7}{2.2} \times 2\,\text{Gy}$

$= 0.64\,\text{Gy}$

Field three $= \dfrac{0.6}{2.2} \times 2\,\text{Gy}$

$= 0.54\,\text{Gy}$

^{60}Cobalt

The calculation of required time is simply the dose divided by the dose rate, i.e.:

$$\text{time} = \frac{TD}{output \times OF \times TAR \times CF}\ \text{mins}$$

where
OF = output factor for equivalent square of collimator setting, in Gy min^{-1}
TAR = TAR for equivalent square of collimator setting (assumes a TAR at dose maximum)

It may also be appropriate to add in a source transit factor – if this is the case the product of the above equation should be multiplied by this factor.

TREATMENT PLANNING AND THE PRODUCTION OF AN ISODOSE DISTRIBUTION

This particular section will not address dose computation models of X-ray and electron beams, or how the treatment planning computer uses such mathematical techniques; this area is adequately covered by Conway (in Cherry & Duxbury 1998), Metcalfe et al (1997) and Bruno

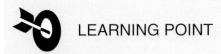

LEARNING POINT

Compare and contrast the concepts discussed in this section with those used in the kilovoltage calculations used in your own department.

Questions
How do kilovoltage time calculations differ from their megavoltage equivalent?

Where is there parity in the method used?

(in Washington & Leaver 1996). Instead, the focus will be on the isodose distribution itself: its production, criteria of acceptability and related quality assurance issues.

An isodose distribution is a two-dimensional graphical presentation of the patterns of dose for a particular set of beam parameters, normally produced through the centre of the planning target volume. Additionally, distributions are also produced in other regions of dosimetric interest, for example at superior and inferior treatment field borders when separation changes throughout the treatment volume are significant.

Treatment volume definitions

In an attempt at standardisation of terminology, ICRU (1993) Report No. 50 provides definitions for a series of concepts relating to the prescribing, recording and reporting of X-ray beam therapy. The main ones of relevance are defined below (terms 1–3 are defined in Ch. 1, see p. 19):

1. Gross tumour volume (GTV)
2. Clinical target volume (CTV)
3. Planning target volume (PTV)
4. Treated volume: the volume enclosed by an isodose surface that is selected and specified by a radiation oncologist as being appropriate to achieve the purpose of treatment (ICRU 1993, p. 16)

5. Irradiated volume: the tissue volume that receives a dose that is considered significant in relation to normal tissue tolerance (ICRU 1993, p. 16)

6. Organs at risk: those normal tissues whose radiation sensitivity may significantly influence the treatment planning and/or prescribed dose (ICRU 1993, p. 18).

Producing the isodose distribution

The first stage of this process is the collation of all required localisation information. This may be CT scans, orthogonal radiographs or DRRs. It is important to initially review the data, and confirm that everything refers to the patient in question, and that information such as prescribed dose, definition of the CTV and required shielding are clearly indicated.

Programming of patient data

Inputting patient data into the treatment planning computer is relatively straightforward with the technology currently at our disposal. CT images can be directly input via a direct computer link, or by the use of a film scanner (which requires correction for image scale). If such a scanner is unavailable, digitising tablets can be used to contour in the patient data.

The next stage is to create patient contours, typically of the body outline, clinical target volume, and critical structures such as spinal cord, rectum, eye, lung, etc. Ideally these should be obtained for as many CT slices as possible. Each contoured organ must have an electron density allocated to it, indicating to the computer algorithm that this particular structure will attenuate the radiation beam in a specific manner.

Isodose distribution

Prior to commencing a treatment plan, it is important to identify exactly what such a plan should achieve. Such aims are termed criteria of acceptability, and these may vary tremendously from department to department. However, each set of criteria will make reference to the following areas, listed in order of priority:

- Dose uniformity across the PTV. ICRU (1993) indicate a range of + 7% to – 5%, and Bomford et al (1993) suggest + 5% to – 5%. In order for this to be achieved, the size, shape and position of the PTV must therefore match that of the CTV.
- Dose to organs at risk must fall within their tolerance levels.
- Hot spots – a definition of a hot spot needs to be unambiguous in terms of size and dose.
- Position of reference point that may be used for normalisation and possibly also dose prescription. ICRU (1993) recommended that this point be representative of the dose throughout the PTV, easily and unambiguously defined, should not be in a region of steep dose gradients, and should be in a position where the dose may be accurately determined.
- Documentation of plan data and patient details should be in the department format and style.
- The plan should be prescribed to the point agreed for that specific treatment site, maximum and minimum tumour doses should be clearly indicated, and the consultant signature should be apparent on the distribution and the treatment sheet.

Isodose plan production for external beam radiotherapy usually commences with the selection of appropriate collimator settings and a technique (in contrast to the concept of inverse treatment planning, see Ch. 5), which is ideally only to be used as a starting point.

The incorporation of wedges to attenuate the isodose profile to match the desired CTV is common. A wedge angle may be defined in one of two ways. It is either the angle which the 50% isodose line makes with the central axis of the beam, or it is the angle defined at a specific depth (usually 10 cm).

Beam weighting (adjusting the relative contribution of one or more fields to the treatment dose) may be applied in order to improve the position of isodoses in relation to the PTV.

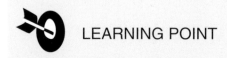

LEARNING POINT

Question
How does this process differ for brachytherapy patients?

Weighting adjusts the dose gradient to improve uniformity of dose around a treatment volume, or to modify the dose outside this volume.

Plan normalisation is where the radiographer allocates a point on the plan to receive 100% of the dose – typically the isocentre, dose maximum or some other predetermined point. This is carried out usually for multiple beam plans, where the summation of isodoses can be in the region of 300–400% for a three or four field plan. This is confusing to the eye, particularly if you then want to ensure that a particular isodose line encompasses the CTV.

Throughout this planning process, the radiographer has the opportunity to use a number of treatment planning tools.

Dose volume histograms (DVHs) present to the observer a graphical representation of the dose distribution data with respect to specific anatomy. The volume or percentage of the total organ volume that receives a specific dose value in a given range of dose levels can then be easily seen for the CTV or organs at risk. Many planning computer packages provide the opportunity to superimpose DVHs of organs and regions of one plan, and to compare them against that of another plan of the same area using a different technique.

Beam's eye view (BEV). This is a particular view of the distribution, with the observer placed to look directly at the PTV from a plane perpendicular to the beam axis. This allows evaluation of the extent of CTV coverage.

3D view. This is a computer generated 3D image of the CTV, organs at risk and body contours. The observer rotates the image using the computer mouse, and can therefore evaluate dose distribution in 360°.

Quality assurance procedures

The treatment planning computer is an integral part of the treatment process, and therefore must be included within the department quality programme. IPEMB (1994) identifies the following areas where potential errors may enter the planning process:

1. *Localisation*. This is the stage where the patient data used as a basis of the isodose plan are produced. Misidentification of the tumour volume, inaccurate data labelling and incorrect or inadequate prescribed fractionation are just some of the potential sources of error.

2. *Receipt and entry of patient data into the treatment planning computer*. Unless the user is comprehensively trained in the complexities of his or her own particular planning system, it is very easy to make errors in scaling CT scans, annotation of scan orientation, allocation of electron density, contouring of structures, etc.

3. *Use of machine data*. There are potential inherent errors in the initial collection of the beam data that are used in the production of the isodose distribution, as well as in how the data are then programmed into the system. How the computer then uses the data to calculate the position of each and every isodose (i.e. the algorithm) is another programming aspect which needs careful consideration.

4. *Verification of calculation accuracy*. There are a number of ways in which the user can confirm the accuracy of the computer calculations. Cross comparison of plans with another centre, or against data verification packages, is one way. Alternatively, hand calculation of point data is equally feasible.

5. *Production of the plan hard copy*. The hardware of the system (plotter, printer, VDU, digitiser, etc.) also contains potentially hidden sources of error. For example, it is relatively simple to check the hard copy against a lifesize patient contour by superimposition of one on top of the other (assuming comparable scaling). Alternatively, digitising in graph paper and verifying the product with a ruler achieves the same end.

6. *Transfer of data to the treatment unit after consultant approval of the treatment plan*. If data are not produced in a format that is compatible with the intended use, then interpretation errors are likely. Consistency is necessary in terminology used, treatment sheet format and documentation of methods of monitor unit calculations.

The above list in designed to stimulate thinking as to where errors are likely to occur. Clearly this is very dependent upon the path that patients and their data typically take from localisation to eventual delivery of treatment. The type of treatment planning system, the variety of health professionals involved in this process, and the efficacy of departmental communication pathways are also of significance. The quality assurance programme developed for the treatment planning system must therefore take all of these aspects into consideration. Further discussion on the principle of quality assurance can be found in Chapter 4.

MANIPULATION OF DOSE AND FRACTIONATION SCHEDULES

The aim of radiotherapy is to eradicate tumour cells by the delivery of a lethal dose of radiation, whilst preserving normal tissue structure and function. Unfortunately the total dose that can be delivered to a tumour is determined by the presence of any dose limiting normal tissue structure that may be in the path of the beam.

The way that tumours and normal tissue respond to ionising radiation is the domain of the radiobiologist, and an in-depth study of the subject of radiobiology is suggested prior to reading this section; authors such as Steel (1997), Tubiana et al (1990) and Hall (1988) address this subject well. It is appropriate, however, to discuss in this text the manipulation of fractionation schedules. Within one radiotherapy department it is not uncommon to see a range of dose and fractionation schedules for a particular disease site. It is of interest to compare such schedules in terms of tumour control and normal tissue complication rates, as well as to consider how fractionation and dose may be changed when a patient is, for some unavoidable reason, unable to continue with the dose prescription initially planned.

The biological effects on tissue from fractionated radiotherapy depend upon the 'four Rs' of radiobiology: repopulation by surviving cell populations, redistribution within the cell cycle, repair of cellular injury, and reoxygenation of the tumour cells.

Repopulation. Repopulation of normal tissue and tumour cells may occur during a course of fractionated radiotherapy. Normal body cells exhibit this feature as a natural response to injury, but it also occurs in some tumour cells during a protracted course of radiotherapy. Allowing normal tissues to repopulate between fractions means that the long-term side-effects of radiotherapy are reduced. Whilst it is a disadvantage for this to happen in the tumour cell population, the rate of repopulation in this group is slower than for cells of normal tissue.

Redistribution. Cell populations that survive previous fractions of radiotherapy are likely to have been in the more radioresistant (e.g. late S phase) stages of the cell cycle during irradiation. Selective killing therefore occurs with each fraction, so that immediately after irradiation the remaining cells attempt to redistribute themselves into the mitotic phase of the cell cycle in order to undergo repopulation. Being able to predict when cell populations are in the more radiosensitive (M and G2 phases) stages of the cell cycle could potentially be of tremendous benefit to the radiobiologist, but this characteristic has yet to be fully exploited.

Repair. Repair of cellular injury to normal and tumour cells is completed a few hours after irradiation, with normal cells having the greatest capacity for repair. The ability to repair is oxygen dependent, and this is the basis for explaining why tumour cells do not exhibit the same speed or potential for repair.

Reoxygenation. Reoxygenation, the process whereby tumour cells gain access to previously unobtainable or limited oxygen, occurs only in tumour tissue. As cell kill with low linear energy transfer radiations such as X-rays is dramatically increased in the presence of oxygen owing to the nature of the cell kill mechanisms, if tumour cells have access to more oxygen they are more likely to be destroyed during the next fraction of radiation.

Some of the implications of these four concepts are indicated below (each is a general statement, and it is important to remember that such assumptions may differ depending upon the tumour type and dose and fractionation schedule prescribed):

- A reduction in the number of hypoxic cells within a tumour owing to cell kill and reoxygenation
- Blood vessels that were compressed by tumour growth may reopen allowing oxygen to reach anoxic or hypoxic cells
- Fractionation exploits the difference between the recovery of normal tissue and tumour cells
- Redistribution will sensitise rapidly proliferating cells
- Fractionation may reduce acute radiation side-effects to tolerable levels, and will minimise the severity of chronic radiation side-effects.

A detailed understanding of the implications of the four concepts has led to the derivation of a number of external beam radiotherapy dose and fractionation regimens; some of the more common ones are listed below:

1. *Conventional fractionation.* Radiotherapy is delivered in daily fractions of the order of 1.8–2 Gy, over an extended period of time.

2. *Hyperfractionation.* More fractions are delivered during the time period (by the delivery of more than one fraction per day) indicated above, but the dose per fraction is lowered slightly. This means that the total overall tumour dose is increased.

3. *Accelerated fractionation.* There is minimal change to the total dose and number of fractions in this schedule, but the overall time is dramatically reduced by treating over weekends and during routine service days.

4. *Accelerated hyperfractionation.* This is a hybrid of hyperfractionation and accelerated fractionation. In CHART (continuous hyperfractionated accelerated radiation therapy), patients

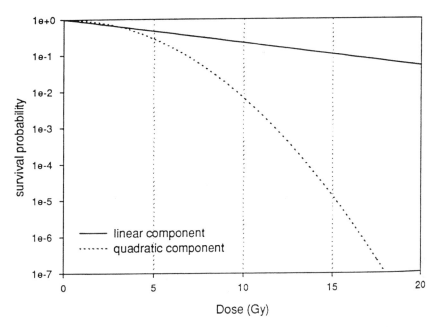

Figure 2.19   An example of a cell survival curve for a single cell population, where alpha and beta components are illustrated separately. Linear component = alpha, quadratic component = beta (from Metcalfe et al 1997, with permission).

are treated three times a day, with a minimum fractionation interval of 6 hours, using lower than conventional fraction sizes, over a total of 12 days.

Tumour control and normal tissue tolerance

Figure 2.19 illustrates the sigmoidal relationship between delivered dose and the probability of tumour control in a tumour cell population. A similar relationship exists between the delivered dose and the incidence of normal tissue complications. The position of these curves on the dose axis is an indication of the sensitivity of the tissue response to radiation, and the steepness of each curve indicates the likely change of response that will accompany an increase or decrease in dose.

The greater the separation of the curves, the larger the therapeutic ratio – i.e. for a set dose of radiation the therapeutic ratio is defined as the probability of curing the tumour against the probability of normal tissue damage.

A number of radiobiological models exist to describe the influence of ionising radiation on living cells; the linear quadratic model is based upon the shape of cell survival curves after irradiation. Figure 2.19 shows a conventional cell survival curve.

Metcalfe et al (1997) and Tubiana et al (1990) then derive the following equation from this curve where:

$S = e^{-\alpha D + \beta D2}$

S = surviving cell fraction

D = dose

α = the size of the initial slope of the cell survival curve, and describes the likely cell kill after a single radiation event (unit = Gy^{-1}

β = the slope of the remaining curve, and describes the cell kill resulting from multiple hits of radiation (unit = Gy^{-2})

Alpha and beta are tissue specific characteristics, and most often the ratio of these two components is used in radiobiology.

Metcalfe et al (1996) describe a derivative of this equation known as the biologically effective dose (BED). This tool is commonly employed to quantify the effect of a fractionation scheme on cell kill. The BED compares the effectiveness of a fractionation schedule against the effectiveness of the same total dose if delivered as a single fraction of radiation, and is written as follows (Metcalfe et al 1996, p. 446):

$$BED = nd\left[1 + \frac{d}{\alpha/\beta}\right]$$

where

n = total number of fractions
d = dose per fraction

This equation can be usefully applied to compensate for a treatment break by changing the daily fractionation to meet the same biological endpoint of the dose and fractionation protocol initially prescribed. Alternatively, it can be used to quantitatively evaluate the therapeutic ratio for a standard dose and fractionation protocol. Derivations of this formula also exist to compensate for tumour growth kinetics and the influence of overall treatment time on the desired biological endpoint.

RECOMMENDED READING

Adeyemi A, Lord J 1997 An audit of radiotherapy patient doses measured with in vivo semiconductors. British Journal of Radiology 70: 399–408

Fraass B A 1998 TG-53 quality assurance for clinical radiotherapy treatment planning. AAPM Refresher Course Handout. San Antonio, Texas

HPA 1983 Revised code of practice for the dosimetry of 2–25 MV X-ray, and of ^{137}Caesium and ^{60}Cobalt gamma ray beams. Physics, Medicine and Biology 28(10): 1097–1104

IAEA 1994 Calibration of dosimeters used in radiotherapy. Technical Report Series No 37. IAEA, Vienna

IPEMB 1994 A guide to commissioning and quality control of treatment planning systems. Report No. 68. Institute of Physics and Engineering in Medicine and Biology, York

IPEMB 1996a The IPEMB code of practice for the determination of absorbed dose for X-rays below 300 kV generating potential. Working party of the Institute of Physics and Engineering in Medicine and Biology. Physics, Medicine and Biology 41: 2605–2625

IPEMB 1996b The IPEMB code of practice for electron dosimetry for radiotherapy beams of initial energy from 2–50 MeV based on an air kerma calibration. Working party of the Institute of Physics and Engineering in Medicine and Biology. Physics, Medicine and Biology 41: 2557–2603

IPSM 1990 Code of practice for high energy photon therapy dosimetry based upon the NPL absorbed dose calibration service. Physics, Medicine and Biology 35(10): 1355–1360

IPSM 1993 Radiotherapy news. Institute of Physical Sciences in Medicine, York

Kron T 1994 Thermoluminescence dosimetry and its applications in medicine. Part 1: Physics, materials and equipment. Australasian Physical and Engineering Sciences in Medicine 17(4): 175–199

Kron T 1995 Thermoluminescence dosimetry and its applications in medicine. Part 2: History and applications. Australasian Physical and Enginering Sciences in Medicine 18(1): 1–25

Royal College of Radiologists 1996 Guidelines for the management of the unscheduled interruption or prolongation of a radical course of radiotherapy. RCR, London

Van Dyk J, Barnett R B, Cygler J E, Shragge P C 1993 Commissioning and quality assurance of treatment planning computers. International Journal of Radiation Oncology, Biology and Physics 26: 261–273

REFERENCES

Ball J, Moore A D 1997 Essential physics for radiographers, 3rd edn. Blackwell Science, Oxford

Bomford C K, Kunkler I H, Sherriff S B (eds) 1993 Walter and Miller's Textbook of radiotherapy: radiation physics, therapy and oncology, 5th edn. Churchill Livingstone, Edinburgh

Cherry P, Duxbury A (eds) 1998 Practical radiotherapy physics and equipment. Greenwich Medical Media, London

Duane S, McEwan M R 1996 Calibration techniques for radiotherapy. RAD Magazine 22(256): 38

Graham D T 1996 Principles of radiological physics, 3rd edn. Churchill Livingstone, Edinburgh

Hall E J 1988 Radiobiology for the radiobiologist, 3rd edn. Lippincott, London

HPA 1983 Revised code of practice of the dosimetry of 2–25 MV X-ray, and of ^{137}Caesium and ^{60}Cobalt gamma ray beams. PMB 28(10): 1097–1104

ICRU 1993 Prescribing, recording and reporting photon beam therapy. ICRU Report No. 50. ICRU, Bethesda

Institute of Physical Sciences in Medicine 1994 Recommendations for the presentation of type test data for radiation protection instruments in hospitals. Report No. 69. IPSM, York

IPEMB 1994 A guide to commissioning and quality control of treatment planning systems. Report No. 68. IPEMB, York

IPEMB 1996 The IPEMB code of practice for electron dosimetry for radiotherapy beams of initial energy from 2–50 MeV based on an air kerma calibration. Working Party of the IPEMB. PMB 41: 2557–2603

Kember N F (ed) 1994 Medical radiation detectors: fundamental and applied aspects. Medical Science Series. Institute of Physics, Bristol

Knoll G F 1989 Radiation detection and measurement, 2nd edn. Wiley and Sons, New York

Leo W R 1994 Techniques for nuclear and particle physics experiments: a how-to approach, 2nd revised edn. Springer-Verlag, Berlin

Meiler R J, Podgorsak M B 1997 Characterisation of the response of commercial diode detectors used for in vivo dosimetry. Medical Dosimetry 22(1): 31–37

Meredith W J, Massey J B 1977 Fundamental physics of radiology. John Wright, Bristol

Metcalfe P, Kron T, Hoban P 1997 The physics of radiotherapy X-rays from linear accelerators. Medical Physics Publishing, Madison

Stanton R, Stinson D 1996 Applied physics for radiation oncology. Medical Physics Publishing, Wisconsin

Steel G S (ed) 1997 Basic clinical radiobiology, 2nd edn. Arnold, London

Thwaites D 1998 Radiotherapy dosimetry: intercomparisons and audits. RAD Magazine 24(280): 35–36

Tubiana M, Dutreix J, Wambersie A 1990 Introduction to radiobiology, translated by Bewley R. Taylor and Francis, London

Washington C M, Leaver D T (eds) 1996 Principles and practice of radiation therapy: physics, simulation and treatment planning. Mosby, St Louis

Williams J R, Thwaites D I (eds) 1993 Radiotherapy physics in practice. Oxford Medical Publications, Oxford

3 Legislation and the principles of radiation protection

CHAPTER CONTENTS

Chapter objectives

On completion of this chapter you should be able to:

- Explain the three key concepts of radiation protection
- Paraphrase the main themes introduced in the 1985 and 1988 Ionising Radiation Regulations
- Propose possible required changes to accelerator working practices once the Health and Safety Commission (HSC) recommendations become legislation
- Define the terms absorbed dose, equivalent dose and effective dose
- Explain the process whereby recommendations from the International Commission on Radiological Protection (IRCP) evolve into UK legislative instruments
- Discuss how the ALARA (as low as reasonably achievable) principle is pursued in the accelerator suite.

INTRODUCTION

The National Radiological Protection Board (NRPB 1994) gives the average yearly dose of background radiation received by the population of the UK as 2.6 mSv – a figure closely supported by Hendee & Edwards (1996). 85% of this results from naturally occurring sources of radiation such as radon gas, gamma rays, cosmic rays, consumer products such as smoke detectors and watches, and food and drink. The remaining

15% arises from artificial sources such as medical investigation or treatment, nuclear discharges, radioactive fallout and occupational exposure. With a growing body of evidence supporting the deleterious effects of even very low amounts of radiation (HSC 1998, Hendee & Edwards 1996, RAD Magazine 1999), it is important to apply the philosophy of radiation protection to each and every accessible source so that individual annual effective dose continues to remain as low as reasonably achievable (ALARA). Currently, radiation protection legislation aims to provide an effective safety standard for radiation workers and the public, without hindering the beneficial applications of ionising radiation. This is achieved through the provision of ionising radiation legislation.

This chapter defines commonly used radiation protection terminology, and discusses in detail the development, content and planned changes to the 1985 and 1988 Ionising Radiation Regulations (IRR 85 and IRR 88). It also reviews the implications of these documents on the design, operation and working practices of a medical linear accelerator. Where radiation protection philosophy for other key pieces of radiotherapy equipment differs significantly from that discussed here, an appropriate subheading is found within the relevant chapter.

RADIATION PROTECTION TERMINOLOGY

Absorbed dose (D_{AB})

The amount of energy deposited, E_D, in a small mass, Δm, by a beam of ionising radiation

$$D_{AB} = \frac{E_D}{\Delta m} \text{ J kg}^{-1}$$

1 J kg^{-1} = 1 gray (Gy)
1 Gy = 100 cGy
1 cGy = 1 rad (non SI unit still in frequent use in North America).

Equivalent dose (D_{EQ})

This unit of dose accounts for the fact that for the same energy different types of ionising radiation

will deposit different amounts of energy in a medium depending upon their specific mass and charge. Consequently each type of radiation is allocated a radiation weighting factor, W_R. Weighting factors can be found in ICRP 73 (1996), and range from a value of 1 for X-rays, gamma radiation and electrons, 20 for alpha particles and an energy dependent value of 5–20 for neutrons.

$$D_{EQ} = D_{AB} \times W_R \text{ sieverts (Sv)}$$

Effective dose (D_{EF})

Different organs exhibit a range of sensitivity to ionising radiation, and consequently each organ of the body is allocated at tissue weighting factor, W_T. These may be found in ICRP 73 (1996).

$$D_{EF} = D_{EQ} \times W_T \text{ sieverts}$$

Stochastic and deterministic radiation side-effects

The occurrence of stochastic side-effects of radiation are predicted by the laws of chance, and there is no safe dose threshold below which such effects do not occur. Whilst the severity of each effect does not increase with dose, its incidence will. They appear in somatic tissue in the form of cancer induction, with a latent period of up to 20 years. Those occurring in germs cells will result in hereditary defects in the offspring, and may be manifested as congenital malformations, or physical and functional impairment. The three principles of radiation protection (see below) are applied where feasible in order to reduce such side-effects to an absolute minimum.

Deterministic side-effects are predictable in that there is a dose threshold below which they will not occur. Typical examples include skin erythema, cataract formation and temporary or permanent sterility. Dose limits are therefore set below the threshold of most deterministic effects.

Half and tenth value layers

The half value layer (HVL) is the thickness of an absorber which will reduce to one half the intensity of radiation incident upon it (see Ch. 7).

The tenth value layer (TVL) is the thickness of an absorber which will reduce the incident radiation intensity by a factor of 10.

Narrow and broad beam spectra

When selecting data regarding the half or tenth value layer of a specific shielding material, it is important to note whether the data were collected under broad or narrow beam conditions.

Narrow beam conditions relate to the situation where the material is subject solely to primary beam radiation, and scatter has been removed by the use of a physical collimator or a device such as a multichannel analyser (MCA).

Where data are collected under broad beam conditions, the absorber is subject to primary and scattered radiation. In this situation the same thickness of absorber becomes less effective than that demonstrated in narrow beam conditions, for the same energy and type of radiation. This is because of the presence of forward scatter which contributes to the primary beam. Broad beam conditions reflect typical working practice, and only data collected under these circumstances should be used in the calculation of clinical radiation barriers.

Primary radiation barrier

This is a barrier which is exposed to radiation emanating directly from the X-ray target and, assuming the ability to perform a gantry rotation of 360°, will include at least four main room surfaces: the floor, the ceiling and two walls. The thickness of each primary barrier must be calculated for the maximum photon energy and dose rate that may be used, with its width determined by the length of the diagonal of the maximum field size.

Secondary radiation barrier

This will receive leakage radiation as well as scatter from the patient, machine or room surface. If designed to attenuate leakage radiation, it will be more than sufficient for the lower energy scattered radiation.

Leakage radiation

In the clinical situation a patient may be subjected to radiation dosage outside a planned treatment volume as a result of leakage and scattered radiation. All radiation escaping from the housing of an accelerator other than through the primary and secondary collimator system is known as leakage radiation, its exposure rate being at a peak for the maximum operating accelerator voltage in X-ray mode. It is likely to be of the same energy as the primary beam and so radiation barriers must be designed taking its presence into consideration. Main causes of leakage include a malfunction in the beam steering or focusing system, or variations in energy of the electrons as they are accelerated along the waveguide, resulting in inadequate focusing and steering.

Leakage through the closed leaves of an independent or symmetric collimator system should not exceed 2% of the central axis dose rate at 1 metre FSD, rising to a maximum of 5% in a multileaf system (Greene & Williams 1997). In the region around the accelerator head, BS 5724 (BSI 1989), paragraph 29.3.3, recommends a maximum limit of 0.5% of the main beam (averaged over 100 cm^2), at a point 1 metre from the path of the electrons. In addition, levels in the patient plane orthogonal to the central axis of the beam, and again averaged over 100 cm^2, should not exceed 0.2%.

Scattered radiation

This is radiation that has undergone a minimum of one interaction (at a point past the target or electron window) in either another part of the treatment head, or the patient, or the surfaces of the room. Whilst of degraded energy and dose rate, at higher energies radiation is classically scattered primarily in a forward direction but uniformly in all directions at lower incident energies. Such a knowledge of scatter characteristics is particularly important for understanding the placement of radiation barriers and for the accurate calculation of barrier thickness.

van der Geissen (1996) acknowledges that different collimator assemblies produce significantly different amounts of scatter due to design variation, but the overall leakage radiation does not tend to exhibit the same fluctuation. Irrespective of manufacturer, BS 4094 Part 2 (BSI 1971) suggests that measured scatter should not exceed 0.1% of the incident radiation per 100 cm^2 of irradiated area.

KEY PRINCIPLES OF RADIATION PROTECTION

In order to address the concept of radiation safety in any environment, the general consensus of opinion is that the following three principles should be applied:

KEY POINTS

- *Justification of practice.* No procedure should be adopted unless the net benefit to the exposed individual or to society outweighs the associated risks of using ionising radiation. This is particularly important when considering screening programmes that employ ionising radiation, or the irradiation of human volunteers for research purposes.
- *Optimisation of protection.* All exposures should remain as low as reasonably achievable, economic and social factors taken into consideration.
- *Implementation of dose limits* for radiation workers and the general public (ICRP 73, 1996).

REGULATORY FRAMEWORK

Since 1950, the primary international radiation protection standards setting body has been an independent organisation known as the International Commission on Radiological Protection (ICRP). The terms of reference of this body are 'to advance for the public benefit the science of radiological protection' (ICRP 1997, Internet reference 1). This is achieved by dealing primarily with basic radiation protection principles and leaving each individual country to construct legislation that incorporates reference to its own social and economic circumstances. The recommendations of the ICRP form the basis of European legislative instruments known as the Basic Safety Standards (BSS) Directive, and the Patient Protection or Medical Exposure Directive. Such directives are developed under the auspices of the 1957 EURATOM Treaty and are binding on the member states of the European Union. Applying to the control of exposure to ionising radiation primarily from artificial sources, the BSS Directive aims to protect the health of workers and the general public against the dangers arising from ionising radiation. The two latest European Union directives are to be implemented into national law by 13 May 2000, and have been produced to ensure that member states incorporate the latest ICRP recommendations (HSC 1998, Moran 1998, ICRP 1996, ICRP 1991).

In the UK the Health and Safety Executive (HSE) is responsible for enforcing and incorporating BSS directives into the national legislatory framework. The statutory instruments known as the Ionising Radiation Regulations are produced by a body of professional organisations headed by the National Radiological Protection Board (NRPB), which reports directly to the HSE.

Minimum standards are then produced for use in the clinical setting by suitably qualified organisations such as the Institute of Physicists and Engineering in Medicine (IPEM), formerly known as the Institute of Physicists and Engineering in Medicine and Biology (IPEMB), the Institute of Physical Sciences in Medicine (IPSM), and the Hospital Physicists Association (HPA). The standard is defined as 'an agreed technical specification, produced by a recognised standardising body, generally based on the results of science, technology and experience, and aimed at the promotion of optimum community benefits' (Lillicrap et al 1998, p. 1225). The IPEM produces its own documentation which recommends minimum performance standards for radiotherapy equipment and which, if followed, allows the radiation user to demonstrate compliance with regulation 33(1) of IRR 85 and regulation 4(3) of IRR 88. Such documentation is also written to conform with the standards laid down by the British Standards Institution (BSI 1989 and 1991), which parallel those laid down on an international level to outline clinically acceptable minimum standards for the installation, operation and maintenance of radiotherapy treatment equipment (IPSM 1988). In the UK, BSI Technical Committee CH/81 is responsible for radiotherapy equipment standards. For further details of the development of standards in the field of radiotherapy, the reader is referred to the paper by Lillicrap and colleagues (1998).

Ionising Radiation Regulations 1985

This statutory instrument became law in the UK on 1 October 1985. It is concerned with the safety of radiation workers and the general public, and implements the 1977 recommendations of ICRP 26 through the incorporation of Directive 80/836/EURATOM (amended by 84/467/EURATOM). Supporting it is an Approved Code of Practice (HSC 1985a) which provides practical guidance in the implementation of these regulations. Of particular relevance to radiotherapy is Guidance Note PM77 (HSE 1998), which gives detailed advice regarding the selection, installation, calibration and replacement of radiotherapy equipment, as well as actions to be taken in the event of the discovery of faulty equipment. The main concepts introduced in IRR 85 are reviewed below:

Restriction of exposure and implementation of dose limits (Regulation 6, 7, 12)

• This requires employers to take all reasonable steps necessary to restrict exposure to employees and other persons from sources of ionising radiation, and reference is made to ways this can be achieved by careful operation and control of such equipment, appropriate shielding and protective clothing, type and position of safety features and warning devices, safe schemes of work, adherence to specified dose limits, and the importance of initial and ongoing training in the principles of radiation protection.

• Annual whole body effective dose limits are described for employees (50 mSv), trainees under 18 years of age (15 mSv), and any other persons (5 mSv); equivalent doses are quoted for female employees of reproductive age (13 mSv in any 3 consecutive months averaged throughout the abdomen), and the abdomen of pregnant females (10 mSv during the declared term of pregnancy). For individual organs and tissues and the lens of the eye, specific equivalent doses are quoted for each category of personnel.

Designation of controlled and classified areas, and classification of personnel (Regulations 8, 9, 13, 16, Schedule 1)

• Defines a controlled area as one where a worker is likely to receive in excess of 3/10 of his or her annual dose limit, or where there is an instantaneous recordable dose rate over 1 minute (IDR) of 7.5 μ Sv h^{-1}. Such limits ensure that the current annual dose limits for radiation workers will not be exceeded for a 40 hour week. Schedule 6 introduces the concept of a time averaged dose rate (TADR) to compensate for the fact that dose rate may not be at a maximum level during a conventional 8 hour working day.

• Supervised areas are those where the worker is likely to receive an annual dose below the limit of a classified worker and above that of the general public – usually in the region of between 1/10 and 3/10 of the annual dose limit of a radiation worker. This equates to an IDR of 2.5 μ Sv h^{-1}. Such areas are likely to be sited around the entrance to a treatment room and the machine controls.

• Each controlled area must be appropriately demarcated using approved signs, warning lights and interlocks, and their extent is to be explicitly described in the local rules.

• Any worker likely to receive 3/10 of his or her annual whole body dose limit is known as a classified radiation worker, and must wear a radiation monitor and undergo annual medical surveillance. Dose records of classified workers must be held by an approved dosimetry service.

• It is recommended that non classified workers who enter controlled areas in their course of work do so under a written scheme of work, and should routinely wear a radiation monitor to ensure that they employ these safe working practices. The wearing of this monitor allows the radiation protection supervisor to subject annual dose records to routine trend analysis. Such analysis will highlight the following: non adherence to or inappropriate schemes of work, ineffective radiation protection, or equipment malfunction not spotted on routine quality assurance testing.

 LEARNING POINT

The study of legislative practice can be extremely tedious unless the concepts are considered in the light of current clinical practice. In other words, you must consider whether these objectives are clinically achievable, and, more importantly, do they work once they are in place?

Questions
What areas of a radiotherapy department are likely to be controlled areas?

Who, from the following, are likely to be classified radiation workers: medical physics staff, patients, radiotherapy radiographers, clinical oncologist, orthopaedic surgeon, nuclear medicine radiographer?

What whole body dose level (Sv) distinguishes a classified radiation worker from a non classified radiation worker?

What are the consequences of not following the advice laid down in the 1985 Ionising Radiation Regulations?

Appointment of a radiation protection adviser (RPA) (Regulation 10)

• Required on designation of a controlled area to ensure that the employer is correctly interpreting the regulations. This person will also be a source of information regarding all health and safety matters concerned with the use of ionising radiation.

• Details of required qualifications, experience and method of appointment of an RPA are described, along with the extent of the role.

Local rules and the appointment of a radiation protection supervisor (RPS) (Regulation 11–15)

• It is the responsibility of the employer to produce written local rules for each source of ionising radiation, setting out safe schemes of work which allow the user to remain in compliance with the requirements of this legislation. The contents of the local rules must be communicated to all employees.

• The role of the RPS, on behalf of the employer, is to implement the procedures documented in the local rules, and to ensure that work in these areas continues to be conducted in this manner. The RPS also monitors the dose records of radiation workers, and investigates any irregularities highlighted within these dose records.

Control of radioactive substances (Regulation 18–21, Schedule 2)

• Where possible, employers must ensure that all radioactive substances used as sources of ionising radiation are appropriately contained at all times, and, where possible, in the form of a sealed source. Leakage tests must be conducted regularly to ensure that the containment remains adequate over time.

• Departments storing radionuclides in excess of those levels documented in column 2 of Schedule 2 must notify the HSE.

• Adequate records must be maintained documenting the quantity and location of each source for at least 2 years from the delivery date, and an additional 2 years from the date of disposal.

Monitoring of ionising radiation (Regulation 24)

- In addition to personnel monitoring, employers must ensure that controlled and supervised areas are adequately monitored to ensure that methods used to restrict exposure to workers is sufficient.
- Such monitors must be appropriately maintained and tested, and records of this testing must be kept for at least 2 years from the date of examination.

Hazard assessment (Regulation 25–27)

- The nature and magnitude of each and every radiation hazard must be identified with the actions to be taken to restrict the occurrence of that hazard. The risk of a hazard occurring must be evaluated. This information should then be communicated to all employees.

Equipment manufacture and maintenance (Regulation 32–34)

- All radiation equipment should be manufactured, installed and maintained in a manner that restricts exposure to employees and other persons.

Ionising Radiation (Protection of Persons Undergoing Medical Examination or Treatment) Regulations 1988 (Statutory Instrument No. 778)

Effective from 1 June 1988, and commonly known as the POPUMET Regulations, this document implements Patient Protection Directive 84/466/EURATOM, which is based on ICRP 26. It relates to the protection of the patient undergoing a medical procedure which results in an exposure to ionising radiation, its

main aim is to limit the exposure of the patient to as low as reasonably achievable. It is accompanied by a detailed set of guidance notes (NRPB 1988) which describe ways in which the user may demonstrate good radiation protection practice.

The main concepts introduced in this document are reviewed below:

Requirement for medical exposures (Regulation 4)

- This requires all medical exposures to be carried out under the responsibility of a clinical director, who must ensure that these regulations are complied with.
- Appropriate guidelines should exist describing acceptable radiation practice, and procedures, at all times, should use the minimal amount of radiation compatible with the desired therapeutic outcome.

Training requirements (Regulation 5–8)

- It is the duty of the employer to ensure that those persons clinically or physically directing radiation exposures are adequately trained, and that records of that training are kept. Minimum training requirements are laid down as a core of knowledge and are contained in the schedule at the end of the document.

Documentation of equipment (Regulation 9)

- An inventory of all medical equipment producing ionising radiation must be kept; the minimum records should include the name of manufacturer and year of manufacture, model and serial numbers, and year of installation.

The provision of expert advice (Regulation 10)

- Those employees clinically or physically directing radiation should have access to a person experienced in the field of radiotherapy physics.

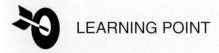

LEARNING POINT

Questions

With respect to the linear accelerator:

Which key personnel clinically and/or physically direct radiation?

What guidelines exist in a radiotherapy department that describe acceptable radiation practice?

How frequently, and in which manner, are these guidelines reviewed to ensure that they remain clinically effective?

Proposals for revised Ionising Radiation Regulations and Approved Code of Practice (HSC 1998)

These proposals aim to raise the profile of the concepts of radiation protection, and by focusing more clearly on these concepts will reduce the need for extensive supporting documentation such as the current Approved Code of Practice. As well as implementing the changes suggested in the BSS Directive described below, it integrates provisions relating to the Outside Workers Directive (90/641/EURATOM), and certain aspects of the Medical Exposures Directive (see below).

The revision arose in response to the following two European directives, which must be implemented in member states by 13 May 2000:

1. The European Union BSS Directive (96/29/EURATOM), which revises document 80/836/EURATOM and gives safety standards for the protection of workers and the general public against ionising radiation (ECCD 1996). The majority of recommendations of this directive are included in the revision to the 1985 IRR.

2. Medical Exposure Directive (97/43/EURATOM) revises the 84/466 EURATOM

Patient Directive dealing with the health protection of patients subject to radiation for diagnostic or treatment purposes (ECCD 1997). The recommendations contained within this directive take into consideration technological and scientific advances in the fields of radiotherapy and diagnostic and radionuclide imaging. The ever increasing use of ionising radiation for medical procedures, particularly with high dose interventional radiology procedures and CT scanning, has meant that patient doses continue to rise. Consequently this directive forms the basis of a revision document to the 1988 IRR.

Both directives evolved from the 1991 and 1996 publications (ICRP 60 and ICRP 73 respectively) which result from a review of the radiation doses received by survivors of the Hiroshima and Nagasaki bombings. This study concluded that the risks to workers of exposure to ionising radiations are significantly higher than previously thought (HSC 1998, Lecomber 1997). At the time of writing, the draft proposals of this new legislation are undergoing review by appropriate UK organisations, and are therefore subject to change. The main concepts presented for review in the revision to the 1985 IRR, and which relate directly to the radiotherapy patient or worker, are as follows:

1. All new classes or types of practice resulting in exposure of the radiation worker, member of the general public or patient to ionising radiation must be justified. The justification procedure must fully consider the medical, economic and social benefit of the new practice in relation to the potential health detriment that it may incur.

2. Current annual dose limits for workers and the general public must be significantly lowered. There are currently two main options under discussion, both of which have direct consequences on the classification of controlled and supervised areas as well as for the classification of radiation workers. The first limits the annual effective dose of a radiation worker to 20 mSv, whilst the second offers a consecutive 5 year dose limit of 100 mSv and requires the worker not to exceed 50 mSv during any one of those 5 years.

3. Following justification of a new class or type of practice, prior authorisation from a competent authority must be obtained before any new practice is introduced. This excludes existing practices unless new evidence should arise indicating that the existing practice is unsafe.

4. The restriction of dose to the general public from patients undergoing diagnostic or therapeutic radionuclide injection. In particular, those individuals who comfort or support any patient undergoing a medical procedure now have any dose received during such procedures credited to their own unlimited medical exposure category, wherein dose constraints are now to be applied. Previously such received dose was included within their annual public dose limit of 5 mSv.

5. Prior authorisation and notification of work involving medical linear accelerators must now be obtained from the secretary of state. Previously this was not a requirement owing to the definition of equipment producing ionising radiation.

6. There is now a detailed requirement for the implementation of a quality assurance programme with equipment used for medical exposures, and the need for the assessment of patient doses resulting from the use of such equipment.

7. The obligation to conduct risk assessment is made clear, and in order to implement adequate measures to restrict staff exposure, as far as reasonably achievable, the identification of the nature and magnitude of any radiological risk is necessary.

8. In the event of accidental or unintended exposure, a clear procedure must now exist to describe subsequent recommended actions following such exposures. Contingency plans indicating prior accident preparedness are also required.

9. Specific areas are indicated where the employer must consult with a 'qualified expert'. Additionally, more explicit statements are made regarding the recommended training and qualifications of such experts.

LEARNING POINT

You will not find the answers to all of these learning points within this chapter. It is important that you read the document and subsequent legislative instruments concerned in detail, and relate these changes to your individual clinical environment. The implications of these proposals will vary significantly depending on individual working practices.

Questions

What are the potential implications of the recommendations on the following:

The definition of controlled and supervised areas?

The use of sealed and unsealed radionuclides in the treatment of patients with cancer?

The implementation of a new external beam radiotherapy technique?

The potential exposure of a relative who physically supports a patient undergoing a procedure on a simulator?

The classification of radiation workers?

The role of the pregnant radiotherapy radiographer?

The external beam radiotherapy treatment of a pregnant patient?

Proposals for the Ionising Radiation (Medical Exposure) Regulations 1999

There are a number of common themes between the BSS and the Medical Exposure Directive; the proposed document echoes this by reiterating the concepts of justification and optimisation of radiation exposure to the patient. The main concepts presented for review are as follows:

• Clinically and physically directing radiation are terms which will no longer be used. Instead the following duty holders are defined: employer, practitioner, referrer and operator. The employer, by the provision of a framework of defined working practices, must ensure that the principles of radiation protection are applied to those employed to allow the safe, efficient and effective delivery of ionising radiation for the medical exposure of patients. The responsibility of the referrer is to ensure that adequate information is passed on to the practitioner, who must justify each medical exposure. Finally, the operator carries out the practical element of the medical exposure.

• Each and every exposure should be justified by the practitioner.

• The principles of optimisation must be applied to diagnostic and therapeutic medical exposures. In particular, all radiotherapy target volumes must be individually planned, in a manner that ensures all tissues outside this target volume receive a dose as low as reasonably practicable and at the same time remaining consistent with the aims of the exposure. Additionally, for diagnostic procedures there is a requirement for the establishment and use of diagnostic reference levels.

• With respect to the diagnostic and therapeutic administration of sealed and unsealed radionuclides, patients (or an appropriate relative or carer) must be provided with written instructions, prior to leaving hospital, explaining in detail how the patient may restrict doses to persons around them. Careful consideration must be given regarding the protection of unborn children and infants where the parent may have undergone medical investigations using ionising radiation.

• Radiation protection in medical and biomedical research, in particular the dose limits extended to those who support and comfort patients, or are volunteers in biomedical research.

• The employer must ensure that a clinical evaluation of the outcome of each medical exposure is carried out and suitably documented, and also that clinical audit is conducted in a manner that reflects national procedures.

• The employer must consult a medical physics expert for every radiotherapeutic practice, and may be consulted in respect to patient dosimetry, dose limitation to the patient, and quality assurance.

• No practitioner or operator may conduct medical exposures without adequate training, and the employer must keep an up-to-date record of all those qualified to carry out medical exposures. Those not trained must be appropriately supervised. Details of the required training are documented in Schedule 2 of this revision.

RADIATION PROTECTION IN PRACTICE

The decision making process

This section concentrates solely on the design of a room to house a linear accelerator safely. It does not address in any detail issues relating to the selection of a new piece of capital equipment (such information can be found in Ch. 6).

Several excellent and current texts (the titles of which are listed in the recommended reading for this chapter) together address in exceptional detail the subject of radiation protection as

KEY POINTS

When calculating the radiation protection necessary to comply with the Ionising Radiation Regulations, the primary clinical considerations are as follows:

▦ What is the available capital?

▦ What is the maximum photon energy of the accelerator?

▦ Will the accelerator be sited in an existing room?

▦ Is a totally new room required?

▦ Will neutrons be produced during accelerator operation?

▦ Ensuring effective communication between the members of the multidisciplinary design team.

applied to a radiotherapy department, and the reader is strongly encouraged to consult these works whilst studying this chapter.

It is often a more challenging project to be faced with redesigning an existing treatment room. Frequently the ideal design is limited by problems such as an inability to reinforce the existing radiation protection beyond a certain point owing to the surrounding architecture, the existing maze being far from sufficient on the installation of a higher energy machine, and an inability to physically install new machinery without having to remove either the roof or a wall.

Designing a totally new room from scratch is the more expensive and time-consuming option, and involves careful consideration of important additional factors such as siting of the room in relation to other treatment areas, access to other essential patient facilities such as the outpatient department and transport services, and the provision of utilities such as power, water, drainage, heating and ventilation. Legislation underpinning the design of treatment rooms is found in Regulation 32.2 of the 1985 Ionising Radiation Regulations (HSC 1985b), which specifies that when equipment emitting ionising radiation is installed in a radiotherapy department a critical examination should be conducted by an RPA to:

1. Establish that all safety features and warning devices are functioning
2. Ensure that personnel are sufficiently protected from exposure to ionising radiation
3. Provide the employer with advice regarding the proper use, testing and maintenance of the equipment.

LINEAR ACCELERATOR ROOM DESIGN

Where to start?

The initial draft of a new room design is usually provided in the form of minimum specifications from the manufacturer. This format should then be reviewed in the light of national and local legislative requirements and recommendations relating to annual whole body doses likely to be received by staff and general public in adjoining department areas during routine accelerator operation. Alternatively, a pre-existing room may provide initial dimensions.

How thick should the walls be?

Prior to calculating the required thickness of a barrier in order to reduce dose rates to an acceptable level, the following must be considered:

• Position of controlled or supervised areas and therefore relative specific annual whole body dose limits. Calculations can be made using time averaged dose rates, or whole body dose limits. If the former is chosen, consideration must be given to values for a 'normal' working week and 'normal' working year.

• Type of radiation barrier; primary or secondary. This will make a difference to the constituents of the wall thickness calculation. If a secondary radiation barrier thickness is required, values of leakage radiation must be substituted for primary beam dose rate values: there is also no need to include a machine orientation factor.

• Typical workload. How much radiation is produced at the isocentre during a typical working day? Typical quoted values from NCRP 49 and 51 (cited in Greene & Williams 1997) are in the range of 10^2–10^3 Gy week^{-1}, but these figures are dated and it would seem reasonable to suggest that they should be calculated for each individual department, taking into consideration possible multiple beam energies and typical workload fluctuations.

• Use factor. This is defined as how frequently the gantry points at a specific barrier during beam on time, and clearly will vary depending on the type of techniques commonly employed on the machine. Quantitative values are 0.42–1 for floors, 0.2–0.25 for walls and 0.12–0.25 for ceilings (Farrow 1985, Moyer 1977, NCRP 1977). Clearly, individual departments would do best to carefully consider the range of techniques likely to be undertaken on this machine, and calculate specific values accordingly.

LEARNING POINT

Definitions as documented in texts are often learned by rote, and without giving consideration to the clinical working definitions of these words and how they may change depending on the number and type of patients routinely treated on the accelerator, and during important and lengthy phases such as installation, acceptance, commissioning and any major maintenance.

Questions

How may use factors vary during the life span of a linear accelerator?

What implications might this have for radiation protection?

• Duty cycle. This factor corrects for how long the accelerator produces a beam during an 8 hour working day.
• Broad beam attenuation data in the form of tenth value thickness (TVT).

Calculation of absorber thickness

The following steps illustrate one method of calculating the required thickness for a primary radiation barrier, and assumes maximum occupancy of all areas adjoining a linear accelerator treatment room. When basing a calculation on annual dose levels, it is advisable to also review the subsequent incident dose rate and time averaged dose rate.

Step 1
Output of the primary X-ray beam at 1 m FSD: 3 Gy min^{-1}

Step 2
Distance to the point of the anticipated wall: 3.5 m

Step 3
Unattenuated dose rate at this same point (applying the inverse square law and converting absorbed dose (Gy) to equivalent dose (Sv):

$$3 \times \frac{1^2}{3.5^2} \times 1 \times 60 = 14.7 \text{ Sv h}^{-1}$$

Step 4
Annual dose at anticipated wall (based upon a duty cycle of 1 hour per day, an orientation factor of one-quarter, a five day working week, and a 47 week year):

$$14.7 \times 1 \times 0.25 \times 5 \times 47 = 863.6 \text{ Sv}$$

Step 5
Desired annual dose at this point (member of the public annual dose limit): 1 mSv

Step 6
Attenuation required of anticipated wall:

$$\frac{1 \times 10^{-3}}{863.6} = 1.16 \times 10^{-6}$$

Step 7
Number of TVT: $-\log_{10}$ of attenuation factor

$$-\log_{10} 1.16 \times 10^{-6} = 5.93$$

Step 8
Subsequent thickness of wall:

Calculated TVT (Step 7) × TVT of specified material at energy of interest. From Table 3.1 (p. 76), at 10 MV X-rays, TVT of Barytes concrete and steel is 25.5 cm and 11 cm respectively:
Therefore,

Thickness of concrete wall $5.93 \times 25.5 = 151.2$ cm
Thickness of steel wall $5.93 \times 11 = 65.23$ cm

In addition, careful consideration should be given to the following:
  Roof and basement areas.   It is rare for there to be any significant occupancy in these areas, and sufficient radiation protection can exist with the judicial application of carefully considered safe schemes of work and the use of an interlock system.
  Skyshine.   This is where scattered X-rays, the result of X-ray interactions in the roof area above

or adjacent to the linear accelerator room, reach areas at ground level either inside or outside the treatment facility. Levels may increase in conditions of heavy rain as raindrops can provide significant scattering surfaces (IPEM 1998), but ultimately the result is an overall increase in background levels of radiation.

Channels through the primary barrier for ducts, cabling and vents. Clearly it is important, where feasible, to ensure that any required channels do not go through primary barriers. If this is the case, then it is important to ensure that channels are cut at an angle to ensure that radiation scatters at least once on its passage through the wall. In addition, they should always be sited as low as possible to the floor.

Entrance maze. This structure prevents primary radiation and first scattered photons from reaching the room entrance. It should be designed so that it is sufficient in length and cross-sectional area to ensure that all X-rays are subject to a minimum of 2–3 scattering surfaces, thereby minimising the structural thickness of a door or perhaps even negating the need altogether. Lillicrap (cited in IPEM 1998, p. 37) states that for primary energies up to 10 MV, as long as the beam has suffered two Compton scattering events prior to reaching the door, the resulting beam spectrum will be equivalent to a beam quality of approximately 300 kVp. A substantial door would be required even at this low energy, and motorised doors are often found in departments when an existing room has been used and it has been impossible to extend the maze sufficiently. Monte Carlo calculations (p. 77) are now commonly used to estimate exposure rates and beam spectra at a maze entrance.

Secondary radiation barriers must be calculated in a similar manner, substituting leakage dose rate for unattenuated dose rate. They will be influenced by the angle of incidence of leakage and scattered radiation as a percentage will pass obliquely through a barrier, thereby increasing its effective attenuation. Once the required TVT has been calculated, the next step is to decide which building material available resources and space will allow.

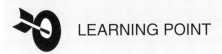

LEARNING POINT

Questions

With respect to radiation barriers, what is the difference between a radiation hazard and a radiation risk?

How may partial or complete occupancy of a room adjacent to your treatment room influence radiation barrier thickness?

What are the implications of always assuming maximum occupancy in adjacent rooms?

What materials should be used?

Material selection depends on the energy of the radiation to be attenuated, available capital and space. Cost is naturally a prime motivating factor for using concrete, since it is cheap, but concrete has a relatively low density and a mid-range atomic number, meaning that thick barriers are required. If space is at a premium it may be necessary to use a denser and therefore more costly material such as Barytes concrete or steel; both have the advantage of greater tensile strength. Lead, being the most expensive option, has the additional disadvantage of creeping under its own weight with time, and so requiring supplemental structural support.

As well as the choice of a suitable material, equal thought should be given to:

• Wall construction when using concrete blocks. It is essential to carefully stagger brick levels to ensure that radiation cannot find a path of least resistance through the lower density mortar.

• Regional variation in concrete density. Concrete density varies considerably across the UK owing to variable aggregate mixes.

• The pouring of concrete when used to make solid walls. The mixture should be poured continuously to prevent the formation of seams.

Table 3.1 Tenth value thickness (TVT) (cm) for shielding materials as a function of X-ray energy (nominal accelerating voltage) (from Greene & Williams 1997, p. 205, with permission)

Energy (MV)	Standard concrete 2350 kg m^{-3}	Barytes concrete 3500 kg m^{-3}	Steel 7800 kg m^{-3}	Lead 11,400 kg m^{-3}
4	29	20	9	5
6	34	23	10	5.5
8	36	24	10	5.5
10	38	25.5	11	5
16	42	28	11	5
25	46	31	11	4

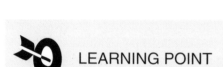

LEARNING POINT

Question
From your knowledge of X-ray interaction processes, explain why the TVT of lead decreases with increasing energy after 10 MV.

• Adequacy of radiation protection around stud and screw holes that are used to fix steel or lead into place and around the wells formed in a wall to house the alignment laser apparatus.

Typical materials include those shown in Table 3.1.

Is neutron shielding required?

An accelerator is capable of producing fast (energy in excess of 0.5 eV) and thermal (energy less than 0.5 eV) neutrons during X-ray or electron mode with a mean energy 1–2 MeV. Electrons produce a neutron yield several orders of magnitude lower than X-rays, so most texts concentrate solely on the management of photoneutrons, or those produced by X-rays. Whichever the source, clearly there are implications for staff and patient safety.

Photoneutron production occurs when the nucleus of a material absorbs energy from a high energy X-ray or electron and produces a neutron as a result, consequently it is referred to as a (γ, n) reaction. With a threshold in the range of 10–20 MeV for most atomic species, this reaction is considered insignificant below 10 MeV. Typical quoted thresholds for commonly used materials are lead 6.7 MeV, tungsten 7.3 MeV and ^{238}Uranium 4.8 MeV. For any specific materials, the neutron yield is very small at the threshold but increases dramatically with increasing photon energy.

The neutron component of dose is stated by the British Journal of Radiology (1983) to be no more than 0.1% of the X-ray component, and 0.4% of the X-ray dose when a radiation weighting factor of 20 is applied (IPEM 1998). BS 5724 Section 2.1 (BSI 1989) requires that neutron dose does not exceed a maximum of 0.05% of the absorbed dose in the useful beam at the isocentre.

Certain materials in the treatment room, such as the walls of the accelerating waveguide, target, beam flattening filter, collimators and shielding, will capture these neutrons and release excess energy in the form of gamma radiation. There can be a delay in the production of this radiation, and this may result in residual radioactivity in the treatment room after the accelerator beam has been terminated. Consequently, at significant treatment energies it is wise to ensure that, where possible, all metals are removed from the path of the beam. With respect to elements in the treatment head such as wedges and inherent shielding, work practices should be such that these elements are not handled until induced radioactivity has decayed to safe levels. The time for such decay will depend on the parameters of the treatment set-up and the length of the exposure, and more detailed advice should be sought from the physics department of each individual radiotherapy centre.

Neutrons are also produced by a process known as photofission or a (n, γ) reaction. Heavy elements such as depleted uranium, which may form part of the shielding within the treatment head, can undergo fission when irradiated by high energy X-rays and electrons. Its incidence is considered negligible below 5 MV (IPEM 1998).

In terms of shielding, fast neutrons are efficiently attenuated by materials with a high hydrogen content; concrete is one such material and it has a TVT of 21 cm for the energy range under consideration (McGinley 1998). With respect to concrete, X-rays are always more penetrating than neutrons at accelerator treatment energies and so shielding that is adequate for X-rays will be sufficient for neutrons. Elastic scattering interactions with the hydrogen atoms cause the fast neutron to lose significant energy and become a thermal neutron. These are then readily captured in materials such as boron or cadmium which have large capture cross-sections for thermal neutrons. Relatively small amounts of these materials are required to absorb a large percentage of the neutron population. Typically boron loaded polythene or borated plaster is used to line the walls of the maze, and maze design should be such as to present as many scattering surfaces as possible to the fast neutrons. Almost always a neutron door is necessary, and this will be a combination of borated polythene to capture the thermal neutrons and steel or lead to absorb any gamma radiation.

Can computer programs be used to calculate room design?

As with many situations in life, where complex calculations are required a computer program can be found to carry out the calculation with greater accuracy and speed than its human counterpart. This is indeed the case with the calculation of typical radiation transport patterns through a material; the majority of available programs stem from what are called Monte Carlo codes.

However, because a computer is able to do the job, it does not mean that one should routinely be used. By the application of the basic principles described above, barrier thickness can be calculated with fairly close approximations to available computer models. In reality, the balance between achievable maximum radiation protection and available budget swings often towards the side of finance and a workable solution to the problem. In addition, computer programs and associated hardware often mean further expenditure, so it is perhaps best practice to calculate the desired protection manually and use technology to confirm the results.

The Monte Carlo simulation of radiation interaction is the most accurate way of predicting how nature transports particles through any medium. It is capable of predicting how particles will scatter, deposit energy and produce secondary particles depending on the type and energy of incident radiation and the characteristics of the media in question. A detailed description of its operation is beyond the scope of this chapter, but Mohan et al (1998) and Metcalfe et al (1997) provide excellent explanations of this subject.

Safety features

Once controlled and supervised areas have been designated, it is important to ensure that they are clearly demarcated by the use of approved radiation warning signs, lights and gamma alarms. An effective interlock system should also be installed.

Local rules can then be composed so that all staff likely to enter any controlled area do so under a written system of work. The rules should be written by a member of departmental staff who is familiar with the normal operating parameters of the individual department, and who has consulted other staff members in the process. Within the rules, clear consideration should be given to documenting the following points:

- Named responsible persons (to include head of department, radiation protection adviser and radiation protection supervisor, with an indication of the extent of the roles of the last two people)

- Acceptable specific equipment uses and general operational procedures
- Extent of controlled and supervised areas, and access to each
- Personnel monitoring
- Procedures to be followed during machine maintenance and repair
- Emergency procedures.

RECOMMENDED READING

Health and Safety Commission 1998 Proposals for revised Ionising Radiation Regulations and Approved Code of Practice. Consultative Document. HSE, Suffolk

Institute of Physics and Engineering in Medicine 1998 The design of radiotherapy treatment room facilities. Report No. 75. IPEM, York

Lillicrap S C, Higson G R, O'Connor A J 1998 Radiotherapy equipment standards from the International Electrotechnical Commission. British Journal of Radiology 7: 1225–1228

McGinley P 1998 Shielding techniques for radiation oncology facilities. Medical Physics Publishing, Wisconsin

Metcalfe P, Kron T, Hoban P 1997 The physics of radiotherapy X-rays from linear accelerators. Medical Physics Publishing, Wisconsin

REFERENCES

British Journal of Radiology 1983 Central axis depth dose data for use in radiotherapy: a survey of depth doses and related data measured in water or equivalent media. British Journal of Radiology Supplement No. 17

British Standards Institute 1971 BS 4094: Part 2 Recommendation for data on shielding from ionising radiation. Shielding from X-radiation. BSI, London

British Standards Institute 1989 and 1991 BS 5724 Medical electrical equipment. Part 1 (1989) IEC 601–1: 1988. General requirements for safety. Part 2, Section 2.1 (1989) Particular requirements for safety. Specification for medical electron accelerators in the range 1MeV to 50MeV. Part 2, Section 2.1, Supplement 1 (1991) Particular requirements for safety. Specifications for medical electron accelerators in the range 1MeV to 50MeV. BSI, London

Department of Health 1999 Proposals for the ionising radiation (medical exposure) regulations. Replacing the Ionising Radiation (Protection of Persons Undergoing Medical Examination or Treatment) regulations 1988. Consultative Document. DOH, London

European Community Council Directive 13 May 1996 96/29/EURATOM. Laying down basic safety standards for the protection of the health of workers and the general public against the dangers arising from ionising radiation. Official Journal of the European Communities No. L159/1

European Community Council Directive 30 June 1997 97/43/EURATOM. On health protection of individuals against the dangers of ionising radiation in relation to medical exposure, and repealing directive 84/466/EURATOM. Official Journal of the European Communities No. L 180/22

Farrow N 1985 The effect of linear accelerator use on primary barrier design. Physics, Medicine and Biology 30: 1151–1153

Greene D, Williams P C 1997 Linear accelerators for radiation therapy, 2nd edn. Institute of Physics Publishing, Bristol

Health and Safety Commission 1985a The protection of persons against ionising radiation arising from any work activity. The ionising regulations 1985 approved code of practice. HSE, Suffolk

Health and Safety Commission 1985b Statutory Instrument SI No. 1333. The Ionising Radiation Regulations. HMSO, London

Health and Safety Commission 1988 Statutory Instrument No. 788. Health and safety. The Ionising Radiation (Protection of Persons Undergoing Medical Examination or Treatment) Regulations. HMSO, London

Health and Safety Commission 1998 Proposals for revised Ionising Radiation Regulations and Approved Code of Practice. Consultative Document. HSE, Suffolk

Health and Safety Executive 1998 Fitness of equipment used for medical exposure to ionising radiation. Guidance Note PM77, 2nd edn. HSE, Suffolk

Hendee W R, Edwards F M (eds) 1996 Health effects of exposure to low-level ionizing radiation. Medical Science Series. IOP, Bristol

International Atomic Energy Authority 1979 Radiological aspects of the operation of linear accelerators. Technical Report Series No. 188. IAEA, Vienna

Institute of Physical Sciences in Medicine 1986 Radiation protection in radiotherapy. IPSM Report 46. Bocardo Press, Oxfordshire

Institute of Physical Sciences in Medicine 1988 Commissioning and quality assurance of linear accelerators. Report No. 54. IPSM, York

Institute of Physics and Engineering in Medicine 1998 The design of radiotherapy treatment room facilities. Report No. 75. IPEM, York

International Commission on Radiological Protection 1991 Recommendations of the International Commission on Radiological Protection. ICRP Publication 60. Annals of the ICRP 21: 1–3

International Commission on Radiological Protection 1996 Radiation protection. ICRP Publication 73. Radiological protection and safety in medicine. Annals of the ICRP 26: 2

Lecomber A R 1997 Revised EURATOM basic safety standards and patient protection directives. British Journal of Radiology 70: 3–5

Lillicrap S C, Higson G R, O'Connor A J 1998 Radiotherapy equipment standards from the International Electrotechnical Commission. British Journal of Radiology 7: 1225–1228

McGinley P H 1998 Shielding techniques for radiation oncology facilities. Medical Physics Publishing, Madison

Metcalfe P, Kron T, Hoban P 1997 The physics of radiotherapy X-rays from linear accelerators. Medical Physics Publishing, Wisconsin

Mohan R, Siebers J, Libby B, Keau P, Hartmann-Siantar C 1998 Monte Carlo methods in radiation dose calculations. AAPM Refresher Course 13 Aug. 1998 (unpublished)

Moran B 1998 Radiation dose reduction in practice. RAD Magazine 24(279): 2

Moyer R F 1977 Analysis of medical usage factors pertinent to radiation protection for a 4 MeV rotational linear accelerator. Health Physics 32: 505–507

National Council on Radiation Protection and Measurement 1977 Structural shielding design and evaluation for medical use of X-rays and gamma rays of energies up to 10MeV. NCRP 49. NCRP, Bethesda

National Council on Radiation Protection and Measurement 1977 Radiation protection guidelines for 0.1–100MeV particle accelerator facilities. NCRP 51. NCRP, Bethesda

National Radiological Protection Board 1988 Guidance notes for the protection of persons against ionising radiations arising from medical and dental use. HMSO, London

National Radiological Protection Board 1994 Radiation doses: maps and magnitudes, 2nd edn. At a Glance Series. NRPB, Oxfordshire

RAD Magazine 1999 Editorial. Stronger evidence provided of exposure risks. RAD Magazine May: 50

van der Geissen P H 1996 Collimator related radiation dose for different cobalt machines and linear accelerators. International Journal of Radiation Oncology, Biology and Physics 35(2): 399–405

INTERNET REFERENCE

http://www.icrp.org 1997

Principles of quality assurance

4

Andy Williams and Samantha Morris

Chapter objectives

On completion of this chapter (and each individual treatment unit chapter) you should be able to:

- Evaluate the role of the quality management system within the radiotherapy department, and consider if, and how, this role may change in future years
- With respect to the patient, evaluate the role of each member of the multiprofessional cancer care team within the quality management system
- Discuss in detail the quality assurance programmes for the following radiotherapy equipment: simulator suite, linear accelerator, treatment planning computer, brachytherapy suite, kilovoltage treatment unit.

INTRODUCTION

The concept of quality concerns how well, and for how long, a service or product meets the requirements of a customer, these requirements varying depending upon the specific situation, individual viewpoint and circumstances. This philosophy of meeting requirements is a continuing theme throughout this chapter since it is important to understand exactly what the requirements of a product are. For example, in the case of a linear accelerator, it can be asked, 'how do we want the machine to perform, what characteristics must it therefore have, and what type of treatment techniques will we need to employ on it?'.

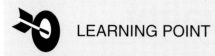

LEARNING POINT

Questions

List what you think the products and services in radiotherapy are, who the customers are and what their requirements are for these products and services.

How have these changed in the last two decades, and how might they vary in the future?

Many quality terms can appear to be confusing; however, in the broadest sense, quality can be defined as fitness for purpose or client satisfaction with a particular product or service. In the case of the linear accelerator, we can ask the question 'is the machine manufactured, installed, calibrated and maintained in such a way as to enable it to function correctly?'. In order to answer this question, a programme of testing must be designed to ensure the following:

- Knowledge of the dose per monitor unit at a specified point within the patient
- Coincidence of the radiation isocentre with the mechanical isocentre over time
- Accuracy and constancy of mechanical and digital indicators of isocentre position
- Consistent and accurate functioning of patient and staff safety systems (Constantinou 1993).

COMMONLY EMPLOYED TERMINOLOGY

Before examining the role of quality and its application to radiotherapy, it is useful to review definitions of some of the terms most widely used in relation to quality.

Client quality. The client or customer view of how well (or otherwise) the service or product provides what he or she expects or requires.

Monitoring. Observing an activity in relation to a defined specification, standard or targets.

Quality assurance. A management system designed to give maximum confidence that a given acceptable level and quality of service is being achieved.

Quality audit. A review of a quality system to find out how well it is operating, followed by recording and documentation of the results.

Quality control. The process by which actual quality performance is measured.

Quality correction cycle. A series of steps which are taken in order to define a problem, gather information to find the cause, and take action to remedy the fault.

Quality management. Those steps that control and improve all aspects of quality using quality methods.

Quality policy. A set of guiding principles that govern how people should act in order to improve quality. Measurable objectives derived from the needs of the supplier and user are key components of this.

Quality system. The structure and organisational responsibilities, procedures, processes and resources for implementing quality management (BSI 1987).

Quality standard. A general statement about the level of performance that needs to be achieved. This needs to be measured by a predetermined accepted method. If there is no measure, there cannot be a standard. When considering quality it is important to think not only in terms of radiotherapy equipment operating on a continuing basis, but also of how well the support activities are functioning, and how well each function relates to others within the entire radiotherapy service. This can be taken a stage further with the question 'how does the radiotherapy service relate to other functions within the much wider field of health care?'

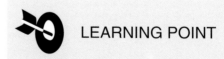

LEARNING POINT

Question

To what extent may these wider aspects of a quality system influence work patterns of a linear accelerator team?

QUALITY SYSTEMS IN RADIOTHERAPY

A good quality system should not only build upon good practice, but should also facilitate the introduction of new procedures. At the same time it needs to place equal emphasis on specification and measurement, while considering the influence of individual attitudes and working relationships. BSI 4778 (1987) defines quality as the 'totality of features and characteristics of a product or service that bear upon its ability to satisfy stated or implied needs'.

An appropriate response to the need for a quality service requires an understanding of the terms outlined above. From this understanding it is possible to examine the relationship between quality assurance and quality control. Although they are interrelated, the most important step is to understand the difference between them.

Quality assurance is an ordered series of procedures and practices providing evidence that the service meets the desired outcomes. Ongoing comprehensive internal and external evaluation is also required to ensure that the desired outcomes continue to be met over time.

Quality control is the term used to describe the detailed activities needed to evaluate the performance of a system over time.

DEVELOPMENT OF PERFORMANCE STANDARDS

Before looking at quality assurance programmes, it is important to know which activities need inspecting, how often they should be inspected, and what the expected level of performance is. The level of performance is normally recorded as a performance standard against which measurement can be made over a period of time.

Once completed, this process allows the specification of a technical standard. It does not, however, record exactly who works within the service and who is responsible for ensuring that standards are achieved. In order to achieve this it is necessary to follow what are known as social steps which allow expansion of the formulated technical standard described above. Once again this can be approached in stages:

- Establish working groups to consider the service provided and to clarify its quality features.
- Each group should propose a set of standards relevant to its own work area.
- Decide which of these standards should be taken as priorities and identify those which overlap or conflict with other work areas.

Having combined the technical and social sections of the standard, the next step is the comparison of what was actually achieved against the intended aims. In other words, a

KEY POINTS

The process involved in the formulation of a standard can be extremely complex and should follow the stages outlined below:

- There should be a general statement of the main requirements for the area being considered. A flow chart can assist in outlining what happens within the process and when. It can also identify who is involved and what the outcome is.
- Pick out the most important or key features of the activity, and for each of them identify

the essential aspects that would indicate whether or not the service is performing well. This stage is important because it moves from being a general statement to something more specific that can be observed or measured.

- Decide how the performance may be measured and documented.
- Specify the standard in terms of the level of performance expected or attained.

measurement of performance in relation to the specified standard. (The process of measurement or audit is covered later in this chapter.)

QUALITY ASSURANCE IN RADIOTHERAPY

In the UK the organisation responsible for preparing standards is the British Standards Institute (BSI). This is an independent body which also provides representation of the UK view on standards at the international level. The practical standard for quality systems is ISO 9000 (IOS 1993a, 1993b, 1994a, 1994b). This identifies the basic disciplines, procedures and criteria to ensure that a product or service meets its requirements.

Bleehan et al (1991) established a framework for applying the methods of ISO 9000 to the field of radiotherapy. This report took the form of a quality standard known as Quality Assurance in Radiotherapy (QART). It is based upon a number of requirements that need to be satisfied in order to ensure that quality is maintained. The quality assurance system as applied to radiotherapy should be a comprehensive series of documents relating to all aspects of the service provided. Such a system is divided into three main categories or levels:

 LEARNING POINT

Each quality system will differ from another, since work practices vary between departments.
If your department has a quality system in place find out what it covers, how it operates, and who is responsible for running it.

Questions
Which professional groups had input into its formulation?

How often is the quality system reviewed in terms of its ability to meet the stated objectives and standards?

1. Level 1, also known as the quality manual, sets out the quality policy for the organisation in terms of which areas and services are included within the scope of the system, a description of the managerial structure of the organisation and identification of those individuals having key responsibility for managing the system.
2. Level 2 sets out the procedures and processes which need to be followed.
3. Level 3 contains the instructions to be followed in order to carry out the identified tasks.

The Clinical Oncology Information Network (COIN) of the Royal College of Radiologists recommended in 1998 that all radiotherapy departments should have a comprehensive quality management system which meets the requirements of QART (Royal College of Radiologists 1998), and should take into account all the relevant national and international approaches to quality as and where appropriate.

This sort of quality system should include clear responsibility for quality management and should also cover multidisciplinary review and audit. The system needs to operate across the entire range of departmental functions and activities, the scope of which will vary from department to department, since the delivery of radiotherapy treatment covers multiple steps and involves a multidisciplinary team. It is therefore essential that the radiotherapy function is integrated into the overall management of the patient. The process of treatment planning and delivery involves the collaboration of a number of professional groups, together with the appropriate information technology and administrative support. The quality management system should ensure and demonstrate a well defined, continuous process for quality and outcome reporting. In practical terms the process begins with the installation and commissioning of a piece of radiotherapy equipment, since all subsequent quality and performance measurements relate back to the initial acceptance and commissioning tests carried out before the unit begins its clinical life.

Installation and commissioning procedures

Precise and consistent performance is required of radiotherapy linear accelerators in order to ensure the accurate, safe and reproducible delivery of external beam treatment. The maintenance of such performance standards over time relies heavily not only on quality engineering, but also on an effective series of tests designed to evaluate such performance.

 LEARNING POINT

There are many effective ways of achieving such an aim, and several texts (Greene & Williams 1996, Constantinou 1993, IPSM 1988) provide excellent examples of a comprehensive range of suitable tests, along with recommended test tools, and the suggested frequency and tolerance for each test.

Questions

Review the quality assurance protocols in your own departments for the following pieces of radiotherapy equipment:

Simulator suite

Treatment planning computer

Linear accelerator

Kilovoltage treatment unit

Brachytherapy unit.

For each piece of equipment, document the extent of the QA programme, the frequency of each of the identified tests, their accepted tolerance, the nature and extent of associated documentation, and identify the member of staff conducting each test. Compare these QA procedures with those described in the textbooks mentioned above, and evaluate areas of commonality and disparity.

When designing and producing new equipment, the manufacturer relies on the specifications stated in British Standard 5724, Parts 2 and 3 (BSI 1991, 1990a, 1990b). After installation BS 5724, Section 3.1 (BSI 1990a, 1990b) details a series of recommended commissioning procedures. The Institute of Physical Science in Medicine (IPSM) produced report No. 54 in 1988, entitled *The commissioning and quality assurance of linear accelerators*, which describes a comprehensive series of such tests and includes suggested frequency and tolerance.

Such testing:

• Ensures that the installed linear accelerator meets the specifications documented by the manufacturer
• Provides beam data collected in the recommended manner
• Defines a baseline performance standard for future quality assurance testing
• Acknowledges that unit performance will vary over the lifetime of the machine, and that it is necessary to determine a clinically acceptable tolerance for each measurement performed.

The actual tests are split into three categories: mechanical, optical and dosimetric. The mechanical and optical tests establish the position of the mechanical isocentre of the accelerator (i.e. verify coincidence of the axes of rotation of the gantry, couch, floor and collimator), and verify the accuracy of devices indicating its position. The dosimetric tests: verify that the position of the radiation isocentre is coincident with the mechanical isocentre; record values for beam quality (X-rays and electrons), output (for a range of field sizes and beam modifying devices), dose rate, flatness, and symmetry; and advise on data collection methods.

Quality assurance programmes

Once acceptance testing is completed, the performance of the unit must then be compared at regular intervals against the baseline standard to ensure performance consistency. This evaluation takes the form of a series of quality control tests (again, examples of these are clearly described in IPSM Report 54, IPSM 1988).

Trend analysis of the quality control test results should demonstrate a pattern of performance that will allow variations to be easily and instantly identifiable. Identification of small variations as they occur can avert the onset of significant problems which may result in machine down time. Such examples demonstrate the proactive benefits of a comprehensive quality assurance programme when conducted on a daily, weekly, monthly, quarterly and annual scale. Typical tests are listed below; requirements and methods will vary depending upon manufacturer recommendations, local needs and the nature of the test tool employed.

A comparison of the performance records for each machine within a department will demonstrate reproducibility and accuracy not only of machine calibration and dosimetry, but also of accuracy in the reproducibility of patient set-up.

Developments in localisation and planning methods require accurate and linear daily performance in order to eliminate variations in patient position. The use, for example, of a laser alignment system that is accurately matched to the mechanical isocentre of the accelerator alongside orthogonal patient skin marks identifying the planning target volume (p. 19) ensures that patient position is accurately established in all planes. Consequently it is vital that data transfer from the simulator and the treatment planning computer to the treatment unit is accurate and of a compatible format.

The comparison of accuracy and reproducibility across a department allows the systematic measurement of activities against specified objectives or service requirements – otherwise known as an audit.

Principles of audit and intercomparison

Audit is the structured and timetabled review of performance, and is therefore an essential part of any quality management system. Its purpose is to:

- Determine whether the quality system (departmental wide), or any of its component parts (e.g. the linear accelerator), comply with the stated requirements
- Provide the opportunity to identify areas of the system which do not comply with recorded procedures and instructions

KEY POINTS

Daily QA requirements:

- Light field alignment with gantry at 0°
- Accuracy of the set-up laser coincidence with the position of isocentre
- Accuracy of optical rangefinder at standard treatment FSD
- Collimator rotation accuracy at 0°, 90°, 180° and 270°
- Dose and dose rate calibration for wedged and unwedged fields at a gantry angle of 0°
- Test emergency power off switches (may be done on a rota basis, one switch tested per day).

Weekly QA requirements:

- Dose calibration at gantry angles 90° and 270°

- Light field alignment at gantry angle 90°
- Optical and mechanical rangefinder check at 80, 90, 110, 120, 130 and 140 cm FSD
- Beam flatness
- Depth dose check (i.e. energy check) for a 10×10 cm field at 5, 10 and 20 cm deep.

Monthly QA requirements:

- Field size accuracy
- Gantry scale accuracy
- Collimator scale accuracy
- Floor rotation accuracy
- Beam flatness and symmetry, and X-ray and optical field coincidence.

• Determine the effectiveness of the system in meeting its stated objectives, thereby allowing changes or improvements to be made within the system.

Audit may be conducted by members from other areas within the department or organisation, or suitably qualified personnel from other similar organisations may be invited in to carry out this role. Recently published reports (DOH 1998) have been aimed at developing national frameworks to ensure that medical care is of a high quality and is consistent in achieving that level of performance. This is to be achieved through the use of service frameworks, and national standards will define a model for a range of service groups including cancer services.

It is therefore necessary to compare performance levels between departments. This appears to be a logical extension of internal audit, since having defined and measured the levels of acceptable performance for each individual unit within a department, consistency between radiotherapy centres can subsequently be evaluated.

Calculation of the recorded radiation dose for a prescribed treatment set-up is a useful way of comparing interdepartmental quality assurance programmes, as described below:

A phantom is selected for use. Usually this is constructed of water equivalent epoxy resin plastic capable of taking interchangeable inserts for variable sizes of ionisation chamber. Additionally, a section that can be either bone or lung equivalent is also desirable. Measurements are then carried out under reference conditions, that is, machine parameters used for beam calibration, plus two separate multi-fied technique set-ups (in one of the latter set-ups the phantom should incorporate the lung substitute section). Results can then be compared intra- and interdepartmentally.

The aim of intercomparison is to determine currently achievable accuracy and precision, and while it does not provide a definitive audit as such, it does constitute a comparison of dosimetry between participating departments.

Experience arising from the first intercomparisons in the UK has demonstrated a growing interest in the development of systems for maintaining regular comparison between radiotherapy centres. A geographical or regional network can provide a relatively cost-effective framework offering various types and levels of audit which may be matched to individual needs and requirements. A number of networks are now in place, with centres being audited by peer professionals from other centres within the group.

Effective intercomparison should consist of a minimum annual audit for checking the beam calibration of at least one megavoltage energy, and testing a three field planned treatment in an appropriate phantom. However, many networks

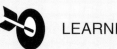

LEARNING POINT

By developing a hierarchy of tests at different levels within the dosimetry chain, it is possible to audit a number of different areas, as indicated below:

Geometric and mechanical performance

X-ray beam and ionisation chamber calibration

Electron beam calibration

Kilovoltage beam dosimetry

Brachytherapy source calibration and dosimetry

Planning methods and quality control

Procedural audit of equipment tolerances, dosimetry records and frequency of checks.

Questions

Does your department participate in an audit network?

What is the timetable and what areas are covered?

How are the results of the audit communicated to all staff members?

have developed systems which include more complex and comprehensive testing using anatomic phantoms in order more closely to reproduce clinical treatment delivery.

Since its introduction, intercomparison has become an integral part of the audit function within the radiotherapy service. It may be considered to be outside the traditional realms of quality system audit in its purest sense; however, it is a vital part of quality control.

RECOMMENDED READING

IPSM 1988 Commissioning and quality assurance of linear accelerators. Report No. 54. IPSM, York

Kehoe T, Rugg L J 1999 From technical quality assurance of radiotherapy to a comprehensive quality of service management system. Radiotherapy and Oncology 51: 281–290

Metcalfe P, Kron T, Hoban P 1997 The physics of radiotherapy X-rays from linear accelerators. Medical Physics Publishing, Madison

Stanton R, Stinson D 1996 Applied physics for radiation oncology. Medical Physics Publishing, Madison

Thwaites D I, Scalliet P, Leer J W, Overgaard J 1995 Quality assurance in radiotherapy. ESTRO. Advisory report to the Commission of the European Union for the 'Europe Against Cancer' programme. Radiotherapy and Oncology 35: 61–73

Williams J R, Thwaites D (eds) 1993 Radiotherapy physics in practice. Oxford Medical Publications, Oxford

REFERENCES

Bleehan N M, Edwards J, Evans R et al (chair) 1991 Quality assurance in radiotherapy (QART) Report of standing sub-committee on cancer. DOH, London

BSI 1987 BS 4778: Part 1: 1987 (EN 28402: : 1991 ISO 8402 – 1986) Quality vacabulary. International terms. BSI online.

BSI 1990a Medical electrical equipment. BS 5724, Part 3. Particular requirements for performance. Section 3.1. Methods of declaring functional performance characteristics of medical electron accelerators in the range 1 MeV to 50 MeV. Supplement 1. Guide to functional performance values. BSI, London

BSI 1990b Medical electrical equipment. BS 5724, Part 3. Particular requirements for performance. Section 3.1. Methods of declaring functional performance characteristics of medical electron accelerators in the range 1 MeV to 50 MeV. BSI, London

BSI 1991 Medical electrical equipment. BS 5724, Part 2. Requirements for safety. Section 2.1. Specification for medical electron accelerators in the range 1 MeV to 50 MeV. Supplement 1. Revised and additional text. BSI, London

Constantinou C 1993 Protocol and procedures for quality assurance of linear accelerators. Constantinou, Brockton

Department of Health 1998 A first class service: quality in the new NHS. DOH, London

Greene D, Williams P C 1996 Linear accelerators for radiation therapy, 2nd edn. IOP, Bristol

Institute of Physical Sciences in Medicine 1988 Commissioning and quality assurance of linear accelerators: Report No. 54. IPSM, York

International Organisation for Standardisation 1993a ISO 9000-2 Quality management and quality assurance standards. Part 2: Generic guidelines for the application of ISO 9001, IOS 9002, and ISO 9003. International Organisation for Standardisation, Geneva

International Organisation for Standardisation 1993b ISO 9000-4 Quality management and quality assurance standards. Part 4: Guide to dependability programme management. International Organisation for Standardisation, Geneva

International Organisation for Standardisation 1994a ISO 9000-1 Quality management and quality assurance standards. Part 1: Guidelines for selection and use. International Organisation for Standardisation, Geneva

International Organisation for Standardisation 1994b ISO 9001 Quality systems: model for quality assurance in design, development, production, installation, and servicing. International Organisation for Standardisation, Geneva

Royal College of Radiologists 1998 Draft report of the generic radiotherapy working group. RCR Clinical Oncology Information Network

5 The linear accelerator

Chapter objectives

When you have studied this chapter you should be able to:

- Describe the main advantages of linear accelerators compared to kilovoltage and ^{60}Cobalt units

- Identify the major components of the linear accelerator structure, and outline the construction and function of each of these components

- Describe the principles of operation of the accelerating structure, and explain how (a) an X-ray and (b) an electron beam is produced

- Discuss the possible structural variations in accelerators produced by different manufacturers, and outline their relative advantages and disadvantages

- Define the term conformal radiotherapy, and explain how the delivery of radiotherapy differs to that of a machine using asymmetric or independent collimation techniques

- Explain the operating principles of an electronic portal imaging device, and compare this to a method using slow radiographic film

- With respect to some of the common machine faults that typically occur during a malfunction of the treatment unit, explain the meaning of each of these and describe the course of remedial action necessary to rectify the fault

- After reviewing the relevant chapter, describe the quality assurance tests undertaken on a linear accelerator with reference to the frequency, accepted

INTRODUCTION

Linear accelerators, more formally known as electron linear accelerators in reference to the particle that is accelerated, have been in use since the 1950s to treat patients with malignant and benign disease. At present the total number of accelerators employed worldwide in radiotherapy exceeds 4000, with several hundred other machines being used in radiobiological and medical research (Valkovic 1997). Since their initial introduction into the medical domain, the increasing range and scope of clinical treatment techniques has led to major changes in the capabilities of these units. We now see equipment with options of dual modality and multiple megavoltage energies, inclusive verification systems, conformal therapy and megavoltage imaging devices, digital platforms providing ease of upgrade and connectivity to accessory equipment, plus vastly improved clinical accuracy and reproducibility.

Such changes have evolved not only from the demands of the medical profession, but also as a result of the requirement of the Ionising Radiation Regulations 1985 and 1988 to reduce all doses received by radiation workers and patients to as low as reasonably achievable. This has led to an appreciation by manufacturers and clinical users of the importance of accurate installation, acceptance and commissioning tests, as well as the development of detailed quality assurance programmes.

In an accelerator, electrons produced from an electron gun are injected into a waveguide in synchrony with a radiofrequency wave produced from a magnetron or klystron. The electrons are accelerated to high speeds in the waveguide and are then fed into the treatment head. Depending upon the components of the treatment head, an X-ray or electron beam will be produced.

Chronological development

1932   The start of the megavoltage era with the development of the 1 megavolt (MV) van de Graaff generator. The maximum obtainable energy reached 2.5 MV in 1946, but production was discontinued in 1959.

1943   The Betatron (a specific type of megavoltage unit) was developed by R Wideroe and D W Kerst, with the first clinical radiotherapy patient treated in 1949. However, owing to its sheer size, low dose rate of 40 cGy/minute and inability to rotate isocentrically around the patient, production was discontinued in the 1970s.

1946   Following the developments in Second World War military radar, the technology of the magnetron and klystron were applied to accelerator design.
Fry, Gray and Miller demonstrated the first low energy travelling wave accelerator.

1950s   The first generation of truly isocentric megavoltage equipment began with the introduction of isocentric ^{60}Cobalt units.

1952   The first stationary linear accelerator (8 MV) was installed at the Hammersmith Hospital in London, England. This was rapidly followed by the installation of 4 MV machines at Newcastle General Hospital in August 1953, and at the Christie Hospital in Manchester in October 1954.

1956　　Varian Associated produced the first low energy isocentric linear accelerator.

1960s　　Design developments led to the appearance of higher megavoltage energy machines, as well as the first dual modality accelerator. However, initial problems included small maximum field sizes and inconsistency in the quality of the electron beam.

1970s–1990s　　This time period produced multiple energy accelerators with smaller mechanical tolerances and larger maximum field sizes, as well as the concepts of conformal therapy, automatic and dynamic wedges, electronic portal imaging devices and computer controlled verification systems (Scharf & Chomicki 1996, Washington & Lever 1996a, Brahme 1987).

THE NEED FOR ACCELERATOR DEVELOPMENT

FUNDAMENTAL CHARACTERISTICS OF X-RAY AND ELECTRON BEAMS

When wishing to calculate absorbed dose at different depths within a patient for a specific type of beam, or compare radiation beams of different quality, it is helpful to consider a diagrammatic representation of how this dose will be distributed within the patient. This is more formally known as the isodose chart. As shown in Figure 5.1, the isodose chart illustrates the dose distribution by a series of curves formed by joining points of equal dose. Isodose curves are characteristic to each quality and energy of radiation, but their shape is also influenced by the design features of individual linear accelerators, specific beam parameters and the homogeneity of the irradiated medium.

Isodose curves are usually evaluated by a comparison of the shape and position of certain common features:

The skin sparing effect

One of the major advantages of megavoltage treatment machines is that they deliver the dose maximum at varying depths below the skin surface of the patient. This is the result of interac-

---

KEY POINTS

Linear accelerators are the most common megavoltage units to be found in the radiotherapy department. They have been developed to replace ^{60}Cobalt and kilovoltage treatment machines for the following reason:

- Greater percentage depth dose
- Variable dose rates
- Enhanced skin sparing in comparison to ^{60}Cobalt units
- Decreased preferential absorption in bone owing to a greater incidence of the compton scatter interaction process
- Multimodalities available in the same treatment machine
- Multiple energies available in the same treatment machine

- A narrower penumbra than that produced by ^{60}Cobalt units
- Larger maximum field sizes
- Network capabilities between the accelerator and the treatment planning computer, simulator, CT/MRI suites, other treatment machines and the automated patient booking system
- Complex computer controlled verification software, reducing the incidence of treatment errors
- Finer mechanical tolerances on the movements of the accelerator leads to greater accuracy and reproducibility of set-up (Bomford et al 1993, Williams & Thwaites 1993).

KEY POINTS

- Central axis depth dose
- Degree of skin sparing
- Width of penumbra
- Shape of beam profile
- Rapidity of dose fall off.

tion processes experienced by the primary X-ray beam and the resultant secondary electrons; these processes are discussed in more detail below. At megavoltage energies, when an X-ray beam is incident upon the surface of a patient the predominant interaction process is compton scatter. This results in the production of a recoil electron and a scattered photon. The energy imparted to these two entities during the initial

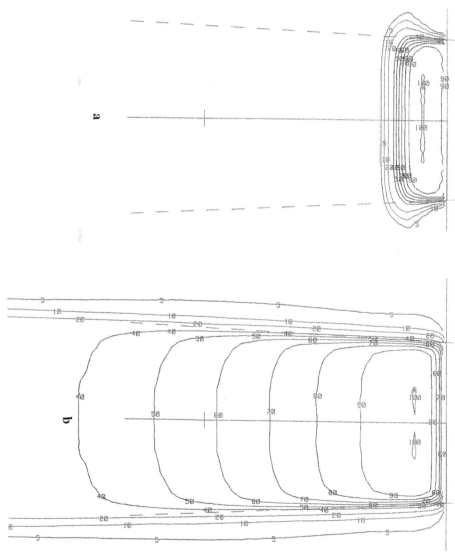

Figure 5.1   **(a)** 9 MeV electron beam isodose curve: 10 × 10 cm @ 100 cm FSD; **(b)** 10 MV X-ray beam isodose curve: 10 × 10 cm @ 100 cm FSD (courtesy of Medical Physics Department, Northampton General Hospital).

interaction will determine the maximum range they may travel in tissue. Absorbed dose in the patient is due to the deposition of energy from the recoil electrons as they travel through the body.

The electron typically loses energy by a large number of collisions, with only a small percentage of its energy lost during each event. As the electron slows down due to this energy loss, it will be involved in more and more collisions so a greater amount of its initial energy is lost towards the end of maximum range. This process is known as the Bragg curve pattern of ionisation. The detail of electron interactions with tissue are grouped into two categories: collision and radiative type interactions (described in detail in Ch. 7).

The amount of energy lost from the electron by collisional or radiative processes is quantified by the use of electron stopping powers. As with attenuation and absorption coefficients for X-rays, density independent terms of mass collision $\left[\dfrac{S}{\rho}\right]_{col}$ MeV cm^2 g^{-1} and mass radiative $\left[\dfrac{S}{\rho}\right]_{rad}$ MeV cm^2 g^{-1} stopping powers are employed (Metcalfe et al 1997, Stanton & Stinson 1996).

The Bethe–Bloch formula (Leo 1994, Knoll 1989) is a complex equation that is considered to be the basic expression to be used for heavy charged particle collisional energy loss calculations. When applying this equation to electrons, the standard formula indicated by the Blethe–Bloch equation must be changed to take into consideration the small mass of the electron, and the fact that the electron interacts in a collisional manner with other electrons that are indistinguishable in terms of mass and charge.

Initially the mass collision stopping power decreases sharply with increasing energy owing to its inverse dependence on the square of the electron velocity, but its value then begins to rise as a result of distant electron charges having a greater influence for higher energy electrons – this is termed the relativistic rise. The magnitude of this subsequent increase is reduced by the number of intervening atoms, particularly for higher density materials, and this is known as the density effect. An understanding of these effects is important in the field of radiation dosimetry and the calculation of absorbed dose. Radiative energy losses are less frequent, but for each interaction will involve a larger energy loss from the electron. In soft tissues, for the energy range of recoil electrons in radiotherapy, the radiative stopping power is approximately 1% (Metcalfe et al 1997) of the collision stopping power. This proportion varies for higher atomic numbers and energies, but for each material it is possible to define a critical energy where the radiative energy loss mechanism and collisional energy loss mechanism are equal. Above this level, radiative energy losses predominate.

In any single Compton scatter interaction, the dynamics of the process dictate that the recoil electron is emitted primarily in the forward direction, whilst the scattered X-ray can be emitted in a range of directions which are determined by the energy of the incident X-ray.

A simplified model of the skin sparing process is illustrated in Figure 5.2, which summarises how these effects contribute to the skin sparing phenomenon:

1. X-rays A–F undergo their first Compton interaction at increasing depths in tissue. From each interaction the resultant recoil electron is assumed to be ejected in a forward direction and will travel in a straight line to the end of its range. In reality electrons travel a very convoluted path in tissue and cause ionisations in all directions; however, the net overall ionisation pattern will be in the forward direction.

2. Assuming each electron receives the same percentage of energy during the interaction process, all recoil electrons will travel the same distance (4 mm in Fig. 5.2), causing progressively increasing numbers of ionisations along their path.

3. The sum number of ionisations per millimeter of tissue is indicated at the bottom

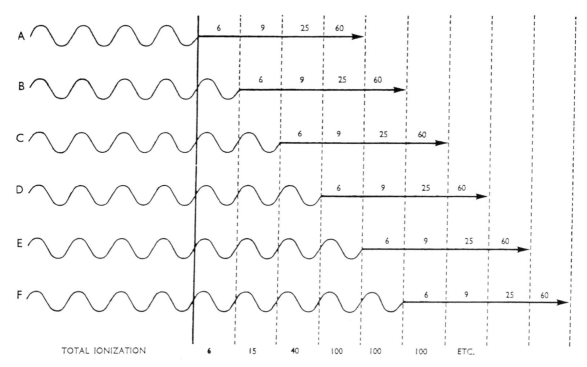

TOTAL IONIZATION   6   I5   40   I00   I00   I00   ETC.

Figure 5.2 A simplified explanation of the skin sparing effect (from Meredith and Massey 1977, reprinted by permission of Butterworth-Heinemann Publishers, a division of Reed Educational and Professional Publishing Limited).

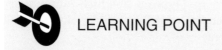

LEARNING POINT

In the clinical setting, tissue equivalent bolus (see Ch. 2) is used to manipulate the distribution of dose within the patient.

Questions

With an 8 MV beam and an FSD of 100 cm to the anterior surface of the bolus, what is the effect of placing a piece of 2 cm thick bolus over the width and length of a treatment field?

Will the effect alter if 100 cm FSD is set to the anterior skin surface?

For a specific X-ray energy, other than the use of bolus what might cause a decrease in the skin sparing effect?

of Figure 5.2; they clearly show a maximum ionisation pattern.

4. This ionisation pattern then tails off after the maximum owing to attenuation of the primary beam as it travels through the patient, and the effect of the inverse square law with increasing distance from the target.

5. The depth of this maximum build-up of ionisation will vary with the energy of the incoming photon beam.

6. This process is emphasised by the fact that very little back scatter occurs to the surface of the patient at these energies, owing to the tendency for the recoil electron and scattered photon to be ejected forward into the patient.

Typical features of X-ray isodose curves

Referring back to Figure 5.1b, it can be seen that linear accelerators produce an X-ray beam where the depth of the dose maximum (d_{max}) is significantly below the skin surface, and the width of

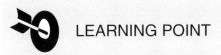

LEARNING POINT

Penumbra is defined as the horizontal distance between the 90% and the 20% isodose lines (see Fig. 5.1b) at the depth of the dose maximum, and at the standard FAD of the accelerator. The width of the penumbra (see Ch. 6) region will decrease with increasing beam energy due to a decreasing contribution of back scatter at higher energies. The exact position of the beam edge can vary in the presence of such scattered radiation. Therefore, field size is conventionally stated to be the horizontal distance between the 50% isodose lines at the depth of the dose maximum and at the same distance from the target (IPSM 1988). This point is in the middle of the defined penumbra region, whilst sufficiently outside the clinically useful limits of the beam. Less frequently, field size is defined as the distance between the 80% isodose lines.

Question
Clinical linear accelerators are available with field size defined to either the 50% or 80% isodose contours. What are the clinical implications of this?

penumbra is characteristically narrow owing to extensive focusing of the accelerated electron beam onto the transmission target.

Within the patient, scatter from all sides of the irradiated volume will increase the dose at the central axis. However, the degree of contributing scatter will naturally lessen toward the edges of an irradiated volume and this causes the shape of the isodose line to curve away from the horizontal. This, along with the influence of the beam flattening filter, produces a relatively square shaped beam profile placed symmetrically either side of the central axis of the beam.

Dose fall off along the central axis of the beam is gradual and this is caused by attenuation of

Table 5.1 Percentage depth dose data for 10 × 10 cm fields at 100 cm FSD (British Journal of Radiology 1996)

Isodose (%)	Depth (cm) 8 MV	Depth (cm) 15 MV
100	2	2.9
80	7–8	9
50	17	20

the primary beam within the patient as well as the influence of the inverse square law.

X-ray beam data for an 8 MV and 15 MV accelerator are presented in Table 5.1.

Typical features of electron isodose curves

Electrons interact very differently in tissue to X-rays. Owing to their charge and mass they will interact with atomic orbital electrons, or positively charged nuclei. Interaction will also occur with particles some distance from their path. The sum effect of these interactions is loss of energy and/or path deflection.

A further form of energy loss from the high energy electron is bremsstrahlung production or the unintentional production of X-rays (see Ch. 7). Typically, an electron will interact with anything in its path, and this type of energy loss results from passing through the electron window, scattering foils and air as well as scattering off any of the major components of the treatment head. This X-ray contamination will form only a small percentage of the beam, but may vary considerably with the design of a treatment head.

As shown in Figure 5.1a, the central axis depth dose is dependent upon the energy of the incident electron beam. Because of the charge and mass of an electron, its linear energy transfer (LET) is higher than an X-ray beam of the same energy. Therefore this densely ionising particle loses most of its energy close to its path through tissue, and characteristically most energy is lost towards the end of its range. Tissue at this point therefore receives a considerable dose. Beyond this point dose is minimal and attributable only

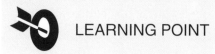

LEARNING POINT

A 6 MeV electron beam specification means the accelerating potential of the waveguide is 6 MV, therefore all electrons have 6 MeV of energy as they leave the waveguide. This implies that the beam spectrum is monoenergetic. In reality, and as described above, the electron beam will interact with a range of materials prior to reaching the patient, resulting in an electron beam spectrum that may be less monoenergetic than would be anticipated.

For X-ray production, a target and other beam modifying devices are placed within the path of the monoenergetic electrons, and interactions with these components result in a continuous spectra of beam energies. Subsequently, the resultant X-ray beam energy is usually quoted as MV rather than MeV.

Questions

What degree of energy variance is found in clinically acceptable electron beams?

Describe how X-ray and electron beam spectra vary in shape.

Table 5.2 Percentage depth dose data for 10 × 10 cm fields at 100 cm FSD (British Journal of Radiology 1996)

Isodose (%)	Depth (cm) 15 MeV	Depth (cm) 25 MeV
100	3.3	3.3
80	5.5	8.5
20	7.3	12.1

to bremsstrahlung. These events result in a markedly more rapid fall off of dose with depth than is seen in an X-ray beam, with the central axis depth dose not reaching zero quite as rapidly as expected owing to the presence of bremsstrahlung radiation. This unusual dose gradient is the main clinical advantage for using electrons, and is typically applied in treating superficial areas to a radical dose whilst sparing the more sensitive critical structure underneath. A common example of this is the delivery of a radical dose to clinically significant lymph nodes overlying the spinal cord.

Beam data for 10 MeV and 25 MeV electron beams are presented in Table 5.2.

Skin sparing does occur with electron beams, but is caused by a different phenomenon. Owing to the presence of electron cones which are placed in contact with the skin of the patient, within the first few layers of tissue most electrons are travelling in a forward direction. This results in a skin dose of approximately 85% (British Journal of Radiology 1996, Washington & Lever 1996b). As the electrons lose energy they begin to scatter in all directions away from the central axis of the beam. The result of the interactions caused by those electrons scattering nearer to the horizontal plane will be the deposition of a greater amount of energy (or absorbed dose) per unit depth than the energy lost per unit depth from those travelling nearer to the vertical plane. Consequently the energy deposited per unit depth of tissue will increase to form a skin sparing effect similar to that seen with X-ray beams. The depth of the maximum will naturally depend upon the energy of the incident electrons.

As shown in Figure 5.1a isodose curves in the 40–10% region balloon outwards because of the propensity of lower energy electrons to scatter sideways. This characteristic decreases with increasing electron energy. The clinical implications of this are significant when considering the matching of electron fields. Overlapping these ballooning edges when field matching can result in hot spots, and this is normally avoided by moving or 'feathering' such junctions throughout a course of treatment.

The width of penumbra is generally greater in electron beams than would be seen for an X-ray beam of the same energy. This is due to a greater 'virtual source' of electrons, as well as the scattering characteristics of the particle itself. The virtual source is defined as the point from which the electrons diverge, i.e. the scattering foils or electron window. An accelerator with a scanning electron beam will have a much finer width of penumbra.

There are three main rules of thumb which are applied for electron beam dosimetry:

1. An electron will lose energy in water at a rate of 2 MeV/cm.
2. The clinically useful treatment depth d_{80} (depth of the 80% isodose) is calculated by the formula E/3 cm, where E is the energy of

the electron beam in MeV. The depth of d_{90} is similarly calculated by the formula E/4 cm.
3. The practical range of the electron beam (considered to be the depth of the 5% isodose line) is calculated by the formula E/2 cm (Bomford et al 1993).

THE PHYSICAL PRINCIPLES OF LINEAR ACCELERATOR OPERATION

The linear accelerator takes its name from its waveguide structure in which electromagnetic radiofrequency waves are used to accelerate electrons to high speeds. The main components of the accelerator are illustrated in Figure 5.4.

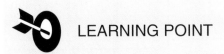

LEARNING POINT

Questions
Which electron depth dose characteristics dictate that the current maximum energy deemed clinically useable for electron beam therapy in radiotherapy practice is approximately 25 MeV?

Why is this so?

KEY POINTS

The physical principles underlying the operation of this piece of equipment are:

- The properties of electromagnetic waves
- Electromagnetism
- The motor principle
- Electromagnetic induction.

Case history

The following information relates to a patient diagnosed with a midline T_1N_1 squamous cell carcinoma of the posterior one third of the tongue.

Dose   60 Gy tumour dose in 25 daily fractions over 5 weeks treating Monday to Friday
Technique Parallel opposed pair of fields
Energy   6 MV X-rays

Figure 5.3a demonstrates the borders of the lateral treatment fields. An anterior field (which is not indicated in this figure) is matched to the inferior extent of these lateral fields, and extends down to encompass the supraclavicular lymph nodes. The prescription for this field is:

Dose   50 Gy applied dose in 25 daily fractions over 5 weeks treating Monday to Friday
Technique Single direct field
Energy   6 MV X-rays

Figure 5.3b indicates the movement of the posterior border of the two lateral 6 MV fields at 40.8 Gy TD. The field placed posteriorly to this border is an electron field designed to treat the palpable lymph

nodes overlying the spinal cord to a maximum of 60 Gy, while limiting the dose to the radiosensitive spinal cord to 40 Gy TD.

Figure 5.3c indicates how a suitable electron energy is chosen:

- The lateral depth of the spinal cord from the right and left lateral field centres is calculated. This information is gained from an AP radiograph taken on a simulator using appropriate skin markers, and in this case demonstrates a right lateral depth of 6 cm and a left lateral depth of 8 cm.

- Using the formula E/2 an electron energy is selected to ensure that the practical range of the electron beam on the right lateral side does not exceed 5 cm, with a corresponding depth of 7 cm for the left lateral side. The selection of a 1 cm margin in this case is simply an example. Such a decision would of course need to be made by a clinical oncologist.

- As can be seen from Figure 5.3c, it may sometimes be necessary to choose a different electron energy for each lateral field if a neck node of significant size is making a difference to the separation on one side of the neck.

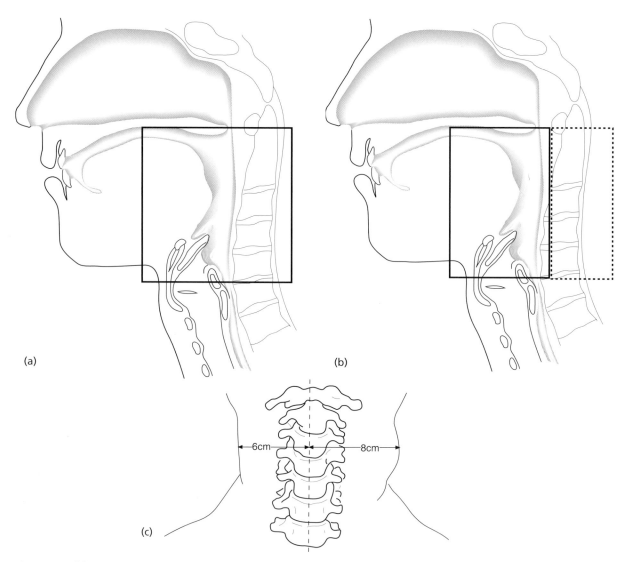

Figure 5.3 **(a)** Field borders of the lateral treatment fields to a maximum dose of 40.8 Gy TD in 17 daily fractions with 6 MV X-rays. **(b)** A diagram indicating the movement of the posterior border of the lateral X-ray fields at 40.8 Gy, and the field borders of the electron field (dotted). **(c)** A diagram indicating the right and left lateral depths of the spinal cord.

Properties of electromagnetic waves

Such waves consist of electric and magnetic vectors perpendicular to each other and to their direction of travel. The strength of both vectors varies in a sinusoidal manner.

Electromagnetism

A moving electron produces a magnetic field about itself. This direction of the magnetic field

will depend upon the direction of the electron's travel. This phenomenon occurs as the electron travels along the waveguide. Because the electron is moving there is a constantly changing magnetic field focused along the path of the electron.

The motor principle

When placed within an electromagnetic field an electron will experience a force upon it. This is

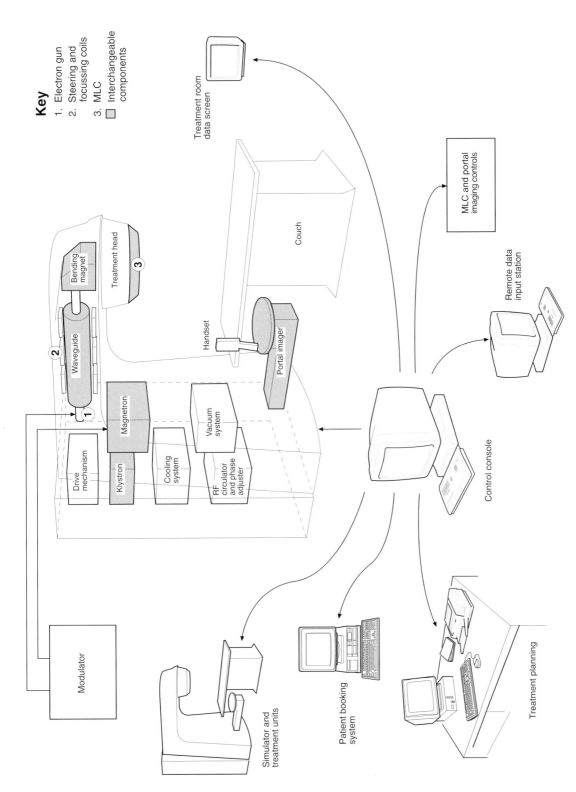

Key

1. Electron gun
2. Steering and focussing coils
3. MLC
   Interchangeable components

Figure 5.4 A schematic diagram indicating the components of a linear accelerator.

because the magnetic field produced around the electron by electromagnetism will interact with the magnetic component of the electromagnetic wave. The resultant vector of these two magnetic fields will be carefully positioned to divert the path of the electrons towards the centre of the waveguide. This is also the same mechanism by which the steering and focusing coils operate to keep the electron travelling along the desired path, as well as the principle underlying the operation of the bending magnet system.

Electromagnetic induction

This is the reverse of electromagnetism and describes the production of electron flow within a conductor when that conductor is placed in a changing magnetic field. The changing magnetic field is the result of the moving electromagnetic wave, and the changing magnetic field produced around the moving electron. The conductor is the waveguide, and, as the electrons pass along it, a transient build-up of areas of positive and negative electric charge occurs on the walls of the waveguide and the iris diaphragms (see p. 104). This charge build-up helps to keep the electrons bunched together on the optimum part of the wave, as well as assisting the forward momentum of these electron bunches.

In summary, the basis of linear propagation of electromagnetic waves is as follows:

COMPONENTS OF A LINEAR ACCELERATOR

The structure and function of each of the components involved in the production of an X-ray or

---

KEY POINTS

- A moving electron produces a magnetic field
- A changing magnetic field produces an electric field
- A changing magnetic field will sustain a changing electric field (Wilks 1987).

---

electron beam (see Fig. 5.4) are discussed below. For a more detailed electronic review of the individual components the reader is referred to the second edition of the excellent text by Greene & Williams (1997) entitled *Linear accelerators for radiation therapy*. In this chapter emphasis is placed on where and why some of these components may be different in machinery produced by different manufacturers.

The pulse modulator

The pulse modulator supplies high voltage negative pulses from a 380–440 V 50 Hz mains supply to the source of microwaves and the electron gun. The output is passed on to the microwave source and electron gun so that high velocity electrons are injected into the waveguide at the same time as the radiofrequency (RF) wave. Varying the pulse repetition frequency from the pulse modulator gives a variable power output; regulation of the dose rate is controlled in this manner.

The microwave source

The selection of a magnetron or a klystron to supply microwave power, also known as the radiofrequency wave, at a frequency of 3000 MHz to a waveguide is purely one of financial and practical convenience. Factors such as cost, size, replacement time and stability, as well as magnitude and range of output, are most often the deciding factors.

The magnetron

Magnetron technology was invented at the end of 1939 and was a development that gave Britain the upper hand in the radar race against Germany. In the medical field, the magnetron is commonly found in low energy accelerators such as the Clinac 600c and the Phillips SL75 series. For acceleration of electrons up to 10 MeV, the magnetron operates at a peak power of 2.5–3 MW. For higher energy accelerators higher peak power levels are required.

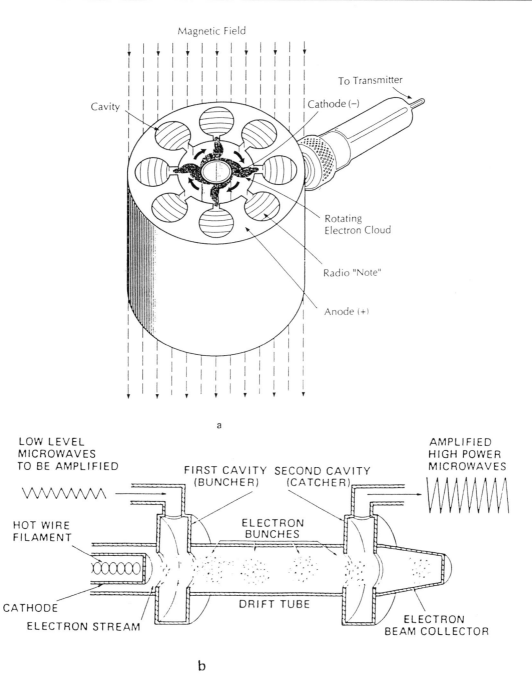

Figure 5.5 **(a)** The multicavity magnetron (from Buderi 1996, with permission). **(b)** A cross-sectional drawing of an elementary two cavity klystron tube (from Karzmark and Morton 1981, with permission).

The magnetron is less costly than the alternative klystron, has a replacement time of 30 minutes and is smaller in size with less electronic circuitry; these latter features mean that it can easily be mounted within the gantry. This advantage is offset by the fact that as the gantry rotates, the magnetron experiences fluctuations in frequency output caused by the influence of the earth's magnetic field and any other external sources of magnetic fields. It also has a shorter life expectancy than the klystron and is less reliable at higher powers.

Principles of operation. As shown in Figure 5.5a, a magnetron operates as a thermionic valve and consists of an anode and a cathode. The anode is a copper block into which is drilled a series of symmetrical resonant cavities which surround a central hole. Sitting within the central hole is an oxide coated cathode. The whole assembly, which is placed within a uniform magnetic field and operated under a vacuum, functions as follows:

- A pulsed DC electric field is applied between the cathode and anode. Electrons are emitted from the cathode and are attracted towards the anode.
- The direction and magnitude of the external magnetic field and the anode–cathode voltage are chosen to ensure that, as the electrons are emitted from the cathode, their path is deflected, and they form a rotating space charge around the cathode, in 'spoke like' bunches. As these spokes of electrons pass by the entrance to each of the resonant cavities, each cavity begins to oscillate at a specific resonant frequency. This process is very similar to air flowing in front of a whistle hole that causes a tone to be emitted.
- Each electron bunch will transfer approximately 60% of its energy to the resonating cavity as it is oscillating. Energy losses form the radiofrequency (RF) wave, which is drawn off and passed into the accelerating waveguide at the required time (Karzmark & Morton 1981, Buderi 1996).
- The output frequency will vary with a change in the volume of each resonant cavity; this variation is deliberately induced by a bellows system when using a magnetron in a dual energy accelerator. Typically, such a magnetron is designed to operate at a selected set of frequencies. In these circumstances it is also necessary to incorporate a way of varying the magnetic field strength; this is usually achieved by the use of a coaxial coil.

- Significant dimensional changes can also occur with temperature variations which result in thermal expansion or contraction of the structure. This will eventually lead to a variation in the beam output, dose rate and flatness, so overall magnetron temperature is stabilised by incorporating the magnetron device into the accelerator water cooling system.
- Magnetron frequency is controlled by a feedback system called the automatic frequency control (AFC). This device maintains the output frequency of the magnetron within ± 20 kHz of the operating frequency of the waveguide (Greene & Williams 1997).

The klystron

The klystron was invented during the summer of 1937 by Varian Associates. It is an alternative to the magnetron. The name is derived from the Greek verb *klyzo*, which means breaking of waves on the beach (Buderi 1996). It is favoured by some manufacturers owing to its greater stability at higher energies, but generally it is more costly to replace owing to the complexity of its design.

Whilst the magnetron produces an RF wave by operating as a high power electron oscillator, the klystron functions differently. It uses a low power oscillator to amplify low energy microwaves. It can produce 5–7 MW of peak power and is therefore incorporated into high energy accelerators such as the Clinac 2100C and 2300C/D, which produce 18 MV and 25 MV X-ray beams respectively. The physical size of the klystron means that it cannot be gantry mounted, and therefore it is not subject to the same frequency changes which occur in the magnetron as a result of the Earth's magnetic field. The higher voltages applied to this device also mean that the cathode end must be submerged in an oil filled insulation tank which contributes to its greater size.

Principles of operation. The klystron consists of a cathode, two resonant cavities, an electron beam collector and a series of drift tubes connecting all these elements together. The klystron illustrated in Figure 5.5b is a simplified version for explanatory purposes – actual klystrons contain three to five cavities overall. This assembly functions as follows:

- The filament of the cathode is energised by a negative voltage pulse of approximately 120 kV, causing it to produce electrons. These electrons accelerate towards the zero potential of the electron beam collector, and pass initially into the buncher cavity.

- The buncher cavity is energised by a low energy RF wave. The electric field component of this electromagnetic wave is positioned so that a potential difference exists between the left and right vertical walls of the buncher cavity. As the strength of this electric field component varies sinusoidally, the electrons that cross this cavity will experience varying electric field strengths. This causes the accelerating force on each individual electron to vary in a sinusoidal manner so that they begin to bunch together as some accelerate and others begin to slow down. The electron bunches are now travelling at a frequency determined by the resonant frequency of the buncher cavity.

- The electrons pass out of the buncher cavity and travel down the drift tube towards the catcher cavity. They remain along the central axis of the klystron under the influence of external focusing magnetic coils. As the electron bunches enter the second cavity it resonates at their arrival frequency, and energy is transferred into this cavity in the form of an amplified RF wave. The frequency of this wave will equal the resonant frequency of the buncher cavity.

- The lower energy electron bunches then pass into the electron beam catcher where their remaining energy is lost as heat, which is removed by a water cooling system. This catcher is also a source of kilovoltage X-rays, and therefore an additional thin walled metal container usually surrounds this end of the device.

- Output frequency can be varied by changing the frequency of the radiofrequency wave applied to the first cavity (Greene & Williams 1997, Buderi 1996, Karzmark & Morton 1981, Internet Reference 1).

Microwave circulator and phase adjuster

Whether a klystron or magnetron is used, it is important to incorporate into the design of the accelerator a device that will prevent the RF power being reflected back to its source. This can be done in a number of different ways.

An isolator is a device that allows the microwave power to travel through it to be fed to the accelerating waveguide and the electron gun, but presents a high impedance to the reflected wave of lower amplitude.

A radiofrequency load removes the excess microwave power at the end of the waveguide by diverting it into a lossy dielectric material that is either water or air cooled.

A circulator is a device that directs the microwave power along one path as it is fed into the accelerator, and along a series of different paths as it exits from the end of the waveguide. The microwaves then pass through a phase adjuster which then recycles the RF power back into the gun end of the waveguide. More commonly they are fed onto a form of RF load where their energy is then dissipated as described above.

Finally, another method of removing excess RF is to make the last few iris diaphragms from a resistive material into which the RF is absorbed.

The electron gun

This is the source of the electron bunches that accelerate along the waveguide. In a linear accelerator the gun is generally a diode or triode type that is supplied by high voltage pulses from the modulator. The main differences between the two are the method by which the cathode is heated and the degree of fine control over this process that can be achieved.

In the simplest form of the electron gun electrons are produced thermionically from a directly heated spiral tungsten filament and are then electrostatically focused onto the central axis of the waveguide. It has a life expectancy of

1–2 years so it is often manufactured as a detachable unit. However, the standing waveguide and the electron gun may be produced as a single component; in this case a greater financial outlay and longer machine down time result from electron gun failure.

In X-ray mode, where the beam current is typically at its highest, rapid changes occur when the temperature of the filament is adjusted and this ultimately leads to changes in the efficiency of X-ray production. It is therefore crucial to keep the beam current as stable as possible. The final electron energy depends upon the amplitude of the RF wave and the electric field strength acting upon each individual electron. The greater the number of electrons, the smaller the electric field strength each is subject to and the less energy each will receive. This leads to a less efficient and lower energy X-ray output.

For a constant electron energy the efficiency of X-ray output is proportional to the electron beam current. However, because there is only a finite amount of energy offered by the RF wave, there will come a point when the amount of energy each electron receives can no longer remain constant if the current continues to increase.

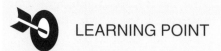 LEARNING POINT

Ensuring optimal output in the form of beam energy, output and percentage depth dose from an accelerator is a carefully controlled balancing act, and it is important that the operator has an appreciation of the complexity of the interactions between the magnetron/klystron output, electron gun current, and the automatic frequency control (AFC) system.

Question
What influence would an undetected rise in electron gun current have upon the percentage depth dose in a patient?

Thereafter each electron will receive less energy and the efficiency of X-ray output will begin to fall. This critical point will depend upon the energy of the bombarding electrons and the target material. The spatial distribution of X-rays is also an influence because with a decreasing average electron energy, fewer X-rays are naturally produced in the forward direction.

The accelerating waveguide

The accelerating waveguide uses an electromagnetic RF wave to accelerate electrons to very high velocities onto a target or an electron window. In this process the electron is able to gain considerable energy from the wave.

The fundamental principle underlying this is simple: an electric field will exert a force upon a charged particle placed within it. In order for the force to continue to act upon the electron, it must move as the electron accelerates and this happens with a travelling electromagnetic wave. The electric field component of the wave is aligned along the long axis of the waveguide, as illustrated by the arrowed electric field lines in Figure 5.6a. The electron gun is positioned at the end of the waveguide to inject electrons onto the optimal point of the wave for maximum acceleration.

The RF source emits the RF wave at a rate of several hundred pulses per second, and this is fed into the waveguide in synchrony with the electrons. As an electromagnetic wave will travel at the velocity of light (c) in free space, in order to position the electrons on the part of the wave where they will experience the maximum force, it is necessary to slow down the RF wave at the beginning of the guide. This is achieved by placing a series of iris diaphragms along the length of the internal aspect of the guide; the spacing and lumen diameter of these will control the speed of the wave.

The principles of acceleration are different in each of the following waveguide designs:

- Travelling waveguide
- Standing waveguide
- Multiple energy waveguides.

which cooling water flows to reduce any dimensional changes caused by thermal expansion or contraction.

In the bunching section, the iris diaphragms are closely spaced to slow down the wave so that it enters the waveguide at approximately 0.4 c. Initially when the electrons are ejected from the electric gun they are spread evenly out across the wave, with typically only one third (Karzmark & Morton 1981) of the electrons being captured onto the optimum part of the wave. However, because the electric field strength of the wave will vary in a sinusoidal manner, each individual electron will experience differing amounts of force. Consequently, those not positioned on the crest of the wave will begin to decelerate and will fall back until they are at the crest of the following point of maximum field strength. This happens along the length of the wave so that the electrons are positioned in bunches at each of the wave crests.

Towards the end of the bunching section the iris diaphragms are less closely spaced so that the wave can begin to accelerate. At the end of the bunching section the wave is travelling at approximately 0.9 c and it enters the accelerating section, where the iris diaphragms are widely spaced, allowing the electrons and the wave to accelerate almost to the speed of light. Because the electron has a finite mass, according to Einstein's theory of relativity it may never reach the speed of light, but will continue to gain energy in the form of additional mass.

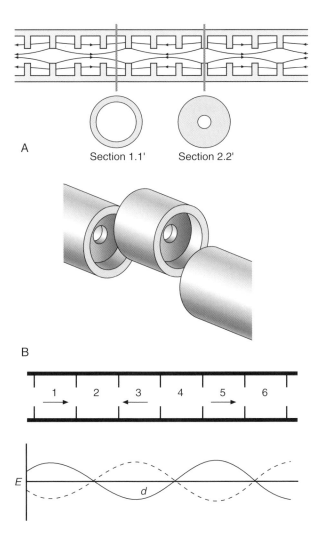

Figure 5.6 **(a)** Sections through a disc loaded waveguide showing arrowed electric field lines, and a perspective diagram of the said waveguide. **(b)** Upper: a standing waveguide; lower: standing waves, the dotted line representing the field one half cycle after the field shown by the dotted line (from Greene and Williams 1997).

KEY POINTS

The final energy of the electron depends upon:

- The position of the electron on the wave
- The length of the waveguide
- The frequency of the RF wave
- The total number of electrons emitted.

Travelling waveguide

A travelling waveguide is a series of adjacent cylindrical, evacuated microwave cavities (see Fig. 5.6a), and is typically found in Philips accelerators. The waveguide is divided into a bunching and accelerating or relativistic section. Along the outside is a water jacket through

Standing waveguide

This is a common alternative to the travelling waveguide and is favoured by manufacturers such as Siemens and Varian. The waveguide construction differs in that the gun and target end are closed apart from small holes to allow the electrons in and out. The design of the bunching and accelerating section is unaffected.

The RF wave is injected into a point at the side of the waveguide, where it is reflected up and down the guide. An induced phase change on reflection means that a standing wave will appear at the resonant frequency of the waveguide, and will oscillate in time.

In Figure 5.6b the cross-section of the waveguide shows arrows which represent the direction of force on the electron from the instantaneous electric field during a positive half cycle of the wave. Owing to the standing wave resonating in time, the evenly numbered cavities will not apply any force to the electron whereas the odd numbered cavities will apply a maximum force.

If the distance between the iris diaphragms is set so that the electron travels from cavity 1 to 3 in one half cycle of the RF wave then, assuming that the electron bunches are already positioned on the optimum point of the wave, each electron bunch will experience an accelerating force in each half cycle of the wave. In essence this means that an electron experiences greater electric field strengths and consequently achieves a greater velocity than it would in the same length of a travelling waveguide. (It is possible to design the dimensions of the waveguide in this manner because the resonant frequency depends upon the diameter of the structure rather than on the length.)

The benefit of a waveguide that produces higher accelerating gradients per metre of waveguide is that it can be used to produce a more compact machine, as seen in the low energy Clinac 600, which has a vertical waveguide positioned in line with the target, reducing the need for an expensive bending magnet system. Alternatively it can be used to produce higher

energy X-ray and electron beams from a standard length of waveguide. Most accelerators operating above 10 MV incorporate the standing waveguide.

Advantages and disadvantages of travelling and standing waveguides can be summarised as follows:

• Standing waveguides produce higher accelerating gradients because, owing to the nature of the standing wave, the electron is accelerated in a field strength of constant amplitude. The electron in the travelling wave system will attenuate the wave it is travelling on as it passes down the waveguide. This results in reduced electric field strength at the target end of the guide and a decreased rate of electron acceleration.

• The standing waveguide will produce a broader electron energy spectrum for a specific peak power, and this can lead to problems with the steering and focusing of some of the lower energy electron bunches. A broader electron spectrum also requires the use of a 270° bending magnet (see p. 108) to reduce problems with resulting beam flatness. The disadvantage of this is that such a magnet will increase the vertical height of the treatment head, leading to an elevated isocentre. Travelling waveguides do not experience this same problem and are fitted with 90° or slalom bending magnets.

• In the travelling waveguide the peak power level of the RF wave is achieved instantaneously at the start of the RF pulse. This means that the energy transferred to each electron will be constant through each RF pulse. In the standing waveguide it takes time for the standing wave to build up to its maximum amplitude and during this time electrons will not be accelerated efficiently. This will result in a broader electron spectrum. This is avoided in some accelerators by delaying the injection of electrons into the system until the wave is of sufficient amplitude.

• The standing waveguide is a highly resonant system and functions efficiently at a fixed frequency. A result of this fixed frequency is a very stable energy output.

Multiple energy waveguides

With the requirement of multiple X-ray and/or electron beams from a single accelerator it is clear that the requirements of such a system will be somewhat more complex than the two previous examples.

In the travelling waveguide the velocity of the wave, and ultimately the stability of the electron energy, depends upon the frequency of the RF wave. Minor frequency changes can cause significant variations in electron energy simply by influencing the position of the electron bunch on the RF wave. This system of varying energy is only acceptable when an electron beam is the required result. Owing to inefficiencies in the system, frequency manipulation is not recommended for X-ray beam therapy, and multiple X-ray energies are produced by operating the system at the optimum frequency but at two or more RF power amplitudes (Greene & Williams 1997).

In the standing waveguide the ultimate energy achieved by the electron depends upon the position of the electron bunches on the RF wave, as well as the amplitude of the standing wave. However, changing electron energy by significantly varying the amplitude of the wave leads to problems with broadening of the electron beam spectrum, as mentioned above.

Consequently, dual electron energies are usually achieved by the use of an energy switch. This switch influences the high energy end of the guide only, whilst maintaining a constant electric field strength in the buncher section. A slight reduction in the amplitude of the electric field strengths in the latter end of the waveguide while keeping the frequency constant will result in a lower energy treatment beam. Other alternatives include a pair of coupled waveguides, the first containing the buncher section and the second the accelerating section. By changing the frequency of the wave as it enters the second guide, the electron bunches will shift to a less optimum wave position and will achieve a lower eventual energy. This is accomplished by feeding the RF wave to both waveguides, but incorporating a phase adjuster into the path leading to the second guide.

The last example of a multiple energy system is the multipass waveguide found in Scanditronix racetrack microtron accelerators. Here the electrons are fed many times through a single waveguide (either travelling or standing wave). The ultimate energy will depend on the number of passes through the waveguide. This system incorporates deflecting magnetic fields at the end of the waveguide to redirect the electron path.

Focusing coils

Focusing coils are aligned along the exterior of the waveguide. They produce magnetic fields with lines of force running parallel to the long axis of the waveguide. The radial component of the RF wave influences the electrons accelerating along the waveguide and causes them to diverge out towards the walls of the waveguide. Focusing coils prevent this divergence, reducing the incidence of unwanted bremsstrahlung (evident as leakage radiation through the acceleration housing), vacuum breakdown and reduced dose rate. Differing electron energies will require different amounts of focusing and consideration must be given to this when selecting a different electron energy. The amount of focusing required will decrease with increasing electron energy; if the focusing is not suitably adjusted, the electrons will be diverted away from the central axis of the waveguide, causing exactly the kind of problems that the system was designed to avoid.

Feedback systems exist between the ionisation chamber in the treatment head and the focusing and steering coils so that adjustments are made automatically to the currents of the focusing and steering coils to ensure that X-ray beam flatness and symmetry remain within clinically acceptable parameters.

Steering coils

Steering coils act independently of the focusing coils but function in the same manner and with a dual purpose. Firstly, they ensure that the electron beam is positioned at the centre of the entrance to the waveguide as it leaves the electron gun and, secondly, they position the electron beam onto the appropriate point on the target or electron window. They are therefore situated at the electron gun and target ends of the waveguide.

The vacuum system

This system maintains the extremely low pressures required for the operation of equipment such as the accelerating waveguide, electron gun, RF source and bending magnet system. The presence of a vacuum prevents electrons from colliding with air molecules which would cause the electrons to lose energy and be deflected from their original path. The vacuum also prevents the breakdown of the high electric fields required during accelerator operation.

The water cooling system

This is required to establish a stable operating temperature throughout the machine. Specific components such as the waveguide, the RF source, and the focusing and steering coils require delicate temperature control to prevent thermal expansion affecting their efficient and accurate operation. Other components, such as the target, require less delicate monitoring and the cooling system simply removes the heat that builds up during normal operation.

It is also important to ensure that the stable temperature is sufficiently high to prevent the build-up of condensation within the accelerator structure.

The bending magnet system

The bending magnet is necessary in a horizontally mounted waveguide in order to project the electron beam onto the target. Accelerators were initially manufactured with vertical waveguides. However, with the demand for higher energy beams, the design of the accelerator became increasingly unwieldy for clinical use, particularly with the advent of arc therapy. In order to balance this need for a more powerful beam with

a clinically compact treatment unit, the bending magnet was incorporated into the unit design to allow isocentric treatment delivery to continue, and also to reduce the height of the working isocentre.

Figure 5.7 shows the three designs of beam bending chamber commonly available: the 90°, 270° and slalom magnet. These angles should not be taken literally – the bending angles found in clinical practice are merely close approximations to these values.

In Figure 5.7a the 90° system deflects the beam through 90° as it leaves the waveguide; this is typically seen in the Philips/Elekta accelerator. The electrons enter a flat vacuum box between the plane parallel poles of an electromagnet and follow a curved path through the system which acts as a spectrometer. The focal spot is approximately 3–5 mm in diameter. Optimal X-ray output is achieved by setting the magnet to accept only electrons of the desired energy and by adjusting the electron gun current and RF power for maximum photon output.

The 270° system is also known as an achromatic magnet (see Fig. 5.7b). The magnets are arranged to subject electrons of different energies to different bending magnetic field strengths, whilst ensuring that the electrons exit the system at the same point and travelling in the same direction. The system produces greater focusing of the electron beam owing to the complex paths that each individual electron travels and produces a smaller focal spot (less than 3 mm). It is often employed with the standing waveguide because it is compatible for use with a broader electron spectrum. The main disadvantage of this magnet is its physical size which results in a higher working isocentre than found in the 90° magnet.

The slalom magnet (Fig. 5.7c) was developed by Philips Medical Systems and is a variation of the 270° system, bending electrons through a total of 112.5°. The ingenuity of its design allows the isocentre to remain at a similar height to that of the 90° system, but it produces a much more focused beam of electrons at the target, resulting in a 2 mm focal spot with minimal penumbra.

Varian have been innovative in returning to the vertical waveguide in their 600C model. This

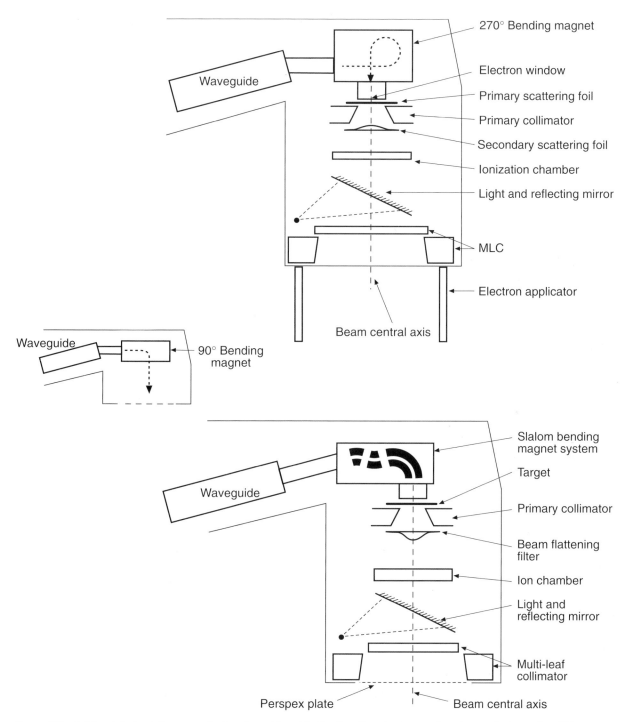

Figure 5.7 **(a)** A minimised diagram of a treatment head indicating the electron path as it travels through a 90° bending magnet. **(b)** The components of a treatment head for the production of an electron beam. This diagram illustrates the path of the electrons as they travel through a 270° bending magnet. **(c)** The components of a treatment head for the production of an X-ray beam. This diagram illustrates the path of the electrons as they travel through a slalom magnet.

incorporates a short standing waveguide which negates the need for a bending chamber. The result is an electron beam flow that is focused directly onto the target with a very small focal spot of less than 2 mm.

The currents in the steering, focusing and bending magnet coils must be carefully regulated to ensure an accurately focused electron beam. Current in the steering coils at the gun end is predetermined by the electron energy selected, whilst current in the target end steer-ing coils depends upon feedback signals from the ionisation chamber in the treatment head.

The X-ray treatment head

The components necessary to produce a mega-voltage X-ray beam are illustrated in Figure 5.7c. The bending magnet systems have been discussed in the previous section so will not be covered here, other than to say that all of the three magnet systems are used clinically for X-ray output.

The target

Once the electrons have left the accelerating waveguide they are fed into and out of the bending magnet by a series of simple flight tubes on their way to the target.

A transmission rather than a reflective target is employed, primarily because the spatial distribution of X-rays at this energy is in the forward direction, with the greatest intensity along the central axis of the treatment head.

When the electron beam strikes the target, X-rays are produced. When the electron interacts with the electrostatic field of the nucleus in an atom of the target material, the resultant X-ray energy will depend upon:

- The maximum electromagnetic field strength the electron may experience (this is related to the atomic number of the target material)
- How close to the nucleus the interaction occurs
- The thickness of the target material.

The resultant continuous spectrum of X-rays will exhibit an energy range that matches the minimum and maximum energies of the incident electrons. Typically, for electron energies up to 10 MeV, a thick tungsten target is employed, with a thick aluminium target being used for energies greater than this. The target is designed to be either retractable so that it can move out of the electron path for electron beam therapy, or mounted on a turntable along with the electron window.

The primary collimator

At the central axis of the beam the inner aspect of the primary collimator is cone shaped and defines the maximum field size available for clinical treatment.

Depending upon space constraints, typical materials used in its manufacture range from depleted uranium and tungsten copper alloys to lead filled steel castings. All aim to reduce the transmitted beam to less than 0.2% of that passing through the central cone.

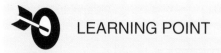

LEARNING POINT

Questions
At kilovoltage energies the efficiency of X-ray production is poor – typically 1% X-rays and 99% heat. How, and why, does this efficiency alter at megavoltage energies and what are the implications of this for accelerator target cooling?

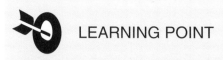

LEARNING POINT

Question
Justify the selection of shielding materials within the treatment head with respect to the X-ray interaction processes.

The beam flattening filter

This is a conical metal filter of a low atomic number material such as aluminium. It is situated between the target and the ionisation chamber. It is thickest at the centre in order to produce a uniform intensity distribution over the central axis of the beam, needed because the X-rays produced at the target have a narrow intensity peak unacceptable in the field of clinical radiotherapy, which demands an equal radiation intensity over the treatment field. Using such a filter reduces the output on the central axis of the beam, but the beam current is sufficiently high in X-ray mode for this not to be a significant problem.

The choice of material for this filter is a balance between the need for it to fit into the space available, and the need for it not to reduce the percentage depth dose values over the range of energies the unit may produce. Choosing a thick layer of a higher atomic number material such as tungsten will harden the beam at energies below 18 MV, and this is a positive feature. However, at higher energies the increasing incidence of pair production (see Ch. 1) will result in the higher energy components of the X-ray beam being attenuated, which softens the beam and thereby reduces percentage depth dose values. A similar problem can also occur when using a single inherent wedge (British Journal of Radiology 1996).

The shape and position of this filter are crucial, as any movement will alter the flatness or symmetry of the resultant beam. Its position is therefore monitored by a feedback loop between the ionisation chamber and the target steering coil. Any changes in beam flatness detected by the ionisation chamber will result in a signal to the steering coil to confirm appropriate alignment of the electron beam. If this alignment is within normal operating parameters the position of the beam flattening filter is then checked and adjusted. If the position of the filter is beyond the range of adjustment tolerated by this feedback system, the accelerator will not continue to function.

An alternative to the beam flattening filter is to scan the X-ray beam across the treatment field.

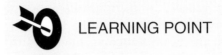

LEARNING POINT

Questions
What is the definition of a flat X-ray beam?

How does this definition vary with depth in the patient, and what might be the clinical implications of this variation?

This technique is discussed further under the heading for the electron beam treatment head.

The ionisation chamber

The dual ionisation chamber system (Ch. 2), which samples points across the treatment beam, will terminate the treatment when the prescribed dose has been given, or if the energy, quality, flatness, symmetry or dose rate of the emitted beam falls outside normal operating parameters. The chambers operate independently of each other in case one should fail, and are sealed ion chambers to prevent variations in the sensitivity of response because of fluctuations in temperature and pressure.

A key design requirement of the ion chamber system is that it causes minimal perturbation of the beam. This is achieved by constructing them from aluminium foil, carbon and plastic. In its simplest form, each ionisation chamber is constructed of parallel plate electrodes forming a large central and two outer D-shaped segments. The greater the number of segments into which the chambers are divided, the more detailed the information received.

The central segment monitors dose and dose rate. The two outer segments are used as dose comparators across the beam profile; their results will appear in the form of a beam uniformity indicator on the treatment control unit when it is operated in the technical mode.

Once currents to the focusing, steering and bending magnet coils have been set, the precise position of the electron beam on the target depends upon the energy of the accelerated electrons. If the electron energy is above or below that required, the focal spot will be incorrectly aligned with the beam flattening filter and the ion chamber will detect abnormalities in the beam uniformity. In order to rectify this, current differences detected between specific planes of the ion chamber are fed to the current supply of the steering coil at the target. The methods for controlling the energy, position and magnitude of the electron beam were covered previously in the section dealing with the accelerating wave-guide (see p. 104). Current fluctuations between other planes of the two D-shaped segments of the ion chamber are used to detect energy differences; these differences are rectified by varying the electron beam current.

The field defining light

This system illuminates the field defined by the collimation system for easy patient positioning. The basic components are a filament lamp and a mirror, and these are carefully positioned to ensure that the visible light beam is coincident with the radiation beam. The mirror does not significantly attenuate the X-ray beam, but its construction is different in an accelerator used for electron beam therapy.

Secondary collimators

Once the radiation has left the ion chamber, its field size is controlled by secondary collimators that are thick enough to absorb 98% of the main beam. The secondary collimators are usually constructed of a high density material such as lead or tungsten alloy and are mounted in pairs either side of the central axis of the beam. They produce significant amounts of secondary electrons when irradiated which, if the patient is close to the treatment head, can impair the skin sparing effect. Most accelerators incorporate a transparent electron filter across the face of the treatment head to absorb these secondary electrons.

Advances in collimator design include greater maximum field sizes of up to 40 × 40 cm at

1 metre from the target, the ability to control each of the four main collimators independently, and multileaf collimation. These advances increase the versatility of the accelerator, providing innovative and simple ways of solving old technique problems while delivering superior dose distributions.

Secondary collimators are designed to reduce penumbra to a minimum by:

- Being placed as far away as possible from the X-ray source
- Matching the shape of the collimator edge to the divergence of the beam.

The three main types of secondary collimator currently available are:

1. Symmetric
2. Independent
3. Multileaf.

The symmetric collimator

This system is generally found in older accelerators. It consists of two pairs of collimators. Each collimator in a pair will move in synchrony with its mate about the central axis of the beam.

The disadvantage of this system is that one pair of collimators is closer to the target than the other pair, and this produces different amounts of penumbra at the beam edges.

The independent collimator

The independent collimator is also known as an asymmetric collimator. The main difference, when compared to the symmetric system, is that each of the four collimators can be moved independently of the other three. Each can generally be moved across the central axis of the beam, but the amount they can move is often determined by mechanical constraints of the system. For financial as well as engineering reasons, quite frequently a machine may be purchased with only one pair of collimators able to move in this manner.

Independent collimators are favoured in treatment techniques requiring the close matching of adjacent treatment fields, as during radical external beam therapy in the patient with a breast or head and neck malignancy. This is because the nearer the collimator is brought towards the central beam axis, the less beam divergence will appear at that beam edge; this is a tremendous advantage in helping to reduce the overdosing difficulties associated with matching to closely adjacent treatment fields.

Case history

Figure 5.8 illustrates the likely irradiation fields for a patient with a breast malignancy. Both the primary site and the regional lymph nodes are to be treated. The technique employed is a tangential pair of fields to the breast, along with a parallel opposed pair of fields to the supraclavicular and axillary nodes.

The tangential pair of fields are treated with the asymmetric collimator facility applied to the field length of the treatment volume. With the superior collimator closed to the central axis of the beam, this same edge is matched to the superior border of the tangential field. The process is then repeated for the other tangential field (Fig. 5.8a).

When treating the supraclavicular and axillary fields, the asymmetric facility is once again applied to the treatment volume length, but this time to the inferior border of the field (Fig. 5.8b). In this way, the incidence of overdosing at the junction edge can be dramatically reduced, and often the traditional 0.5–1.0 cm gap between such fields may be significantly reduced or removed altogether.

Multileaf collimation

Conformal therapy using a multileaf collimator was developed to match more closely the shape and size of the individual treatment volume and produce a carefully shaped three-dimensional high dose volume; this has helped to reduce the use of heavy and labour intensive straight edged lead or divergent custom-made blocks that have traditionally been used to produce non standard treatment field shapes. Multileaf collimation (MLC) systems currently available are either tertiary collimator systems (attached below the secondary collimator sub-system), or a partial or total replacement of the upper or lower jaws of the conventional collimator system.

The advantage of a tertiary collimator system (as produced by Varian) is that it can be purchased as an addition to an existing unit, and so is an extremely cost-effective way of upgrading the accelerator. However, the tertiary collimator does reduce the distance between the patient and the accelerator, which can lead to potential head clearance problems with some forms of immobilisation devices.

An upper jaw replacement (found in the Elekta accelerator) lends itself to a compact head design as a result of beam divergence, and therefore facilitates maximum head clearance. In order to

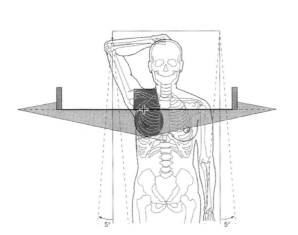

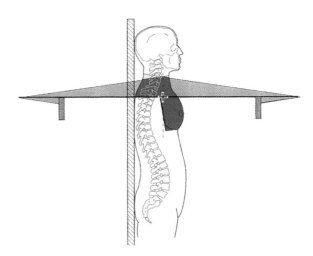

Figure 5.8 **(a)** Asymmetric collimator facility as applied to a tangential pair of fields treating the right breast. **(b)** Asymmetric collimator facility as applied to the supraclavicular and axillary parallel opposed pair of fields (from Chism et al 1994, with permission).

augment the attenuation provided by the individual leaves of the MLC, an additional set of back-up diaphragms is provided. Lower jaw replacements are typically found in Siemens accelerators.

Multileaf collimation and principles of conformal therapy

Stereotactic radiosurgery and radiotherapy are applications of conformal therapy that have been around for some time (see Ch. 6). The term stereotactic radiosurgery refers to treatment delivered in a single fraction with the intention of obliterating the tumour volume, whereas stereotactic radiotherapy describes a fractionated delivery of the total dose in an attempt to preserve function in the treated area. With respect to cranial irradiation, the former requires the use of an invasive head frame which is attached to the skull under a local anaesthetic. Such a method would not be practical for fractionated treatment, and other specialised head frames have been devised (Bentel 1999).

When an accelerator is used to deliver such treatment, multiple arcs and simultaneous couch rotations are employed to deliver a high tumour dose whilst dramatically minimising the dose delivered to surrounding structures. The technique is characterised by a finely collimated and focused beam resulting in a highly spherical tumour volume that demonstrates sharp and significant dose fall off. The average planning target volume (see p. 19) is in the region of 3 cm^3 and currently these techniques are used to manage conditions where significant complications arise with conventional treatment methods (e.g. arteriovenous malformations, small localised brain tumours, epilepsy and recurrent disease).

The first British MLC for clinical use was installed at the Royal Marsden Hospital, but the principle of conformal therapy was understood as early as 1959, when Shinji Takahashi looked at the feasibility of creating irregular treatment volumes. Unfortunately the practical technology to deliver his ideas was not developed until the 1980s with the advent of microprocessor technology.

Conformal therapy is usually applied in one of two ways:

1. To deliver a higher dose to the treatment volume without compromising surrounding tissue
2. To deliver a standard dose to the tumour volume while delivering a considerably lower dose to the normal surrounding tissue. This helps to reduce the side-effects in radiosensitive tissues.

True dose conformity requires the technical capability to control dynamically the treatment couch, the MLC jaws, back-up collimator system, the head twist mechanism and gantry rotation. However, practicalities such as time, resource constraints and patient position do limit the maximum number of fields that may be delivered in this manner.

Additionally, the problems of verifying the position of all of the moving parts of the accelerator in relation to the planning target volume have yet to be resolved effectively. Greenberg & Kalend (cited in Elekta Oncology Systems 1999) are currently studying the use of artificial intelligence and artificial vision for the verification of patient position and detection of patient movement. Their work aims to evaluate whether surface anatomy is comparable to conventional methods of treatment verification (see Ch. 1).

There are disadvantages associated with the use of conformal therapy, the main one being that a decrease in the size of the average planning target volume increases the possibility of a geographical miss. In order to deliver the idea of conformal treatment to its true potential, much work is needed on improving the accuracy of current immobilisation techniques, as well as in the accuracy associated with defining the tumour volume. Internal organ movement also presents significant problems that have yet to be satisfactorily resolved, and even with current advances, the quality of on line imaging could still be improved further.

The technology required for the delivery of this method of treatment is complex, and the software currently available on the market is diverse. In addition to an accelerator equipped with a multileaf collimator and a portal imaging system (see p. 121) for verification, the following are required:

• Multileaf configuration computer system to allow the desired field outline to be translated into MLC leaf positions. This may be by the use of a manual digitiser and light box, a digital image from the simulator of sim CT (see Ch. 1), or CT simulator software. These positions are then communicated to the MLC control and file system.

• Multileaf control and file systems to enable accurate positioning and control of each leaf, detection of that position in real time, and leaf calibration.

• Storage system using either a network link to a file saver, CD or floppy disk, or a hard copy produced by laser printer. The former is advantageous in that only a single copy of the patient data is resident within the system, significantly reducing potential errors associated with multiple copies, but it is only effective if regular system back-up occurs.

The collimator itself consists of anywhere from 20 to 80 pairs of tungsten leaves arranged in two opposing banks (see Fig. 5.9a). Each leaf projects a 1–2 cm width at the isocentric plane and has the ability to move individually. The accuracy of positioning is in the region of 1 mm, and obviously the complexity of controlling many individual leaves requires the use of specific programming software, as indicated above.

The edge of each leaf as it projects into the beam is curved in the vertical plane but blunt ended in the horizontal plane. Whilst this design reduces penumbra at the beam edge, it does make it difficult to closely match the tumour edge and the formation of a 'stair case edge' is a significant problem. The micro MLC now available helps to reduce this effect, with enhanced volume definition (Sharrock & Read 1998).

Each leaf must be thick enough to provide the attenuation afforded by conventional secondary collimators. Problems with leakage between adjacent leaves means that back-up collimators analogous to conventional secondary collimation are always provided. Leakage also occurs between opposing banks of leaves which, when closed, demonstrate a gap of approximately 2 mm. The amount of leakage between the leaves varies between manufacturers because of the way in which the leaves are designed to fit together.

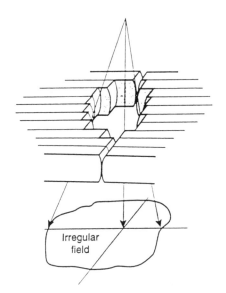

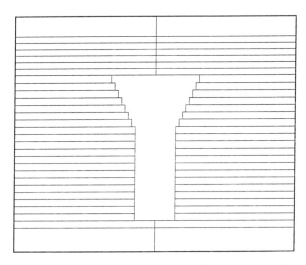

Figure 5.9 **(a)** A simplified diagram of an MLC (from Greene and Williams 1997, with permission). **(b)** A patient specific arrangement of leaves (from Siemens 1996, with permission).

After simulation, the radiographs of the area to be treated are marked with the required volumes. These are then digitised into a treatment planning computer. An individual treatment plan is produced, usually via the inverse treatment planning method (see below), and the digitised information is converted into a series of signals which are then sent to the multileaf collimator positioning system. Alternatively, patients may be CT simulated (see p. 21) and the concepts of virtual simulation used to produced the desired planning target volume. After passing to the MLC positioning system on the treatment unit, the individual leaves can be moved into place (see Fig. 5.9b).

Inverse treatment planning

Owing to the nature of conformal therapy, and the anatomical sites around which it is commonly employed, this method of treatment planning is frequently used. The treatment planning software is designed to allow the user to program optimal isodose contours around the tumour volume, while at the same time prescribing maximum doses to be delivered to the tumour volume and any adjacent critical or radiosensitive structures. Using complex mathematical algorithms, the required beam arrangement is then calculated to deliver the desired distribution.

It is important to stress that computer software systems such as these may deliver clinically impractical solutions to the problems posed – the judicial application of common sense must always be applied during the approval and verification process!

Beam intensity modulation

Traditionally practised in principle for many years by the timely application of customised remote tissue compensators, the advent of multiple field planning and the time taken for manufacture of these devices has led to significant clinical developments in the principles of tissue compensators.

In beam intensity modulation, accelerator beam intensity is varied during treatment by a continuous unidirectional sweep of some or all of the MLC leaves, with the intention of creating a highly conformal dose distribution even in the case of concave tumour volumes. Treatment delivery may be dynamic or static; in the latter each individual field consists of a number of static fields delivered consecutively at the required gantry angle.

One implication of this technology is the potential of being able to wrap dose around a planned target volume while at the same time protecting adjacent critical structures, making it possible to use external beam radiotherapy to treat targets not geometrically well separated from critical structures. Trials currently ongoing are examining the implications of beam intensity modulation in malignancies of the head and neck region, breast, prostate and lung.

Quality assurance of MLC systems

The principles of acceptance, commissioning and routine quality assurance testing for an MLC are very similar to those of conventional secondary collimator systems. Galvin (1998) recommends that consideration should be given to testing the following:

1. Leaf position readout and isocentricity (different tolerance for beam intensity modulation)
2. Penumbra width as a function of leaf position
3. Light and X-ray field coincidence
4. Collimator leakage
5. Interlocks
6. Collimator rotation and speed
7. Interleaf leakage and leakage through any back-up collimators
8. Leakage at the point where opposing banks of leaves meet and overlap (usually known as the tongue-and-groove overlap)
9. Interlocks of back-up collimators
10. Generation of leaf shapes and file transfer mechanism
11. Dose distribution at the stepped edge
12. Leaf speed control (for dynamic dose delivery only).

The frequency and complexity of each test may vary during the three separate stages of testing, and the type of test and its tolerance limits must be determined by each individual department. For specific details of these tests consultation of the paper by Galvin (1998) is recommended.

Dosimetry of MLC systems

Dosimetry for accelerators with an MLC facility is complex, and careful consideration must be given to areas such as field size dependence on output factors, depth doses, isodose distribution, penumbra and leaf transmission data (Palta & Kim 1998).

The change in output factor with field shaping of irregular fields produces the most significant impact on the accuracy of the dose delivered to the patient, with characteristic scatter emanating primarily from the tertiary collimator, the beam flattening filter and any other beam modification device placed between the target and the patient.

Minimal changes occur to depth doses and isodose distributions when compared to those produced by conventional collimator systems. Scatter and electron contamination potentially may influence percentage depth dose (particularly in the build-up region), owing to the proximity of a tertiary collimator to the skin of the

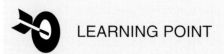 LEARNING POINT

The new technologies discussed above have many advantages over conventional methods of delivering external beam therapy. However, it is far from simple to translate theory into practice.

Question
Evaluate the feasibility and implications of implementing such advances in treatment delivery and working practices into your specific department.

patient. Palta & Kim (1998) have also reported undulating 50% isodose contours produced from the staircase effect of the leaf edges.

Penumbra and leaf transmission factors are individual to each accelerator, and as such will be established during the commissioning process.

Wedges

Wedging techniques currently in clinical use fall into three main categories:

1. Fixed wedges
2. The inherent wedge
3. The dynamic wedge.

Fixed wedges

Fixed wedges remain in the treatment beam through the delivery of dose to an individual treatment field. They are generally stored in an interlocked wedge filter bank, and are available in an array of commonly used wedge angles (15°, 30°, 45° and 60°). Several wedges of the same angle will be available to adequately cover the range of likely field sizes.

Wedges mounted externally to the treatment head are generally heavier and larger than internally mounted fixed wedges and will obscure the field defining light. Their advantage is that the radiographer can clearly see the wedge orientation in relation to the patient set-up. Alternatively, they are mounted within the treatment head, positioned just above the mirror of the field defining light system. Because of the divergence of the beam these wedges are physically smaller and lighter.

The inherent wedge

The inherent wedge is also known as the motorised wedge. It enables the selection and treatment of wedged fields having any angle between 1° and 60°. Commonly in radiotherapy practice wedged fields are employed with open fields at different gantry angles, and this principle is extended to the single gantry angle in this application of field wedging. This practice can be employed using fixed wedges, but this is a somewhat laborious procedure which extends the time the patient is on the couch. With the use of microprocessor control it is possible to conduct such practice automatically.

As the wedge is located above the optical field it does not obscure the field light, and interlocks confirm that the wedge is in place or fully retracted. Treatment machines with this equipment routinely provide two sets of monitor units for each field; one set for the wedged portion of the field and the other for the unwedged portion. A disadvantage of the inherent wedge is that because it must be used for the full range of field sizes that may be selected it is physically larger than the comparable fixed wedge for the same machine parameters. This means that it tends to have a greater attenuation factor than its fixed wedge equivalent.

The dynamic wedge

The dynamic wedge is a wedge angle produced by the rapid movement of the collimator during treatment delivery, with the field size changing constantly to generate the desired wedge angle. The main advantage of this wedging technique is that the quality of the beam will not be altered as it is with traditional wedge materials. However,

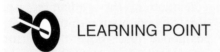

LEARNING POINT

There are two definitions of the term wedge angle:
The first is the angle at which the 50% isodose crosses the central axis of the beam.
The second is the angle that crosses the central axis of the beam at a depth of 10 cm.

Question
What are the implications of the difference between these definitions?

such a method of generating a wedge angle gives rise to complex dosimetry problems in calculating the exact array of collimator positions to reproduce a specific beam angle. This method is employed in multileaf and independent collimator systems.

The electron beam treatment head

The components required for the production of an electron treatment beam are illustrated previously (Fig. 5.7b). In the electron mode the beam current must be reduced by a factor of approximately 100, along with a matching adjustment to the frequency of the RF source. This prevents the production of dangerously high dose rates of high energy electrons. This alteration of electron gun current dictates a need for similar modifications to the currents supplying the bending magnet system, and the steering and focusing coils.

The target is removed and replaced with an electron window. This is necessary to prevent bremsstrahlung production in the target and to contain the system vacuum. Any inherent wedge is retracted out of the electron beam.

The beam flattening filter is replaced with electron scattering foils, made from thin sheets of metal of high atomic number. One foil widens the narrow electron beam, and the second acts in a manner similar to the X-ray beam flattening filter in an attempt to improve the flatness of the beam. Unfortunately these foils act as sources of bremsstrahlung radiation, contaminating the purity of the electron beam, so care must be taken in the design of this collimation system to achieve the desired angular spread by the scattering foils with the lowest amount of bremsstrahlung contamination. Secondary diaphragms are retracted to their maximum setting to reduce their bremsstrahlung contribution, and electron collimators are fitted. These take the form of cones or trimmer bars which are attached to the accessory ring of the treatment head. Cones are available in standard field sizes, while trimmers can be used for a whole range of different field sizes. Collimation is necessary as the electrons undergo significant numbers of

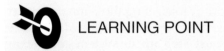

LEARNING POINT

Questions

Why is the wall thickness of an electron cone usually less than the practical range of the maximum electron energy?

Are electron trimmers as efficient collimators as electron cones?

interactions between the electron window and the patient, giving a very scattered beam that needs focusing onto the treatment area. In this manner electron cones prevent the delivery of dose to areas outside the treatment volume and sharpen the beam edges at the skin surface. Individual customised cutouts are available to allow non standard field shapes to be used; these generally fit inside the patient end of the collimator.

Finally, it is important to calibrate the machine and, in doing so, confirm the energy, output and dose rate of the machine prior to treating the patient.

Scanned electron beams

One of the problems associated with the traditional electron beam treatment head is the unacceptable levels of bremsstrahlung contamination routinely experienced with some collimator designs. The problem is considerably reduced in machines which use a magnetic deflection system to scan the electron beam across the required treatment field, thereby negating the need for electron scattering foils. This also produces a flat beam which can compensate for an irregular body contour by the generation of a non uniform distribution. A helium atmosphere also reduces the incidence of electrons scattered by collisions with air molecules and produces a more defined beam edge.

This technology can also be applied to X-ray beams, where the beam may be deflected in a similar manner. Scanning also eliminates the

need for a beam flattening filter, thereby reducing the beam quality problems caused by such filters. When in X-ray mode, the use of a purging magnet removes the troublesome secondary electrons produced on the patient side of the target (Brahme 1987, Washington & Lever 1996b).

The disadvantage of electron beam scanning accelerators is the consequence of failure of the beam scanning mechanism. A large dose delivered to a very small area can cause significant problems for the patient.

COMPUTER CONTROL AND VERIFICATION SYSTEMS

Linear accelerators are extremely complex pieces of machinery, and an adequate explanation of control systems is really beyond the scope of this book. The information that follows is a brief introduction to the basic principles of computer based verification and record systems; for a comprehensive review of these and computer control systems the reader is advised to consult Chapter 10 of the excellent text by Greene & Williams (1997).

Verification of the treatment parameters prior to irradiating the patient can be achieved in a number of ways. These methods range from the simple to the very complex, and are described below:

1. *Manual*. The radiographer positions the patient with respect to the data recorded on the treatment sheet and isodose distribution, and manually sets all treatment parameters inside the room. The required monitor units and time, beam modality and energy, dose rate, and any beam modification interlocks such as wedges are set or selected on the treatment control panel. All machine parameters should then be confirmed visually by a second radiographer before the unit is switched on. The machine terminates treatment when the monitor units have been delivered.

2. *Manual select and confirm*. The computer will confirm basic machine parameters such as wedge angle, monitor units, energy and modality, whilst the radiographer continues to

manually set and visually verify the remaining set-up parameters. Data are then manually set and selected on the treatment control panel, and the machine will only commence radiation delivery if the measured and entered parameters coincide.

3. *Automatic select and confirm.* All treatment parameters are manually pre-programmed into the computer, delivered via a DICOM link from the planning computer or simulator suite, or automatically acquired on the first day of treatment. Thereafter the patient data are called up using either the patient name or a bar code placed on the front of the treatment sheet. The radiographer ensures that the patient is in the correct position on the treatment couch and manually sets the remaining parameters. The machine will not operate until the programmed and selected parameters coincide within a defined tolerance limit. A radiographer should

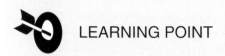

LEARNING POINT

There is no doubt that the incorporation of such systems into commercially available accelerators has reduced the incidence of treatment errors. Radiotherapy departments have a professional duty to develop working practices and safe schemes of work that ensure treatment errors are kept to a minimum, and in quality driven systems the benefits speak for themselves. However, there has been debate among radiotherapy radiographers regarding the extent to which such systems should be used and relied upon in the clinical setting.

Question
Using examples of verification systems that you are clinically familiar with, discuss the advantages and disadvantages of the four types of verification system listed above.

then visually confirm the data against the treatment sheet prior to selecting the beam on button.

4. *Automatic and assisted set-up (ASU) systems.* This is the next step up in system complexity from the previous option. If desired, and once the identity of the patient has been confirmed and he or she is lying in the correct position on the treatment couch, the radiographer can choose to allow the machine to automatically program itself to the desired settings. Parameters such as field size and beam energy can be automatically set, whereas with other parameters it would be unwise to rely on this facility since factors such as couch height, lateral and longitude depend on the patient being on the exact same part of the couch every day. This is unlikely to happen, even when the chosen position of the patient is reproduced on a daily basis.

MACHINE FAULTS

It is not the intention to provide a comprehensive list of all the types of machine error likely to terminate treatment or prevent it from starting. Causes of individual errors can be, and often are, numerous, and it would be of little use to attempt to list them here. In addition, fault messages will vary depending on the manufacturer.

The intended emphasis of this section is to highlight the sources of common fault messages that you may be presented with and suggest principles of management. Naturally any comments expressed here must be viewed in the light of your own individual departmental protocols relating to the recognition, management and documentation of machine faults. Such protocols should have been carefully written taking into account the history of the accelerator, and after detailed consultation between medical physics and the in-house maintenance team, superintendent radiographers and the manufacturer concerned. An additional starting point for information is the user manual for the accelerator in question. Manuals can provide extensive information relating to the error message, its cause and suggested solution.

The monitor and control system of the accelerator is designed to observe the operating systems and ensure that their performance remains within specific parameters in order to effect the safe delivery of treatment to the patient. In the event of a malfunction this system will either produce a fault message, or will terminate machine output.

Common fault messages usually relate to one or more of the following elements of the system:

Dosimetry. These include errors relating to beam output, energy, dose rate or flatness, dose channels one and two, timers and the ionisation chamber. Potential sources of a fault can originate in any of the systems that influence beam production, such as the modulator, magnetron/klystron, AFC, waveguide and components of the treatment head.

Modulator cabinet. This provides power to the microwave source and electron gun.

Vacuum system and electronic ion pump. These provide the low pressures required for the effective operation of the electron gun, waveguide and bending magnet system.

Cooling system and temperature control. A large majority of accelerator components must operate within an optimum temperature range. This is particularly critical for the waveguide. Thermal expansion can lead to detuning which seriously impairs its ability to accelerate electrons.

Pressure system. This pressurises the waveguide with an insulating gas that helps prevent electrical breakdown from the electric component of the electromagnetic wave.

Automatic frequency control (AFC) system. This detects the operating frequency of the accelerator structure and then adjusts the output of the magnetron/klystron to ensure optimum radiation output. It influences the focusing and steering of the electron beam as it travels from the electron gun and into the bending magnet system (Karzmark & Morton 1998).

Certain departments operate protocols whereby a specific fault peculiar to their individual accelerator can be rectified, and treatment continued, by a nominated person activating the reset switch. These procedures should be agreed prior to any fault occurring, and should be clearly documented in a place accessible to,

and regularly viewed by, all accelerator staff. Some error and fault messages do not require any action other than to document their appearance in the accelerator fault book. Such documentation should be examined on a regular basis by maintenance staff and should be subject to trend analysis. On the appearance of other fault messages and errors, the following actions are suggested:

1. Pause treatment and notify supervising radiographer of fault
2. Inform patient of situation, and reassure them during the delay or remove them from the treatment room
3. Inform accelerator maintenance team, and document fault and machine performance prior to fault appearing
4. Once the fault message has been cleared by the maintenance staff, ensure that they record the action taken to rectify the fault in the accelerator operating manual
5. Inform staff of any recommended changes to required operating procedure, and modify work protocols where appropriate
6. Reassure patient, confirm patient position and continue treatment delivery.

ELECTRONIC PORTAL IMAGING

Portal imaging has been used for many years in the verification of treatment fields. Using radiographic film, the treatment volume can be visualised with respect to bony anatomical landmarks. Field borders can be confirmed in this manner, as can the accuracy of shielding placement. However, image quality is generally poor in comparison to the simulator radiograph, owing to the predominance of the compton scatter interaction process at megavoltage energies. The main advantage of using radiographic film, often enhanced by copper filters, is that the facilities are available in any radiotherapy department for minimal additional cost.

Electronic portal imaging devices (EPIDs) capture the image in a digital format and provide a real time image. In this way, sophisticated image processing technology can be applied to improve its quality. Additional software can also be used to superimpose these images over the initial simulation film to confirm the accuracy of field placement. Other options include establishing a relationship between the digital image brightness and absorbed dose. It then becomes possible to calculate the exact exit doses from a particular field and thereby verify the treatment plan and its inherent factors such as tissue electron density. Routine daily monitoring of the patient position is now feasible quickly and without delivering unnecessary additional dose to the patient.

For the first time it has also become possible to view the influence of organ movement during treatment. As well as being able to capture an image using very little dose, it is also possible to capture a series of images throughout the course of a treatment field. These images can then be played back in cine format, and any changes in field placement with breathing can be observed.

There are two main types of EPID available:

- Fluorescent screens
- Radiation detector arrays.

The fluorescent screen is placed in the exit beam of a field. It is coated in a material that converts the perpendicular scattered X-rays to secondary electrons, as well as absorbing very low energy scattered radiation which would otherwise reduce the image quality. These electrons are absorbed in the fluorescent material and the amount of light emitted will be proportional to the absorbed radiation dose. This optical image is then collected by a mirror system and picked up by a camera that stores the image. Ionisation chambers and silicon diode detector arrays operate in a similar manner and are positioned to replace the fluorescent screen. They are arranged as very wide, thin arrays which absorb dose as it is emitted from the patient, and consequently have a very fast acquisition time.

QUALITY ASSURANCE, TREATMENT CALCULATIONS AND RADIATION PROTECTION

Information relating to quality assurance, treatment calculations, radiation protection and room

design will not be discussed discussed in this chapter. Because of the importance and predominance of linear accelerators in the radiotherapy department, it is appropriate for each of these subject areas to be discussed in detail in its own chapter (see Chs 2, 3 and 4).

All other pieces of treatment equipment are discussed in the relevant chapters, with an examination of how the principles and practice of these areas differ from those of the linear accelerator.

RECOMMENDED READING

Galvin J M 1998 Acceptance testing, commissioning and routine quality assurance for multileaf collimator systems, AAPM refresher course, Aug 8–10, San Antonio, Texas
Greene D, Williams P C 1996 Linear accelerators for radiation therapy, 2nd edn. Institute of Physics Publishing, Bristol
Institute of Physical Sciences in Medicine 1988 Commissioning and quality assurance of linear accelerators. Report No. 54. IPSM, York
Karzmark C J, Morton R J (eds) 1981 A primer on theory and operation of linear accelerators in radiation therapy. US Department of Health and Human Services, Maryland
Palta J R, Kim S 1998 Multileaf collimator dosimetry, AAPM refresher course, Aug 8–10, San Antonio, Texas

REFERENCES

Bentel G 1999 Patient positioning and immobilisation in radiation oncology. McGraw-Hill, New York
Bomford C K, Kunkler I H, Sherriff S B (eds) 1993 Walter and Miller's Textbook of radiotherapy, radiation physics, therapy and oncology, 5th edn. Churchill Livingstone,. Edinburgh
Brahme A 1987 Design principles and clinical possibilities with a new generation of radiation therapy equipment. Acta Oncologica 26: 403–412
British Journal of Radiology 1996 Central axis depth dose data for use in radiotherapy. Supplement 25. British Institute of Radiology, London
Buderi R 1996 The invention that changed the world: the story of radar from war to peace. Little Brown, London
Chism S E, Chism D B, Kalsched M, Yakoob R, Oline D 1994 Breast cancer. Medica Mundi 39(3): 115
Elekta Oncology Systems 1999 Wavelength: News and Advances in Precision Radiation Oncology 3: 1
Galvin J M 1998 Acceptance testing, commissioning and routine quality assurance for multileaf collimator systems. AAPM refresher course, Aug 8–10, San Antonio, Texas
Greene D, Williams P C 1997 Linear accelerators for radiation therapy, 2nd edn. Institute of Physics Publishing, Bristol
Institute of Physical Sciences in Medicine 1988 Commissioning and quality assurance of linear accelerators. Report No. 54. IPSM, York

Karzmark C J, Morton R J 1998 A primer on theory and operation of linear accelerators in radiation therapy, 2nd edn. Medical Physics Publishing, Madison

Karzmark C J, Morton R J (eds) 1981 A primer on theory and operation of linear accelerators in radiation therapy. US Department of Health and Human Services, Maryland

Knoll G F 1989 Radiation detection and measurement, 2nd edn. Wiley, New York

Leo W R 1994 Techniques for nuclear and particle physics experiments: a how-to approach, 2nd revised edn. Springer-Verlag, Berlin

Meredith W J, Massey J B 1977 Fundamental physics of radiology. John Wright, Bristol

Metcalfe P, Kron T, Hoban P 1997 The physics of radiotherapy X-rays from linear accelerators. Medical Physics Publishing, Madison

Palta J R, Kim S 1998 Multileaf collimator dosimetry. AAPM refresher course, Aug 8–10, San Antonio, Texas

Scharfe W H, Chomicki O A 1996 Medical accelerators in radiotherapy: past, present and future. Physica Medica 12: 199–226

Sharrock C, Read G 1998 The present status of conformal radiotherapy. Rad Magazine (March). Kingsmoor Publications, Essex

Siemens 1996 Siemens multileaf collimator data sheet. Siemens Medical Systems, Concord, California

Stanton R, Stinson D 1996 Applied physics for radiation oncology. Medical Physics Publishing, Madison

Valkovic V (ed) 1997 International atomic energy agency accelerator Newsletter 4:2. Analysis and Control Technologies, Zagreb

Washington C M, Leaver T (eds) 1996a Principles and practice of radiation therapy, vol. 1: Introduction to radiation therapy. Mosby Year Book, St Louis

Washington C M, Leaver T (eds) 1996b Principles and practice of radiation therapy physics, simulation and treatment planning. Mosby Year Book, St Louis

Wilks R 1987 Principles of radiological physics, 2nd edn. Churchill Livingstone, Edinburgh

Williams J R, Thwaites D I (eds) 1993 Radiotherapy physics in practice. Oxford University Press, Oxford

INTERNET REFERENCE

Varian Associates: an early history. 30.8.97 http://www.varian.com/

⁶⁰Cobalt units

Chapter objectives

On completion of this chapter you should be able to:

- Evaluate the role of the teletherapy ⁶⁰Co unit in the management of malignant disease
- Discuss the implications of errors in the calculation of patient dose
- Describe the role of the multidisciplinary team in the selection of a new piece of external beam radiotherapy equipment.

INTRODUCTION

⁶⁰Cobalt units have been used for the treatment of cancer for several decades, and were the first machines to produce a beam with significant percentage depth dose that also delivered the dose maximum below the skin surface of the patient, resulting in dramatically reduced skin reactions. However, their position in the radiotherapy department has been superseded by the linear accelerator for a wide variety of reasons discussed later in this chapter. At present, although its use is declining in the UK, the isocentric cobalt unit still has a significant role to play in the treatment of the palliative patient, mainly because of its mechanical reliability, short warm-up procedure and low maintenance requirements.

Despite the decline of this isocentric teletherapy machine, the isotope has reappeared in a device known as the gamma knife. This development is not new, but has been supported by recent interest in the concept of stereotactic radiosurgery.

^{60}COBALT PRODUCTION

^{60}Cobalt is an isotope produced by bombarding its stable form, ^{59}Co, with neutrons.

^{59}Co + ^{1}n = ^{60}Co

^{60}Cobalt then attempts to gain stability by the emission of beta and gamma radiation.

^{60}Co $\Rightarrow$ excited ^{60}Ni + β (0.31 MeV)

excited ^{60}Ni $\Rightarrow$ stable ^{60}Ni + γ (1.17 MeV) + γ (1.33 MeV)

For convenience, the energy of a cobalt unit is usually quoted as 1.25 MeV, and it has a half life of 5.26 years. This length of half life means that during a typical course of radical external beam treatment (i.e., approximately 30 daily fractions) the treatment calculations will need to be corrected for a decay of approximately 1% per month. Whilst this can be simply incorporated into a monitor unit calculation, it should always be remembered that any additional correction factor will increase the possibility of error in the calculation of absolute dose. The activity of radionuclides is quoted in terms of the curie (Ci) or the SI unit of the becquerel (Bq).

1 Ci = 3.7×10^{10} Bq
1 Bq = 1 disintegration sec^{-1}

PENUMBRA AND FIELD SIZE

Radiotherapy students commonly believe that there is no radiation outside the field defining light used to align the patient during daily set-up. This is not the case.

In normal clinical practice radiation does exist outside the field light edges, and this is the result of the penumbra. Exactly how much exists is individual to each department and its specific definition of field size (see p. 95).

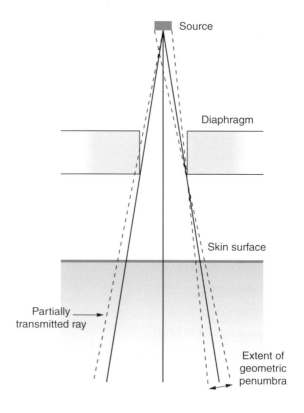

Figure 6.1 A schematic diagram of a ^{60}Cobalt beam emerging through a diaphragm from a source of finite size. Geometric penumbra and a partially transmitted ray are shown on the right and left edges of the beam respectively (from Jayaraman & Lanzl 1996 with permission from Lewis Publishers, an imprint of CRC Press).

Penumbra is the result of three main elements:

1. *Geometric penumbra.* As demonstrated in Figure 6.1, a lack of sharpness appears at the edge of the radiation beam. This is caused by the source of radiation having finite size. It can only truly be demonstrated on a radiograph, and if a theoretical point source of radiation is used, penumbra will be insignificant. The cobalt capsule has considerable size and produces significant geometric penumbra. Reducing the source size so that penumbra is acceptable will reduce the total source activity, thereby increasing overall treatment time.

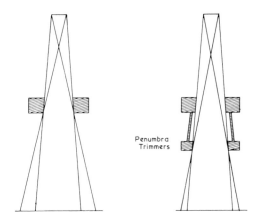

Figure 6.2   The reduction of geometric penumbra by the use of penumbra trimmers (from Bomford et al 1993, with permission).

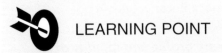

LEARNING POINT

Questions

What implications may penumbra have when planning a patient's treatment?

How may we reduce the influence of geometric penumbra in the clinical situation?

2. *Scatter penumbra*. This contributes to existing penumbra and is caused by radiation backscattering to the surface of the patient.

3. *Transmission penumbra* is caused by radiation not travelling through a complete collimator or diaphragm leaf (see Fig. 6.1), and consequently not being reduced to the desired intensity. Its incidence is directly proportional to the size of the field, and may also occur when shielding blocks are placed in the path of the main beam. It is reduced by the use of multilevel vertical collimation and penumbra trimmers. As Figure 6.2 shows, the latter are attached to the head of the treatment unit, and act to define the edge of the beam more clearly.

THE REQUIREMENTS OF A RADIONUCLIDE SUITABLE FOR TELETHERAPY USE

KEY POINTS

Any radionuclide to be used in a teletherapy treatment unit ideally should demonstrate all of the following characteristics:

- A long half life. This has two benefits; firstly minimising costly and time-consuming source replacements, and secondly removing the need for a decay correction factor in the treatment calculation.

- A small volume to reduce any geometric penumbra produced. Typical source sizes range from 0.5 cm to 2.0 cm in diameter.

- A high specific activity so that the source size can be as small as possible. Specific activity is defined as the number of transformations per second per gramme of material. Clinically, total source activity ranges from 3000 to 9000 Ci, which gives a specific activity in the range of 75–200 Ci g^{-1}. As well as reducing the penumbra, a high specific activity also gives a reasonable dose rate at 1 metre from the source. The latter point benefits the treatment set-up in terms of stability of patient position with time. The higher the dose rate the shorter the treatment time and the easier it is for the patient to remain in a stable position. Figures quoted above will produce an average dose rate at 1 m of approximately 1 Gy min^{-1}.

- Suitable radioactive emissions. This isotope produces gamma radiation with an average energy of 1.25 MeV. This is an ideal energy for the areas routinely treated on this machine; head and neck, breast and thorax all have mid-range separations ideally matched to the percentage depth doses produced from ^{60}Cobalt. The maximum energy of 1.33 MeV requires minimal expenditure on radiation protection in comparison to a low energy accelerator.

KEY POINTS (continued)

■ Readily available and cost-effective. This is no longer the case, as the cost of a source replacement is now prohibitive for the budgets of most radiotherapy departments. Legislation also places restrictions on transport and disposal.

Table 6.1 Percentage depth dose data for 10×10 cm field at 80 cm FSD (British Journal of Radiology 1996)

Isodose (%)	Depth (cm)
100	0.5
80	4–5
50	11–12

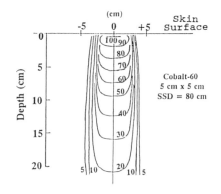

(a)

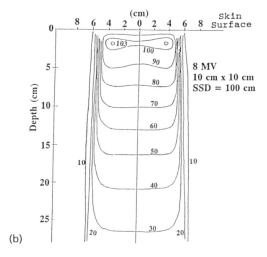

(b)

Figure 6.3 **(a)** Isodose curves for a [60]Cobalt beam. **(b)** Isodose curves for an 8 MV X-ray beam (from Jayaraman & Lanzl 1996, with permission from Lewis Publishers, an imprint of CRC Press).

BEAM CHARACTERISTICS

The cobalt isodose distribution has distinct features in comparison to a megavoltage beam produced from a linear accelerator:

Central axis depth dose and degree of skin sparing

Beam data for a [60]Cobalt unit are shown in Table 6.1.

Width of penumbra

For equivalent beam parameters, [60]Cobalt has a wider penumbra than any megavoltage beam produced from a linear accelerator.

Shape of beam profile and rapidity of dose fall off

As shown in Figures 6.3a and b, the cobalt isodose has a less flattened beam profile in comparison to an accelerator owing to the absence of a beam flattening filter. Dose fall off is comparable.

COMPONENTS OF AN ISOCENTRIC [60]COBALT UNIT

An isocentric [60]Cobalt unit is extremely simple in design, consisting of a radioactive isotope, a source housing and method of collimation, and an isocentric mechanism. Figure 6.4 illustrates that certain aspects of the appearance of a cobalt unit are very similar to that of a linear accelerator.

Source design

The radioisotope can be in the form of discs, pellets or powder, and is double encapsulated in stainless steel to prevent leakage of the radioisotope and to absorb the beta emissions (Meredith & Massey 1977). It is then placed into a treatment head (Fig. 6.5) containing adequate shielding

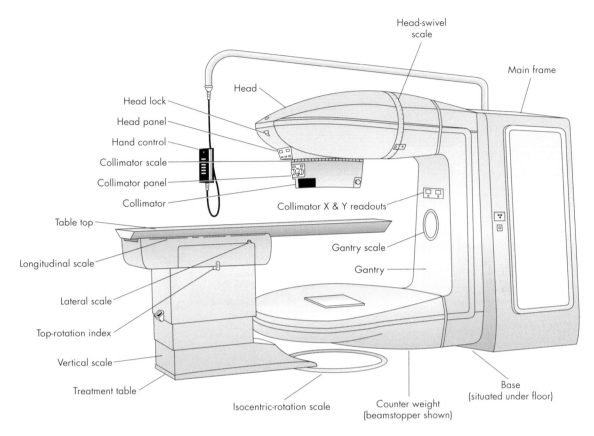

Figure 6.4 An Atomic Energy of Canada Limited Theratron 780C 60Cobalt unit (from Washington & Lever 1996, with permission).

which may consist of lead, tungsten or depleted uranium.

There were formerly five main mechanisms for placing the source at the 'beam on' position, but only two of them are now in common use.

A mercury shutter employed liquid mercury which was taken during treatment from a reservoir in front of the source. This clearly had significant health and safety implications and was soon withdrawn from use. Moving lead jaws located below the source were unwieldy and not particularly effective, and a chain driven sphere containing a stationary source that was rotated through 90° for treatment was superseded by a more effective rotating wheel mechanism.

The rotating wheel mechanism has the source placed on a turntable, very like the beam flattening filter turret in an accelerator. When the 'beam on' mode is required, the wheel rotates through 180° to place the source in front of the collimators.

The moving drawer version operates by the use of compressed air (see Fig. 6.5). The source capsule containing the radioisotope is held within a source drawer. This is pushed horizontally over the collimators by compressed air. When the radioisotope is in the correct position a source position indicator protrudes from the head of the machine and can be used to push the source back into the 'beam off' position. This is necessary, as the source can stick in the 'beam on' position because of particles of dust and dirt which collect over time within the path of the source drawer and prevent it from retracting back into the safe position. If this should happen during routine use a procedure known as the 'source stick protocol' (see p. 000) should be

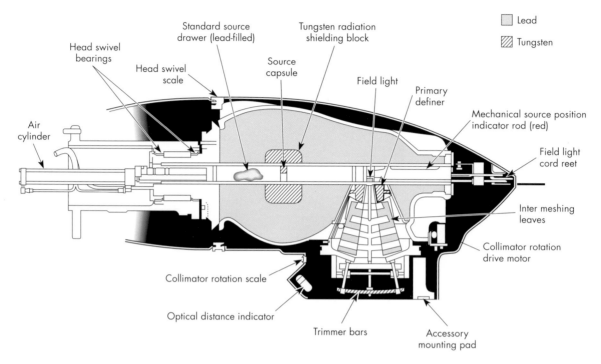

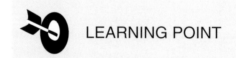

Figure 6.5 A cross-section of typical ^{60}Cobalt components (from Washington & Lever 1996, with permission).

followed. In the event of a power failure, the mechanism will automatically return the source to the safe position.

An additional correction factor also needs to be applied for ^{60}Cobalt treatment calculations, owing to the fact that the source travels from the safe housing to the 'beam on' position. At any time when the source capsule is not in its safe housing, radiation will be emitted. Levels increase as the source moves nearer to the collimator, and so a source transit factor needs to be applied to compensate for this, otherwise an inaccurate calculation of patient dose will result.

Collimation

This is divided into primary and secondary collimation. The primary collimator or primary definer is fixed, and defines the maximum available field size. The secondary collimator system is a complex set of interleaved lead blocks (see Fig. 6.5) which aims to reduce geometric

LEARNING POINT

Question
Secondary electrons will also be produced in the electron filter, so why is it still used?

penumbra. One disadvantage of this design is an increase in scatter produced from the secondary collimators; a large number of secondary electrons are produced by these interactions. If these electrons reach the skin surface of the patient they will contribute to skin dose, and destroy the minimal skin sparing effect characteristic of this machine. Increasing the distance between the collimator and the patient is one solution, but this also increases geometric penumbra. A compromise has been to introduce a thin sheet of perspex to act as a filter, and to ensure that the distance between the patient and the collimator remains greater than 15–20 cm.

LEGISLATION

In addition to the Ionising Radiation Regulations, two other pieces of legislation are of particular significance for ^{60}Cobalt machines.

Radioactive Substances Act 1993 (RSA 93) (Department of the Environment 1993)

This act places stringent controls on the storage, handling and disposal of radioactive materials at any establishment. A licence must be obtained so that the department is listed as a registered holder of radioactive substances (Section 6a); this licence specifies exactly how much of each radionuclide the department is entitled to hold, describes how each radionuclide may be administered and by whom, and how waste products should be disposed of. Enforcement of the act is the responsibility of Her Majesty's Inspectorate of Pollution at the Department of the Environment.

In a situation where it is necessary to dispose of a ^{60}Cobalt source, special precautions for its safe disposal need to be taken by the local authority responsible for the waste site. Such activity sources can only be disposed of at carefully selected sites, and site selection involves the chief inspector (appointed by the Secretary of State) consulting with the public and local authority before granting authorisation for disposal (Section 18, para. 1). It is becoming increasingly difficult to find appropriate sites. Contractors who accept responsibility for removing and disposing of the source under the auspices of RSA 93 now charge prohibitive amounts, as potentially they may be unable to gain authorisation to dispose of the ^{60}Cobalt in this country. Ultimately, all disposal costs must be paid by the holder of the licence (Section 18, para. 2a).

In the light of the recently issued Basic Safety Standard Directive, a consultative document has been produced asking for comments on the technical aspects of RSA 93.

Radioactive Material (Road Transport) (Great Britain) Regulations 1996

This relates to the road transport of radioactive materials in the UK, making new provisions for such transport from that required by previous legislation such as the Radioactive Material (Road Transport) Act 1991, and the Radioactive Substances (Carriage by Road) (Great Britain) Amendment Regulations of 1985. Collectively these documents make reference to:

- The design, manufacture and maintenance of packaging acceptable for such transport
- Approved labelling format
- The preparation and storage of radioactive materials during transit and delivery
- Vehicle placarding
- Record keeping and the provision of information
- Recommended transport indices for each category of packaging
- Required licences for the transit of sealed and unsealed radioactive materials.

Similar legislation exists for the carriage of radioactive materials by air, sea and rail, for example the Packaging, Labelling and Carriage of Radioactive Material by Rail Regulations 1996. Access to these and other documents mentioned above may be obtained via the excellent virtual book store produced by Her Majesty's Stationery Office (Internet reference).

ASPECTS OF RADIATION PROTECTION

Source stick protocol

The source stick protocol is the procedure to be followed in the event of the ^{60}Cobalt source remaining in the 'beam on' position. It is a carefully planned series of events designed to remove the patient from the room safely and with as little dose as possible to all concerned. Its conception should involve the radiation protection supervisor as well as the radiographers who are likely to be involved in such a situation. Once a consensus of opinion has been reached, the protocol must be included in the local rules for the machine.

On failure of the source to return to the safe housing, typically the following should occur:

1. Start a stop-watch – it is important to be able to calculate the amount of dose to both patient and staff.

2. Reassure the patient via the intercom, and attempt to return the source to the safe position. This may be achieved by hitting the emergency stop, turning the shutter supply key to the off position, or removing the mains supply by use of a wall isolator switch. If none of these work, and there is a patient on the treatment couch, someone has to go into the room and attempt to return the source to the safe position manually.

3. Inform the chief physicist of the machine fault.

4. A member of staff must go into the treatment room. The protocol for selecting a member of staff should be written in the local rules, but preferably the member of staff should be someone who is no longer of reproductive age. In the event that this does not apply, the most senior member of staff present should be nominated.

5. Depending on the source mechanism, it may be necessary to collect a piece of equipment designed to push the source indicator rod, and therefore the source, back into the treatment head. This device should be positioned on the wall of the maze just inside the entrance.

6. On entering the treatment room it is extremely important to note the time on the stop-watch. In addition, it is wise to continue to reassure the patient. Remaining in the maze if possible, collimate the beam down to its smallest setting and rotate the gantry away from the intended path into the room. This relies on developing a working practice to bring the control pedestal as near as possible to the start of the maze every time the radiographers leave the treatment room. If there is a ceiling mounted pendant, then it should be possible to swing the control near to the same position.

7. Walking around the back of the treatment head, return the source to the safe housing. Assist the patient off the treatment couch and leave the room.

8. Close the door to the maze, ensuring that signs clearly indicate the machine is not for further use.

9. Note the time on the stop-watch.

10. Reassure the patient. Explain that prior to his or her next treatment any extra dose caused by this incident will have been calculated, and treatment times will be adjusted as necessary.

11. Document the incident in the machine fault log.

12. Calculate additional patient dose where appropriate, and inform the consultant oncologist.

13. Hand the machine over to maintenance staff for fault investigation.

14. Send the radiation monitor of the staff member to be read, and replace it with a new one.

15. Prior to using the machine once the fault has been rectified, or the machine has been declared safe for use, it is important to repeat routine quality assurance tests.

16. Because of the risk of a source stick, it is wise to ensure that only patients physically capable of getting themselves off the treatment couch unaided should be treated on this machine. Unfortunately this is no longer happening as the main emphasis of the machine's work tends to be palliative treatments. Indeed, it is possible that two people may have to enter a treatment room under these circumstances. Strictly speaking this is not adhering to the ALARA (as low as reasonably achievable) principle.

The ^{60}Cobalt unit is continually emitting radiation, even when in the 'beam off' position, resulting in a higher background level of radiation than is typical in a treatment room. Working practices should therefore dictate that:

- Patients and staff should only be in the treatment room for the actual treatment set-up. All patient preparation and discussion should be conducted outside the treatment room in a private area.
- Pregnant members of staff, or those trying to become pregnant, should not work on this machine.
- At the end of every day the collimators should be wound down to their smallest setting.

Why are isocentric ⁶⁰Cobalt units being phased out in the UK?

Technological advances such as the development of the magnetron and klystron during the Second World War, and increasing computer sophistication have provided us with the ability to produce very high energy megavoltage accelerator beams with increasing accuracy and reproducibility. The Ionising Radiation Regulations have also required us to stringently practice principles of radiation protection. A constantly emitting source of radiation that cannot be switched off does not fit in with this philosophy, as staff and patients are being irradiated even when the source is retracted into the 'beam off' position. In addition, RSA 93 and the transport regulations have placed considerable restrictions on the movement and disposal of this isotope, making the linear accelerator a more desirable option.

KEY POINTS

Low activity ⁶⁰Cobalt sources are being replaced with accelerators for the following reasons:

- The requirement to keep doses to staff and patients as low as reasonably achievable
- The difficulty in disposing of spent sources has pushed up the cost of replacement sources to prohibitive levels
- Few haulage experts with the appropriate radiation transport licences exist in the UK
- Accelerator treatment calculations do not require a decay correction factor. Minimal correction factors ultimately minimise errors in treatment calculations
- In addition, see page 91 for a detailed list of the technical superiority of accelerators.

Quality assurance protocol

In addition to the tests described in Chapter 4, there are additional inclusions to a QA programme associated with ⁶⁰Cobalt units:

• Wipe testing needs to be conducted on a regular basis, to ensure that radioactivity on the surface of the unit and the collimation system does not rise to unacceptable levels (e.g. as a result of the source capsule having fractured). The test requires that a damp cloth be wiped around the treatment head and in the collimation system, and then a radiation monitor used (scintillation or Geiger counter) to measure levels of radioactivity. When carrying out this test it is important to correct for background radiation levels (BSI 1993).

• Confirmation of the accuracy of the stopwatch is also important, and this can be confirmed by checking the watch against any other form of timer on a regular basis.

• Finally, regular practice of the source stick procedure is necessary to ensure such responses are automatic in the event of such an incident.

SELECTION OF A NEW TREATMENT UNIT

It was decided to place this subject into this particular chapter because it is increasingly common to see cobalt units being replaced by megavoltage or dedicated brachytherapy units. The principles of the following paragraphs do, however, apply to any of the treatment units discussed in this text.

The main factors to be considered when purchasing a new accelerator are as listed below. The list is by no means exhaustive, and has assumed that the standard method of progressing capital investment projects in the UK National Health Service will be followed (HM Government 1994):

1. Establish the capital available, and the source of staff, maintenance and running costs.

2. Develop a business plan to justify the need for the purchase based on current and projected workloads, stating clearly the aims and objectives of the project, the management process and how progress will be monitored. It is essential to ensure that the piece of equipment selected is what is required to meet projected service requirements in the most efficient and effective manner.

LEARNING POINT

Calibration errors relating to sealed sources (teletherapy and brachytherapy) have arisen in the past, to the considerable detriment of the patient and the reputation of the profession. The following scenario is designed to make you consider the implications of such an incident to the patient, the department and the profession as a whole.

You are the senior radiographer responsible for the ^{60}Cobalt unit, and in recent weeks you have become increasingly concerned about the severity of radiation reactions in several of your patients. After expressing your concerns to your superintendent radiographer, it is discovered that a calibration factor has been incorrectly added twice to the source activity calculations.

Question
What immediate and long term actions should be taken by those concerned?

3. Involve representatives from a multiprofessional pool when appointing a selection committee; at the very least include a radiographer, oncologists, medical physics staff, a radiation protection adviser, an architect and estate and finance personnel.

4. Answer the following questions:

- Will the machine be housed in a new facility, and if so where will this be placed? What are the implications of siting the new facility at this position?
- If the machine is a replacement for an existing accelerator, what additional radiation protection will be required?
- If this purchase is to replace another accelerator, how will the patient load be managed during the installation, acceptance and commissioning process?

- Will it be compatible with other equipment in the department – in particular simulator and network equipment.
- Will current external beam techniques need to be retained, or will this purchase provide the opportunity to evaluate current techniques?
- Are additional staff required to operate this unit? If so, how will they be funded?
- How will the staff rota need to be adjusted to ensure that all staff develop the required skills on the new unit?

5. Compile required machine specifications.

6. Invite manufacturers to submit tenders.

7. Establish if there is a tender that exactly meets the required specifications. If not, how might specifications be adjusted to match the tenders submitted whilst meeting the requirement?

8. Monitor project progress and adjust as necessary.

PRINCIPLES OF CALCULATIONS

See Chapter 2.

STEREOTACTIC RADIOSURGERY AND THE GAMMA KNIFE

In this method of external beam radiotherapy, multiple beams of radiation converge on one point where their summative values result in a tumorocidal dose. By delivering dose in this manner, surrounding structures are spared (see Principles of conformal therapy, p. 114). The term radiosurgery refers to the delivery of a single large dose of radiation to a lesion. Stereotactic radiotherapy delivers a fractionated course of treatment in a similar manner.

Radiosurgery was developed in the 1950s using kilovoltage equipment. The gamma knife, which is a direct development of this earlier work, is favoured for treating lesions which are surgically difficult to access in a non invasive manner (e.g. brain lesions) without causing significant damage to surrounding critical structures.

The use of the gamma knife was pioneered by Lars Leksell in the 1950s and 1960s. Today,

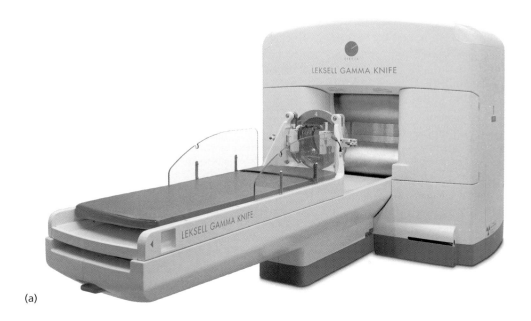

(a)

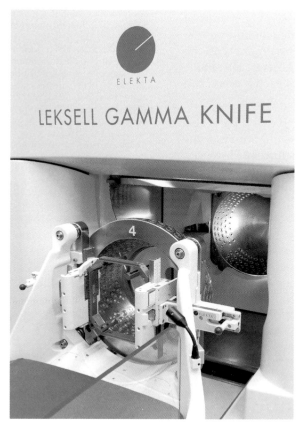

(b)

Figure 6.6 **(a)** Leksell gamma knife – C. **(b)** Close-up image of the Leksell gamma knife – C, collimator helmet (courtesy of Elekta Instruments AB).

commercially available machines consist of 201 collimated ^{60}Cobalt sources in a hemispherical arrangement. They are used in the treatment of a range of benign and malignant conditions, including arteriovenous malformations (AVMs), metastatic brain tumours, meningiomas, uncontrollable epilepsy, acoustic neuromas, pituitary adenomas, craniopharyngiomas, Parkinson's disease (Goldman 1998) and other tumours of the base of skull and pineal gland.

The accuracy required in such treatments clearly demands the use of superior immobilisation techniques, precise 3D angiographic and CT localisation procedures, and highly focused beam delivery in order to achieve a suitable dose differential between the tumour and surrounding normal tissue. Typical planning target volumes are in the region of 8–18 mm. As shown in Figures 6.6a and b, the patient is fixed inside a metal helmet containing 201 appropriately positioned holes and the whole assembly is moved into the head of the machine containing the cobalt sources. Stereotactic treatment can be delivered by either a gamma knife or a suitable equipped linear accelerator, but each method has its own merits (listed below):

• The gamma knife has few moving parts and demonstrates extremely precise alignment of the helmet and the radioactive sources. However, capital costs are high, and the problems of background radiation and source replacement (6–8 years post installation) result in high running costs.

• The linear accelerator method is more flexible, allowing a larger range of field sizes and more precise beam shaping for irregular volumes. Initial outlay is cheaper, but there is considerably more machine down time owing to the complexity of its design. In addition, mechanical tolerances are not as fine as the gamma knife, leading to less overall accuracy.

RECOMMENDED READING

Friedman W A, Buatti J M, Bova F J, Mendenhall W M 1998 Linac radiosurgery. Springer-Verlag, Berlin
Ganz J C 1997 Gamma knife surgery. Springer-Verlag, Berlin

REFERENCES

Bomford C K, Kunkler I H, Sherriff S B (eds) 1993 Walter and Miller's Textbook of radiotherapy, radiation physics, therapy and oncology, 5th edn. Churchill Livingstone, Edinburgh
British Journal of Radiology 1996 Central axis depth dose data for use in radiotherapy. Supplement No. 25. British Institute of Radiology, London
British Standards Institute 1993 Medical electrical equipment. Part 2: Particular requirements for safety, Section 2.11, Specification for gamma beam therapy equipment. Supplement 2. Methods of test for radiation safety. BSI 5724, BSI, London
Department of the Environment 1993 Radioactive Substances Act. HMSO, London
Goldman H 1998 Gamma knife to replace surgery for patients with Parkinson's? Rad Magazine (Jan): 41
HM Government 1994 Capital investment manual. HMSO, London
Jayaraman S, Lanzl L H (eds) 1996 Clinical radiotherapy physics: treatment planning and radiation safety. CRC Press, Boca Raton, Florida, vol. 2
Meredith W J, Massey J B 1977 Fundamental physics of radiology. Wright, Bristol
Washington C M, Lever D T (eds) 1996 Principles and practice of radiation therapy: physics, simulation and treatment planning. Mosby Year Book, St. Louis

INTERNET REFERENCE

http://www.hmso.gov.uk

7 Radiotherapy equipment operating at kilovoltage energy range

Chapter objectives

On completion of this chapter you should be able to:

- Compare the structure, function and associated filtration of the X-ray tube assembly within a kilovoltage therapy treatment unit with that found in a conventional radiotherapy simulator

- Evaluate the role of the kilovoltage treatment unit in the radiotherapy department of the 21st century.

INTRODUCTION

X-ray equipment up to approximately 300 kV have been used to treat benign and malignant disease since the early 20th century. However, a wider range of lower energy units were used prior to the increasing incidence and use of ^{60}Cobalt units and subsequent development of linear accelerators in the late 1950s. Grenz rays operate in the energy range 10–300 kV but are rarely used in clinical practice today, whilst the more frequently seen contact therapy delivers beam energies of 40–70 kV (Barish & Donohue 1994, Williams & Thwaites 1993) and, as the name implies, operates at greatly reduced treatment distances. By manipulating the inverse square law, contact therapy delivers larger than average fractions of radiation in a very short space of time, with limited radiation side-effects to surrounding normal tissue.

Historically, the kilovoltage energy range has been traditionally divided into two categories:

1 Superficial therapy: energy range of 50–150 kV, HVL (see p. 144) of 1–8 mm Al, and an FSD of 10–30 cm
2 Orthovoltage or 'deep' therapy: energy range of 150–300 kV, HVL of 0.5–3.0 mm Cu, and an FSD of 50 cm.

Kilovoltage units are used for the delivery of non isocentric appositional set-ups, and the advantages of this equipment are the same today as they were when they were first used: the machinery is relatively inexpensive, is simple in design, demonstrates straightforward principles of operation, has simple warm-up and quality control procedures, and provides quick and easy methods of collimation and irregular field shaping. The depth dose profile is excellent for the management of external superficial lesions such as skin tumours, and intracavitary rectal (also known as the Papillon technique), oral and vaginal lesions (Barish & Donohue 1994, Papillon 1994, Podgorsak & Evans 1987, Cummings 1983). However, there are two significant disadvantages: the down side of having superficial depth dose values is the inability to deliver adequate dose to areas of considerable separation, and there is no demonstrable skin sparing characteristic. Furthermore, owing to the nature of compton scatter, considerable scattered radiation is demonstrated outside the radiation beam. Additionally, the percentage of photoelectric absorption occurring in this energy range results in a differential absorption of dose in high atomic number tissues such as bone, with a subsequent increased incidence of early and late radiation side-effects in these tissues. Differential absorption is, however, exploited to make kilovoltage X-ray therapy particularly effective for the management of metastatic bone deposits and for certain primary bone lesions.

THE CLINICAL SIGNIFICANCE OF KILOVOLTAGE THERAPY

Despite the disadvantages indicated above, there is still an important place for this equipment in

the radiotherapy department of today. Whilst the advantages of treatment using megavoltage X-rays or electrons are irrefutable, consideration must be given to the fact that the aims of treatment are not the same for all patients. Precision in radiotherapy delivery is crucial for both radical and palliative intent alike, whilst the opportunities of control over patient positioning and directional delivery afforded by the linear accelerator cannot be surpassed. However, for many patients, speedy access to treatment, simplicity of set-up, less oppressive and intimidating technology and reduced systemic radiation side-effects are equally important. Kilovoltage treatment planning is straightforward and only on very rare occasions is it necessary to use a planning computer. Megavoltage electrons are the alternative mode of treatment for superficial lesions, but they do demonstrate a skin sparing effect. Consequently, unless a tissue equivalent mate-rial is used as bolus on the skin surface it can be difficult to deliver a radical dose to a superficial lesions (Lovett et al 1990). Access to the treatment site can also be technically challenging when using bulky electron applicators as opposed to slender and shorter kilovoltage applicators, particularly around the medial canthus of the eye. Practically it is also simpler, quicker and cheaper to make templates for the treatment of very small field sizes on a kilovoltage unit. Careful consideration by the oncologist of the required treatment modality and energy is therefore crucial. At a managerial level the selective prescription of kilovoltage X-rays, where appropriate, will significantly improve departmental efficiency and cost-effectiveness of overall treatment delivery through better use of available resources (Thomas & El-Sharkawi 1996).

THE INTERACTION OF THE ELECTRON BEAM WITH THE TARGET

It is important to understand the interactions that occur in the target of an X-ray tube, as the very nature of the processes occurring in the target is the key to explaining the efficiency of X-ray production and why heat deposition at the point of interaction varies with incident electron energy, the latter clearly having implications for the design of effective coolant systems.

The way in which electrons interact with, and lose energy to, matter is characterised by the interactions each electron may experience with the atomic electrons and nuclei of the target material. Each charged particle will, as a result of its charge and mass, collide many times before losing all energy reserves. At each interaction only a very small amount of energy is lost. This is in direct contrast to X-rays (see Ch. 1) which experience far fewer interactions in comparison, and during each interaction a significant amount of energy is transferred away from the X-ray. X-rays are therefore able to penetrate much further into matter compared to electrons of a similar energy.

Energy loss from the electron is divided into two main categories: radiative and collision:

Radiative energy loss

This is more commonly known as bremsstrahlung (German for 'braking radiation'), and is one of three main interactions occurring in the target of the X-ray tube.

As shown in Figure 7.1, an electron of kinetic energy E_k passes very close to a nucleus of the target material and is subject to the electromagnetic forces that surround nuclei. This results in the electron slowing down; owing to the

law relating to the conservation of energy, this energy loss manifests itself as a bremsstrahlung X-ray. The incident electron continues on a diverted path, with reduced kinetic energy equal to its original energy prior to this interaction minus that transferred to the bremsstrahlung X-ray (E_k – hv). The greater the energy of the incident electron, the more likely that the resulting bremsstrahlung X-ray will be emitted on a path in line with that of the incident electron before it interacted with the field around the nucleus.

The maximum energy appearing as bremsstrahlung cannot exceed the energy of the incident electron, and below this limit a range of bremsstrahlung energies will be apparent. In other words, a continuous spectrum of X-rays is produced when electrons interact in this manner (see Fig. 7.2). The probability of bremsstrahlung occurring is directly related to the square of the atomic number of the target material and the square of the unit charge of the incident electron. It is inversely proportional to the square of the electron mass.

Bremsstrahlung may also occur when an electron passes close to the field surrounding an orbital electron, but the contributing component to the total amount of bremsstrahlung is small.

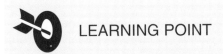

LEARNING POINT

Questions

Why does the bremsstrahlung interaction result in a continuous energy spectrum, unlike the line spectra appearance of characteristic radiation?

During an electron beam treatment on a linear accelerator, what percentage of bremsstrahlung is produced

- in the patient?
- in the head and applicator of the treatment unit?

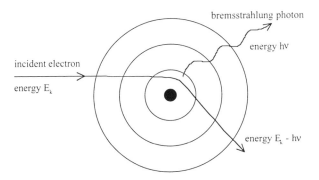

Figure 7.1 Bremsstrahlung X-rays emitted as an electron interacts with the electromagnetic field around the nucleus (from Metcalfe et al 1997, with permission from Medical Physics Publishing).

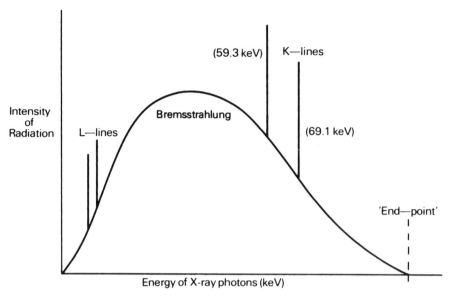

Figure 7.2   An X-ray spectrum emitted from the target of an X-ray tube (from Wilks 1987, with permission).

Collision energy loss

Within the kilovoltage energy range, there are several types of collision interactions that may occur when an electron interacts with the target material. The electron may interact with an orbiting electron, resulting in either excitation or ionisation of that atom. The end product of these two types of interaction is the production of heat and/or the production of characteristic radiation at the target. Alternatively, the electron may be attracted by the positive charge of the nucleus, such that its path is slightly diverted as the result of a very small energy transfer to the nucleus. Finally, it may interact in a similar manner with an orbiting electron. In this final case, the incident electron does not lose energy and this interaction is considered insignificant at radiotherapy energy ranges.

As shown in Figure 7.3a, excitation occurs when an electron passes close to an orbital electron of the target material and transfers sufficient energy to temporarily elevate the latter electron to a higher orbital shell. The orbital electron has insufficient energy to maintain this position, and falls back to its original position. The potential energy difference between the two orbits is

lost in the form of heat, which increases the target temperature.

Ionisation occurs when (see Fig. 7.3b) the incident electron transfers enough energy to the orbital electron to permanently remove the latter from the atom by exceeding the binding energy of the orbital electron. The ejected electron is often termed a delta ray, or secondary electron. The kinetic energy of the incident electron is reduced by a figure equal to the sum of the kinetic energy of the secondary electron plus its orbital binding energy. As a result of this process, an outer orbital electron falls down into the space left by the secondary electron, and the potential energy it loses as it falls down into the new position appears as characteristic radiation. It is termed 'characteristic' because the energy of the radiation is directly related to the energy difference between the two orbits, and this figure is specific to the target material. For example, when considering the energy difference between two orbital shells such as the K and L orbits, different materials produce characteristic radiation of different values. Characteristic radiation appears as single lines of energy superimposed on top of the continuous bremsstrahlung spectrum (see Fig. 7.2).

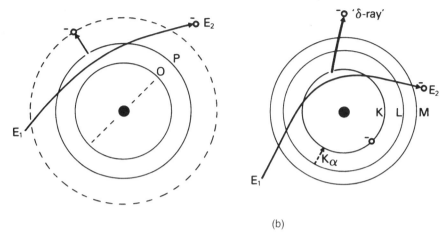

(b)

Figure 7.3 **(a)** Excitation, and **(b)** ionisation as a result of an electron interacting with an orbital electron (from Wilks 1987, with permission).

It should also be remembered that the secondary electron may possess significant energy, potentially allowing it to interact with surrounding target atoms in a collisional or radiative manner.

X-ray production efficiency

At the energies commonly used in diagnostic radiography there is 1–5% X-ray production in the target, and 99–95% heat production. For a linear accelerator this ratio is much nearer to 50:50. Because there is less heat produced the cooling system requirement of a linear accelerator target is much less complex than those of a diagnostic X-ray tube target.

The reason for this relates to something known as the critical energy. This is defined as the point at which the percentage of collisional energy losses that an electron will experience equals the radiative energy losses. The critical energy is material-specific and relates to the energy of the incident particle (Leo 1994). Above this critical energy radiative losses dominate. Consequently, more X-rays and less heat are produced in the target of an accelerator in comparison to a diagnostic X-ray tube, where collisional type losses dominate.

Why do X-ray tubes feature a reflective target, while linear accelerators employ a transmission target?

This can be explained by the concept of the spatial distribution of X-rays produced in a target (see Fig. 7.4a). When an incident beam of electrons hits a very thin target, the X-ray intensity at a fixed distance from the target can be measured. If the energy of the electrons is varied, a range of intensities will appear at specific angles around the target. It can be seen that at low energies, maximum X-ray intensity is produced at approximately right angles to the path of the incident electrons, and there-fore a reflective target is used in low energy X-ray machines (Fig. 7.4b). As the energy of electron increases, maximum X-ray intensity is produced in the same direction as the path of the incident electron beam. Consequently, accelerators are fitted with transmission type targets (see Fig. 7.4b).

Target angle and the anode heel effect

The target angle is the angle between the central axis of the X-ray beam and the face of the

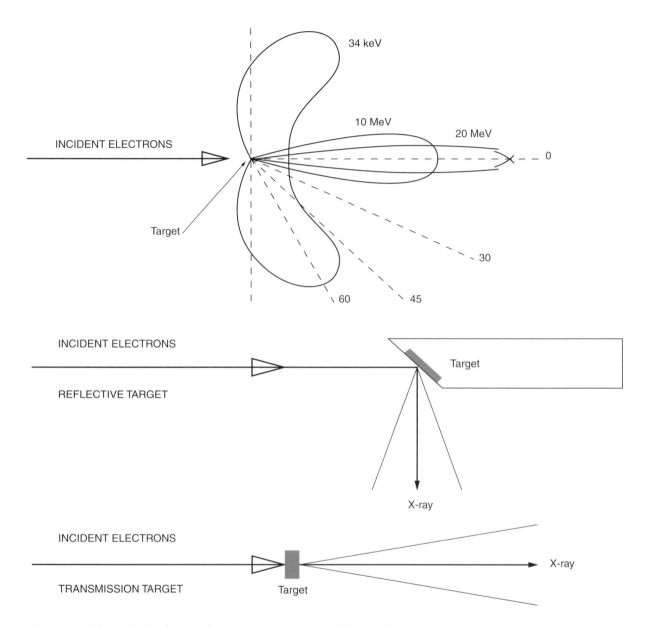

Figure 7.4 **(a)** Spatial distribution of X-rays around a target. **(b)** The reflective and transmission target (from Leung 1990, with permission).

reflective target. In therapy X-ray tubes this is approximately 20° (Pantak product specifications, Internet reference), and the selected angle will govern the maximum available field size for treatment. Additionally, the larger the area the electron beam bombards, the smaller the temperature rise in the anode. However, real

focal spot size and its relationship to target angle has other implications for the design of the therapy X-ray tube.

Electrons hitting the target material will interact to produce bremsstrahlung X-rays. Some electrons will travel further into the target before interacting in this manner, and therefore will have more target material to pass through before being emitted. This means that the intensity of the resultant X-ray will vary depending upon the point of each electron interaction in the target. In X-ray tubes this mechanism produces a distinct pattern, such that the intensity profile of an X-ray beam as it exits from the tube is lower at the anode end of the tube when compared to the cathode end. This is known as the anode heel effect.

This effect is more pronounced as the target angle is reduced, and with older tubes as a result of pitting of the target with use. This in theory could become a significant problem if attempting to match kilovoltage treatment fields. If the intensity profile of the beam dips significantly at the anode end of a field, but still remains within acceptable QA parameters, then it would be prudent to ensure that the cathode end of the field was used at the field junction.

The anode heel effect is not the only factor to influence the X-ray intensity distribution across a treatment field. In comparison to the intensity at the central axis, measurements at the anode and cathode ends of a field will be less, due to the influence of the inverse square law. Clearly this will become significant only at large fields, which are rarely seen in kilovoltage therapy, but this effect can be compensated for by the use of filters. Finally, intensity measurements at the cathode end of a field will be less than the intensity at the anode end as a result of the spatial distribution of X-rays around a target (see p. 141).

COMMONLY USED TERMINOLOGY ASSOCIATED WITH KILOVOLTAGE EQUIPMENT

X-ray spectrum

An X-ray tube will produce a continuous bremsstrahlung spectrum, superimposed on top of which are single energy characteristic lines. Graphically these are usually represented by a plot of X-ray intensity as a function of energy (Fig. 7.2), or wavelength. The use of wavelength

 LEARNING POINT

Consideration of the above three factors leads to the design requirement of a balanced tube for a specific energy of radiation in order to produce a homogeneous intensity profile – in other words, to result in a flat beam of radiation hitting the patient.

Question
If you have a multi-energy kilovoltage unit in your own department, review the intensity profiles for at least two energies and evaluate the clinical implications of any differences you may see.

can be confusing to the student, as it has to be remembered that the wavelength and energy of an electromagnetic wave are inversely related. The following equation is derived from the knowledge that the energy of the X-ray is related to its frequency by Planck's equation (Wilks 1987, p. 358). As the energy of the maximum X-ray is the same as the kV_p, it can be said that:

$$\lambda_{min} = \frac{1.24}{kV_p} \text{ (nm)}$$

where λ_{min} is the minimum wavelength, and 1.24 is the sum of Planck's constant and the velocity of electromagnetic radiation in a vacuum.

The energy of X-rays emitted from an X-ray tube depends upon the energy of electrons in the stream bombarding the anode. This electron energy is determined by the peak kilovoltage (kVp) used, which will therefore determine the maximum X-ray energy produced. The average energy of the beam is typically between one third to one half of the maximum.

Half value layer (HVL)

The HVL of a kilovoltage unit provides direct information regarding the penetrative characteristics of the X-ray beam. It is defined as the thickness of a specified absorber that will reduce the incident beam intensity to 50% of its original value. Common absorbers used are aluminium for superficial X-ray beams, with copper and tin for the orthovoltage range. Although this information is also obtained from the kVp of the X-ray beam, HVL is the preferred indicator simply because the relationship of kVp with changing external filtration is of a complex nature.

For a clear explanation of the conditions under which HVL should be measured, see Wilks (1987) and Williams & Thwaites (1993).

Finally, the term 'lead equivalent' is commonly used in place of HVLs or TVLs. The lead equivalent of an absorbing material is defined as the thickness of lead which would absorb the same amount of radiation as the given material under equal radiation exposure conditions.

Tube rating charts

The rating of an X-ray tube is the combination of exposure settings the structure can withstand without incurring damage that will result in either temporary or permanent tube failure. Such failures are usually the result of thermal damage, caused either by tube malfunction or by a lack of knowledge regarding the heating and cooling rates of the anode in question. Ratings charts are produced for each type of X-ray tube (fixed or rotating anode), the range of kVp values each tube is likely to be subjected to, broad and fine focal spot use, and single or multiple exposures. Modern X-ray tubes are fitted with a device that automatically assesses the exposure factors selected and calculates whether the recommended tube rating will be exceeded.

Thermionic emission

Certain materials will release electrons when heated. This process is known as thermionic emission. When the cathode is heated outer shell electrons in the atoms at the surface of the material forming the filament of the cathode gain enough kinetic energy to escape from the parent atom, and in effect 'boil off' the surface. This will only happen if the electron can exceed the work function of the specific material (i.e. the amount of work that must be performed by the electron to escape from the body). Thus materials with a low work function are efficient thermionic emitters. Thermionic emission is influenced by:

1. The temperature to which the material is raised
2. Surface area (cathode filaments are coiled to increase surface area)
3. Work function of the material selected
4. The cleanliness of the surface of the material.

Focal spot: effective (apparent) and real (true)

The real or true focal spot is the area on the anode that is bombarded by electrons. For a stationary anode, the target is angled so that as large an area as possible is bombarded by electrons in order to limit the temperature rise and subsequent thermal damage at this interaction point.

The central axis of the X-ray beam projects down onto the patient, and owing to the angle of the face of the target the projected beam area on the surface of the patient will demonstrate smaller dimensions than the area irradiated on the target. These new dimensions are termed the effective or apparent focal spot. The relationship between the effective and real focal spot is known as the line focus principle.

BEAM CHARACTERISTICS

The isodose distribution for a 200 kV (1.4 mm Cu HVL) orthovoltage unit is shown in Figure 7.5. As demonstrated in their respective chapters, it is very different to the isodose curves of a linear accelerator and ^{60} Co unit.

Central axis depth dose and skin sparing

In comparison to megavoltage units, clearly percentage depth dose is poorer for kilovoltage

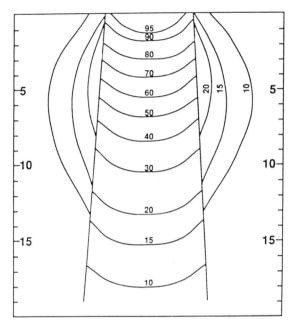

Figure 7.5 A 200 kV (1.4 mm Cu HVL) isodose distribution for field parameters of 15 × 6 cm and 50 cm FSD (from Williams & Thwaites 1993, by permission of Oxford University Press).

Table 7.1 Percentage depth dose data for a 250 kV (1.1 mm Cu HVL), 10 × 10 cm field at 50 cm FSD, orthovoltage unit (Ontario Cancer Institute 1992, p. 13)

Isodose (%)	Depth (cm)
100	0
80	3.5
50	7.25

X-rays. This is due not only to the lower accelerating voltage, but also to the direction of scatter produced at this energy during the compton scatter process.

The 100% isodose is at the skin surface, resulting in absence of the skin sparing effect. This is why these units are tailored for treating superficial skin and subcutaneous lesions. However, care must always be taken to define the term 'skin surface'. This is usually considered to be the point in layers of skin at which radiosensitivity is first demonstrated – i.e. below the epidermis at a level of approximately 0.1–0.15 mm (Williams & Thwaites 1993). Research by Aldrich et al (1992) describes high surface doses, with increases in the range of 64–400% from orthovoltage X-rays as a result of photoelectrons scattering from the inner surfaces of the treatment applicators and lead cut-outs placed directly onto the skin surface. Aldrich and colleagues advise that this problem can be reduced by using applicators with a plastic end piece, coating the inside of the applicators and lead cut-outs with a thin layer of paint, or enclosing the cut-out in a plastic film.

Width of penumbra

There is wide geometric penumbra evident in kilovoltage isodose curves, owing to the size of focal spot and target angle used. In addition, there is an abrupt discontinuity on the skin surface at the edges of the field. This is due to the applicator used to direct the X-ray beam.

Shape of beam profile and rapidity of dose fall off

The curves are noticeably rounded, and distended sideways. This reflects the nature of the compton scatter interaction process occurring within the patient.

COMPONENTS OF A KILOVOLTAGE TREATMENT UNIT

A multi-energy unit consists of the following components:

- High voltage generator and associated circuits
- X-ray tube, tube housing, cooling system and method of collimation
- Filtration
- Control panel.

This chapter is not intended to provide the basics of X-ray tube structure and function, a subject covered well in texts by Graham (1996) and Bomford et al (1993). Instead the chapter focuses on the clinical application of the technology.

High voltage generator

The general X-ray circuit consists of a filament circuit and a high voltage circuit. The filament circuit contains the electrical components necessary to generate the heat required for electron emission from the filament. This is achieved by the use of a step down transformer to reduce the mains voltage to a level sufficient to generate stable thermionic emission.

In the high frequency generator circuit, AC mains voltage is rectified and smoothed and then converted to high frequency pulsed DC. This is fed to the primary side of the high voltage transformer, and the output from the secondary side of the transformer is once again rectified and smoothed to provide an almost constant potential to the X-ray tube.

KEY POINTS

The basic principles of X-ray tube circuits are well documented in many texts (Cherry & Duxbury 1998, Graham 1996, Thompson et al 1994), and include detailed discussion on the need for:

- The conversion of low voltage mains to a kilovoltage supply to the X-ray tube
- A filament circuit controlling the temperature of the filament and subsequent thermionic emission of electrons
- Timers to control the period of X-ray production
- A method of measuring and compensating for variations in the incoming mains voltage
- Rectification to convert mains AC to a DC supply across the X-ray tube
- Meters to monitor tube current and voltage.

A constant potential power supply to the X-ray tube is highly desirable as it results in a stable and reproducible X-ray output, and at any point in time the maximum X-ray energy and beam spectrum relates to the potential applied across the tube. The advantage of using high frequency generators is that owing to their more efficient operation at higher frequencies, less bulky transformers can be incorporated into the circuit, resulting in smaller and more compact units.

Control console

Modern equipment features a microprocessor controlled digital control console which acts as a message centre to inform the user of the current status of the operating system.

Additionally, a treatment interrupt button, emergency stop and mains power switch will be present. Other features include visual and audible indicators of system faults and system status during delivery of treatment. It is important to remember that there should be at least two, and preferably three, stages of delivering mains power to the control console. This is to ensure that the unit cannot be activated simply by the selection of a mains on switch on the console.

KEY POINTS

Digital displays of the following parameters should be apparent:

- kV and mA
- Filtration to be selected via a select and confirm mechanism (once selected, kV and mA are automatically set)
- Dose rate in monitor units per minute
- Set time and dose, elapsed time and backup time. The last will terminate the delivery of treatment if the elapsed time exceeds the set time by a predetermined value, which should not exceed 10% of the set time (NRPB 1988, reg. 33{2}, para. 7.52).

X-ray tube, tube housing, cooling system and method of collimation

One of the most recent developments in the design criteria of kilovoltage X-ray tubes has been the evolution of the metal ceramic tube (see Fig. 7.6).

KEY POINTS

The advantages of this design are summarised below:

▓ For a comparable energy, the weight of the tube is approximately 25–35% less

▓ Overall physical dimensions are less

▓ Lack of electrical discharges, or 'sparking'

▓ Improved reliability of operation

▓ Physically more robust (Williams & Thwaites 1993).

This design eliminates the weakest link, and a common cause of traditional X-ray tube failure – the glass insert containing the vacuum. The technology provides superior mechanical strength and improved electrical insulation characteristics, allowing the manufacturer to construct a lighter and smaller tube housing. In addition, there is an increase in the maximum operating voltage and subsequent output energy. Traditional X-ray tube assemblies with glass tube inserts are limited in voltage range by the strength of the insulating high voltage connector(s). In order to adequately insulate at energies in the region of 200 kV, such a connector needs to be in the region of 18 cm in the horizontal dimension (Thomson TTE, Mendon product spec, n.d.). Increasing the voltage merely increases the required length of this insulator, leading to larger overall dimensions and reduced tube manoeuvrability. This issue is addressed in the metal ceramic tube by the use of a ceramic insulator which operates in a radial rather than a horizontal dimension.

The tube design consists of an outer alumina body which supports the cathode and contains the vacuum. The tungsten target sits embedded in a copper and ceramic anode at the opposite end of the tube, directly overlying the beryllium window which is integrally welded into the outer sleeve.

BASIC TUBE OPERATION

Electrons are produced from the tungsten filament which is kept at the required temperature by the filament current circuit supplying it. Increasing the filament current will increase the number of electrons released by thermionic emission from the filament, which subsequently increases tube current (mA), the latter being defined as the number of electrons flowing from the cathode to the anode. The shape of the cathode is such that the ends of the device nearest to the anode are curved and negatively charged; this is known as the focusing cup. It repels the negatively charged electrons, and focuses them towards the central point of the target.

As the electrons are released they form a cloud around the filament, and are attracted towards the target by the potential difference (kVp) existing between the cathode and the positively charged anode. The tube should be operated under saturation conditions whereby the number of electrons bombarding the target equals the number released by the cathode structure. The greater the potential difference across the tube, the greater the force of attraction between the anode and cathode. Consequently, electrons will strike the target with more force to produce X-rays of a higher energy. The vacuum within the tube prevents the electrons from interacting with anything between their point of production and desired end destination, in doing so preserving electron energy for bremsstrahlung production. During bremsstrahlung production, considerable amounts of heat are produced in the tungsten target. This energy needs to be quickly dispersed from its point of origin to prevent thermal damage, and the main mechanism of heat loss is via conduction through the target and into the anode structure. The back of the anode incorporates a water or oil cooled mechanism. To facilitate cooling the anode structure around the

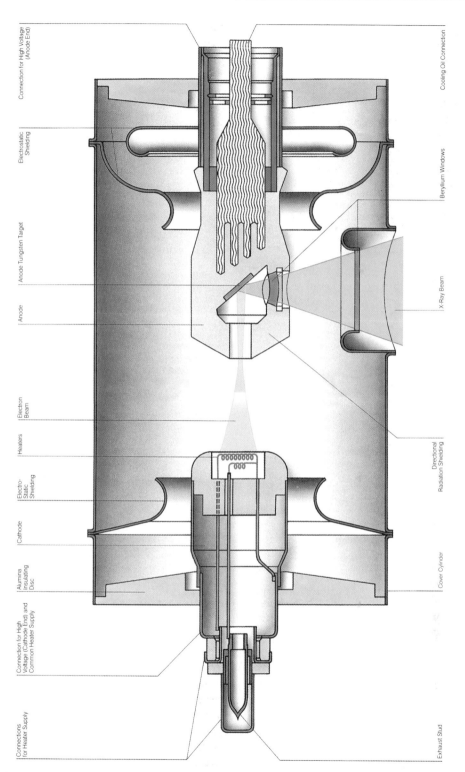

Figure 7.6 A schematic representation of a metal ceramic X-ray tube (with permission from Thomson TTE – Mendon).

LEARNING POINT

Main beam, scattered and leakage radiation will emanate from an X-ray tube during routine use.

Questions

What are the sources of each of the above types of radiation?

What are the implications of scattered and leakage radiation for

- the patient?
- radiotherapy staff?

How can we limit the magnitude of scattered and leakage radiation, and to what level do we aim to reduce them?

LEARNING POINT

Many kilovoltage treatment units are supplied with applicators of significantly different FSDs, but a similar range of available treatment fields. However, in some of the older treatment units still in use it is possible to treat a patient using the wrong applicator length.

Question

How will this influence

- percentage depth dose?
- field size?
- dose rate?

tungsten target is made of a material of high thermal conductivity. In addition, the anode block is designed to have a large cross-sectional area, and is short in overall length; both of the latter features facilitate heat loss by the conduction method (Graham 1996).

The anode of a stationary X-ray tube used for radiotherapy purposes is usually 'hooded' in nature. In other words the target is completely surrounded by shielding apart from two portals; the first is aligned with the beam of electron focused onto the target; the second is at 90° to the face of the target and its purpose is to permit the useful beam of radiation to exit the tube. The latter portal is covered by a low atomic number material – usually beryllium. The X-ray beam then leaves the anode structure and passes through a second beryllium window in the outer casing and into the collimation system. The hooded anode provides very effective radiation protection to the patient and the user by attenuating a high percentage of the bremsstrahlung produced outside the dimensions of the useful beam, as well as absorbing any secondary electrons produced from electron interactions at the target. Leakage through the anode is then

attenuated to permitted levels (BSI 1998) by the lead layer lining the outer casing of the tube.

Typically, removable applicators are used in kilovoltage therapy as the main method of collimation. Applicators range in FSD from 15 to 50 cm, and may be provided in square or circular geometry with field sizes up to a maximum of approximately $20 \, \text{cm}^2$. In addition, contact applicators are available for specialist techniques.

Applicators are standard in design, and are constructed of divergent metal walls with a plastic end piece that aids treatment set-up. At the point of attachment to the X-ray tube is a large lead plate which contains a hole through which the primary beam passes and defines the maximum field size that can be obtained with this applicator.

Anode or centre earthed tubes

For tubes up to 150 kV, the tube is usually anode earthed (i.e. at zero kilovolts) with a high negative voltage supply to the cathode. The advantage of this is that the anode can be water cooled, which is a far simpler and cheaper option that the oil cooled alternative. The water cooling mechanism is integrated into the external radiation protection housing (not shown in

Fig. 7.6) which envelops the anode end of the tube. This housing is lined with lead to attenuate the leakage radiation emanating from the target.

In addition, there is only one high kV (high tension (HT)) cable connected to the tube. This is an advantage because a cable carrying a high kV needs to be insulated to carry and withstand the full 150 kV. It is therefore bulky and inflexible. From the point of view of the operator, overall tube manoeuvrability is increased if only one HT cable is attached.

Anode earthing is insufficient for voltages above 150 kV, and so these tubes are centre earthed. This means that both the anode and the cathode are at high positive and negative voltages respectively, so the anode is also supported by a ceramic insulator. With two HT cables attached, the tube becomes far more difficult to manoeuvre around the patient. For safety reasons, cooling can no longer be carried out by a water based mechanism, and so oil coolants and associated oil-to-water or oil-to-air heat exchangers are employed.

Dose monitor

For kilovoltage units operating below 150 kV it is sufficient to terminate treatment by the use of a timer, rather than by a dose rate monitor. In such a situation the machine output must be checked at least once every working day (NRPB 1988, reg. 33{2} para. 7.48). For energies greater than this, a dose monitor is required, and a calibrated parallel plate ionisation chamber (Ch. 2) is incorporated into the unit between the external filtration and applicator base plate. It produces a signal that is evident on the control panel as an accumulated number of monitor units, with the machine calibrated in such a way that one monitor unit (mu) equals one centigray (100 mu = 1 gray (Gy)). Once this value equals the number of monitor units initially programmed, the machine will terminate treatment delivery.

Filtration

X-ray units are classically operated with filters placed in the path of the beam to modify the energy of radiation reaching the patient. When reviewing the X-ray spectrum demonstrated in Figure 7.2, it can be seen that there are a number of very low energy components to the beam. These 'soft' X-rays contribute little to the prescribed treatment as they are of insufficient energy to penetrate to the required depth. They merely interact superficially in the patient, causing radiation side-effects with few associated benefits. Consequently, filters are used to absorb these low energy X-rays and remove them from the beam before they reach the patient.

The removal of these low energy components will increase the average energy of the remaining beam by a varying degree depending on the type of filter used. This is known as beam hardening, and changes the HVL of the resultant beam spectrum. This feature is exploited by the use of a specific range of filters designed to elicit a series of HVLs so that multiple beam energies can be produced from one X-ray tube.

Filtration is divided into two categories: inherent and external:

Inherent filtration is a fixed characteristic of the tube and cannot be varied. It is the attenuation experienced by the X-ray as it passes through tube components. For a ceramic metal tube this filtration is produced by two beryllium windows and is equivalent to 2 mm beryllium. In the conventional stationary X-ray tube, the inherent filtration is greater than this as it is formed by the glass tube insert, the beryllium exit window and any cooling oil that may be in the path of the beam.

External filtration is the beam attenuation produced by filters placed in the path of the beam, but external to the X-ray tube, their material is specific to the shape and intensity of the beam spectrum required to treat the patient. Aluminium (Al), copper (Cu) and tin (Sn) are commonly used materials – for lower energy units these materials tend to be applied as single elements, whereas at higher energies composite filters are usually employed.

The Thoraeus filter is a well known composite of tin, copper and aluminium. The amounts of each material will vary from centre to centre

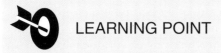

LEARNING POINT

The selection of a filter material is not straightforward. It is imperative to choose a material with an atomic number that produces significant beam hardening without an equally significant reduction in beam intensity. It should also be mechanically stable at the required thickness, and not produce absorption edges within the useful beam spectrum.

Question
What intensity of radiation is suitable for treating a patient?

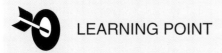

LEARNING POINT

The filters are kept in an interlocked filter bank inside the treatment room, and the operator must make a filter selection on the control panel prior to switching the machine on to deliver treatment. Each filter must be carefully marked with the element(s) it contains, and the total filter thickness.

Questions
In the clinical situation, how do we reduce the possibility of an incorrect filter being used?

If an incorrect filter is used, what subsequent actions may be taken to reduce the magnitude of this error?

depending on the output required, but values for a 300 kV unit will be in the region of 1.2 mm Sn, 0.25 mm Cu, and 1 mm Al (Siemens 1984). These filters are carefully constructed so that the higher atomic number material, (Sn), is nearest to the X-ray tube, and the lowest atomic number

material, (Al), is nearest to the patient. This order is important because in addition to the required beam hardening, lines of low energy characteristic radiation are produced as the X-ray beam interacts with the tin. This is undesirable and is as harmful to the patient as the 'soft' X-ray components that the tin removes from the beam. Copper is therefore placed in front of the tin, to selectively remove this harmful characteristic radiation, with a final layer of aluminium added to remove the even lower energy characteristic radiation produced by the copper.

CALCULATION OF DOSE

The Code of Practice for the determination of absorbed dose for X-ray below 300 kV generating potential was introduced by the IPEMB in 1997. It describes the recommended method for the calculation of absorbed dose, and explains in detail the methods and equipment to be used. It is based upon an air kerma calibration of the ionisation chamber, mass energy absorption coefficients for air and water, and backscatter factors (BSFs) for the stated energy. Values for the last two components are published in the Code of Practice.

Depending on the set-up used during commissioning for the measurement of output values for each individual applicator, it may be necessary to apply inverse square law corrections within the monitor unit calculation to correct for any applicator stand off.

ROOM DESIGN AND RADIATION PROTECTION

The principles of room design for kilovoltage therapy are very similar to those described in Chapter 3. Typically, concrete is the material of choice for wall construction, but if space constraints are an issue, Barytes concrete, lead lined brick walls or barium plaster may be used. None of the alternative materials offer simple solutions – Barytes concrete is more costly, lead lined walls are expensive and difficult to hang and barium plaster is scarce and requires the services of an experienced and skilled plasterer.

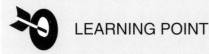

LEARNING POINT

At kilovoltage energies, the photoelectric absorption process will occur preferentially in lead as a result of the dependence of this interaction process on atomic number, thereby making lead an effective absorber.

Questions

For a set thickness of lead, how will the amount of photoelectric absorption occurring within it vary as incident energy increases from 150 kV upwards?

Why are lead and concrete equivalent absorbers at megavoltage energies?

Doors are usually lead lined and radiation emitting equipment must be installed so that the doors are not directly in line with the primary beam. Lead glass viewing windows used to be common, but in these technological times closed circuit television is a more versatile and cheaper option.

Chapters 7 and 8 of the guidance notes associated with the 1988 Ionising Radiation Regulations (NRPB 1988) provide detailed advice and recommendations regarding room design, interlocks and warning signs, installation and operating requirements, the use of protective clothing, and machine calibration and maintenance. If followed, the guidance allows the user to comply with the aforementioned legislative documentation. Furthermore, British Standard BS 5724-2-8 (BSI 1998) is an excellent source of information relating to the requirements that manufacturers must currently conform to with respect to the design and manufacture of radiotherapy kilovoltage equipment in this energy range.

QUALITY ASSURANCE

The extent and range of tests which should be conducted will depend very much upon the clinical objectives of the use of kilovoltage therapy and the range of beam qualities likely to be in use. As with any other equipment emitting ionising radiation, newer machines are developed with the characteristics of complex technology. Consequently the range and extent of quality tests will differ. Tests specific to kilovoltage equipment not considered in Chapter 4 are reviewed in detail in Williams & Thwaites (1993).

RECOMMENDED READING

Aldrich J E, Meng J S, Andrew J W 1992 The surface doses from orthovoltage X-ray treatments. Medical Dosimetry 17: 69–72
British Standards Institute 1998 Medical electrical equipment. Part 2. Particular requirements for safety. Section 2.8. Specifications for therapeutic X-ray equipment operating in the range of 10 kV to 1 MV. BS 5724–2–8. BSI, London
Graham D T 1996 Principles of radiological physics, 3rd edn. Churchill Livingstone, Edinburgh
IPEMB 1996 The IPEMB code of practice for the determination of absorbed dose for X-rays below 300 kV generating potential. Working Party of the Institute of Physics and Engineering in Medicine and Biology. PMB 41: 2606–2625
Thomas D W, El-Sharkawi A 1996 The clinical significance of kilovoltage therapy in the modern radiotherapy department. RAD Magazine (Sept): 41–42
Williams J R, Thwaites D I (eds) 1993 Radiotherapy physics in practice. Oxford University Press, Oxford

---

REFERENCES

Aldrich J E, Meng J S, Andrew J W 1992 The surface doses from orthovoltage X-ray treatments. Medical Dosimetry 17: 69–72
Barish R J, Donohue K E 1994 Modification of a superficial X-ray therapy machine for rectal contact therapy. Preliminary results. Medical Dosimetry Spring 19: 11–3
Bomford C K, Kunkler I H, Sherriff S B (eds) 1993 Walter and Miller's Textbook of radiotherapy, radiation physics, therapy and oncology. 5th edn. Churchill Livingstone, Edinburgh
British Standards Institute 1998 Medical electrical equipment. Part 2. Particular requirements for safety. Section 2.8. Specifications for therapeutic X-ray equipment operating in the range of 10 kV to 1 MV. BS 5724–2–8. BSI, London
Cherry P, Duxbury A (eds) 1998 Practical radiotherapy physics and equipment. Greenwich Medical Media, London
Cummings B J 1983 Colorectal carcinoma. Canadian Journal of Surgery 26(3): 271–274
Graham D T 1996 Principles of radiological physics, 3rd edn. Churchill Livingstone, Edinburgh
IPEMB 1996 The IPEMB code of practice for the determination of absorbed dose for X-rays below 300 kV generating potential. Working Party of the Institute of

Physics and Engineering in Medicine and Biology. PMB 41: 2606–2625

Leo W R 1994 Techniques for nuclear and particle physics experiments: a how to approach, 2nd edn. Springer Verlag, Berlin

Lovett R D, Perez C A, Shapiro S J, Garcia D M 1990 External irradiation of epithelial skin cancer. International Journal of Radiation Oncology, Biology, Physics 19(2): 235–242

Metcalfe P, Kron T, Hoban P 1997 The physics of radiotherapy X-rays from linear accelerators. Medical Physics Publishing, Wisconsin

NRPB 1988 Guidance notes for the protection of persons against ionising radiations arising from medical and dental use. HMSO, London

Ontario Cancer Institute Princess Margaret Hospital 1992 Clinical physics handbook. OCI, Toronto

Papillon J 1994 Intracavitary irradiation of early rectal cancer for cure: a series of 186 cases. Dis Colon Rectum 37(1): 88–94

Podgorsak E B, Evans M D C 1987 An endocavitary rectal irradiation technique. International Journal of Radiation Oncology, Biology, Physics 13(12): 1937–1941

Siemens 1984 Medical engineering: data, formulas and facts. Siemens, Berlin

Thomas D W, El-Sharkawi A 1996 The clinical significance of kilovoltage therapy in the modern radiotherapy department. RAD Magazine (Sept): 41–42

Thompson M A, Hattaway M P, Hall J D, Dowd S B 1994 Principles of imaging science and protection. W B Saunders, London

Wilks R 1987 Principles of radiological physics, 2nd edn. Churchill Livingstone, Oxford

Williams J R, Thwaites D I (eds) 1993 Radiotherapy physics in practice. Oxford University Press, Oxford

INTERNET REFERENCE

Pantak X-ray tubes specifications:http://www.pantak.com 18.8.99

Small sealed source afterloading equipment

CHAPTER CONTENTS

Chapter objectives

By the end of this chapter you should be able to:

- Contrast the localisation and planning procedures of a patient receiving treatment solely by external beam therapy or brachytherapy
- Consider the role of the small sealed afterloading unit in the cancer centre
- Discuss in detail the principles underlying the Manchester and Paris dosimetry systems, explaining why the latter has evolved from the former
- Evaluate the quality assurance system in place for the small sealed afterloading unit in your own particular department.

INTRODUCTION

The delivery of radiotherapy by small sealed source afterloading equipment is usually referred to as brachytherapy, a process employing radioactive sources placed directly into, or immediately adjacent to, the area to be treated. In order to do this, a small amount of radioactive material is contained within a metal capsule, and these sealed sources are then placed within the patient. A high dose of radiation can thus be delivered directly to the tumour or planning target volume, without the delivery of a high dose to the surrounding normal tissue (Williams & Thwaites 1993). The National Council on Radiation Protection (1972) defined the term brachytherapy as 'a method of radiation therapy in which an encapsulated source or a group of such sources is utilised to deliver gamma or beta radiation at a distance of up to a few centimetres, either by surface, intracavitary or interstitial application'. When sources are used interstitially they are placed directly into tissue via surgical intervention, and this is seen typically for breast boosts, lesions in the anterior two thirds of the tongue, rectal and prostate tumours. Intracavitary, intraluminal or endovascular brachytherapy (where sealed sources are placed within natural body cavities or vessels) are used in the management of gynaecological, oesophageal and lung tumours respectively. Sealed sources within surface, plaque or 'mould' type applicators demonstrate an extremely rapid fall off of dose, and are therefore ideal for treating superficial tumours overlying normal but radiosensitive tissue. The latter method is rarely employed today, for a number of reasons. The availability of megavoltage electron and kilovoltage X-ray therapy provides a cheaper and simpler method of treatment, neither type of therapy involving exposure of staff to ionising radiation. However, the cosmetic result of correctly planned surface or 'mould' brachytherapy is exceptional, and its declining use is a loss to the field of brachytherapy. The prefix 'brachy' simply means short range delivery of radiation as opposed to 'tele' or distance therapy.

Since the discovery of radium, brachytherapy has played a significant role in the management of malignant disease. Initially, the live sealed source was implanted directly into the patient in the operating theatre. The safe and accurate placement of the brachytherapy source relied on the skill of the doctor conducting the procedure. However, even in the best possible scenario, staff doses remained significant. With the advent of the ALARA concept (see Ch. 3), the need to find safer methods of source implantation was paramount, and remote afterloading equipment was soon a commonly employed technique. Even so, in the last 3–4 decades the role of brachytherapy has declined, and Joslin (cited in Mould 1989) lists the following reasons for this:

- Significant technological advances in the equipment available for delivery of external beam radiotherapy
- An awareness of the dangers of exposing staff to ionising radiation
- The need for a homogeneous dose distribution across the planning target volume.

In the last decade the role of brachytherapy has continued to evolve. With the advent of sophisticated automatic afterloading equipment, 3D computerised treatment planning offering dose optimisation and other sophisticated treatment planning tools, plus a range of low to high dose rate radionuclides, brachytherapy is being routinely used in the management of a range of conditions from gynaecological malignancy to vascular restenosis (Nag 1997, Waksman et al 1996).

HISTORICAL REVIEW

This entire chapter assumes a basic understanding of the radioactive decay schemes, and the reader is referred to basic radiotherapy physics text books for a detailed explanation of these processes. In the early days of brachytherapy, the choice of radionuclide was limited. ^{226}Radium was one of the first encapsulated sources available, and it was favoured mainly for its very long half life of 1620 years. As it could be reused, the required treatment times for specific techniques rarely changed owing to an activity decay rate of approximately 1% in 17 years (Trott 1987). However, its disadvantages are numerous, and are summarised below:

- The daughter nuclides of ^{226}Radium are alpha emitters. One particular decay product of ^{226}Radium is ^{222}Radon gas. If the encapsulated sealed source ruptures, radon gas can be released into the environment. Absorption or inhalation of radon by either patient or staff can result in serious radiobiological consequences. The possibility of these sources rupturing also has financial consequences for the design of the radiation store, as it needs to incorporate a ventilation system that exhausts out into the environment.

• ^{226}Radium emits a maximum gamma energy of 2.4 MeV. This results in a tenth value layer of approximately 44 mm of lead, resulting in costly radiation protection.

• The specific activity of the source is low, which means that for a high dose prescription, bulky and impractical sources are needed.

With a wide range of radium substitutes now available on the market, many of which have none of the disadvantages listed above, departments are faced with the problem of having to retain ^{226}Radium within the hospital environment. Problems of disposal are very similar to that described for ^{60}Cobalt and as a result of its long half life it is likely to remain a significant storage problem for many years to come.

In the 1950s the ability to create artificial radionuclides extended the number suitable for clinical applications. ^{137}Caesium, produced in a nuclear reactor, has largely replaced ^{226}Radium in the UK. Many other man-made radionuclides are also available; some of the more commonly seen examples employed in brachytherapy work are included in Table 8.1.

Some less frequently used alternatives to ^{125}Iodine for permanent implants include:

• ^{103}Palladium, with a maximum gamma emission of 0.5 MeV and a half life of 17 days
• ^{169}Ytterbium, with a maximum gamma emission of 0.3 MeV and a half life of 32 days
• ^{145}Samarium, with a maximum gamma emission of 0.06 MeV and a half life of 340 days.

THE STRUCTURE OF A SMALL SEALED BRACHYTHERAPY SOURCE

Sources suitable for brachytherapy use consist of small amounts of radionuclide which are totally encapsulated by a non toxic and inert material, such as stainless steel or platinum (see Fig. 8.1). This encapsulation prevents leakage of the radionuclide under the stresses and strains associated with routine use.

Additionally the outer capsule should not significantly attenuate any gamma emissions, but should be thick enough to absorb the majority of beta emissions and any characteristic radiations that may be produced.

The source may be produced as a wire, needle, rod or sphere. Whichever the form, it is important that each individual source carries an identification number, and that its structure and form comply with the International Organisation for Standardisation (ISO) requirements for safety of such sources.

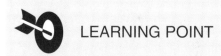

LEARNING POINT

Questions

Can ^{192}Iridium wire be classified as a sealed source?

What mechanism has resulted in the production of the above mentioned beta particles, and characteristic radiation?

Table 8.1	Radionuclides used in brachytherapy				
Radionuclide	Gamma energy (MeV) maximum	Half life	Specific activity	Atomic number	Attenuation in lead TVL mm
^{60} Cobalt	1.33	5.26 years	High	27	45
^{137} Caesium	0.662	30 years	Low	55	22
^{192} Iridium	0.61	74 days	High	77	12
^{198} Gold	1.09	2.7 days	High	79	12
^{125} Iodine	0.043	60 days	Low	53	0.04

CHARACTERISTICS OF AN IDEAL RADIONUCLIDE FOR BRACHYTHERAPY USE

Obviously 'ideal' characteristics of a radionuclide depend primarily upon its intended application – for imaging, unsealed radionuclide therapy, or sealed radionuclide therapy. Traditionally, the physical properties of the material concerned have been used to select suitable sources, but lately radiobiological implications have developed a significance in the management of malignant disease (Ch. 2), and so are often used as additional selection criteria.

KEY POINTS

For brachytherapy use, all or most of the following characteristics are desirable:

▪ For a temporary implant *a long half life* is preferred. This has cost implications as the source can be reused many times within its active lifetime. The shorter the half life, the greater the chance of having to include decay correction factors. Any factor included into a calculation merely increases the possibility of a calculation error. However, if a permanent implant is needed, a shorter half life (in the order of a few days) is preferred in order to reduce the overall dose to the patient.

▪ *Suitable gamma energy*. The term 'suitable' has a dual definition in this particular instance. Firstly, the gamma energy should be sufficiently high to deliver the required depth dose within the patient (and avoid differential bone absorption of the primary beam of radiation). Conversely, it should not be so high as to require enclosing the patient within significant and costly radiation protection barriers. Secondly, using a radionuclide that emits a monoenergetic spectrum will simplify the dose calculation –

however, with modern computing technology the use of a radionuclide emitting a range of gamma energies is no longer a significant problem. Usually, in the latter case the average energy is used as a basis for the dose calculation, and the maximum energy is used for calculation of radiation protection barriers.

▪ A *high specific activity* results in a higher dose rate. This impacts upon the range of size and shape of the sources that can be manufactured, thereby increasing the diversity of use of a particular radionuclide. It may also reduce the length of time that the sources need to remain in situ.

▪ *Cost-effective*. In today's health care system this is a particularly important factor.

▪ *Charged particle emission should be absent*, or absorbed within the source container.

▪ *Reasonable atomic number and density*. Source verification is an essential part of treatment planning, and radiographs (or occasionally megavoltage port films) are used to obtain this information.

 LEARNING POINT

Questions
How might this list of idea characteristics change when selecting a radionuclide for

• imaging?

• treatment by the use of an unsealed radionuclide?

PRINCIPLES OF AFTERLOADING

The loading of live radioactive sources directly into body tissue or cavities by a surgeon in an operating theatre was an extremely hazardous procedure in respect of the radiation dose received by theatre staff. Afterloading was introduced in the 1960s, and takes a number of forms.

In conventional, or manual, afterloading, hollow guides of plastic or stainless steel are inserted into the desired position. Radiographic verification of the catheter position ensures

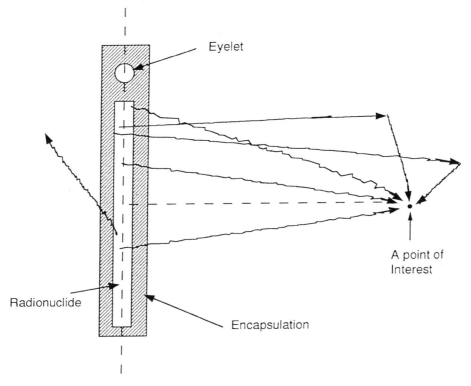

Figure 8.1 A schematic diagram of a sealed brachytherapy source (from Nag 1997, with permission).

optimal positioning prior to the manual place-ment of the sealed sources, and subsequently improved accuracy in the resultant isodose distribution. The verification process may occur in theatre or in the patient's room, reducing staff exposure to a minimum.

In remote, or automatic, afterloading the catheters are positioned within the patient as described above, but once the patient has left the theatre and returned to the ward the catheters are connected to a safe containing the radioactive sources. Source transfer is then conducted automatically, once all staff have left the patient's room. When any nursing care is required, the source is remotely retracted by the use of a remote control panel, and the nursing intervention can be carried out without staff exposure to radiation. Options include the ability to monitor source position during treatment, rectal and bladder dose monitor facility, and

safety interlocks and associated features such as failsafe return. Low (0.4–2 Gy h^{-1}), medium (2–12 Gy h^{-1}) and high (0.2 Gy min^{-1} and above) dose rate afterloading equipment is available, but there is no general consensus between texts regarding the dose rates which delineate the borders between these three categories.

High, low and pulsed dose rates

The selection of dose rate depends upon projected patient case load, clinical demand and required support and ancillary facilities.

High dose rate (HDR) afterloading equipment clearly has a major advantage in that the patient can usually be treated on an outpatient basis. Although a designated room is required in the radiotherapy department where anaes-thetic may be administered if necessary, the short treatment time means that the risk of catheter movement during treatment is small and a higher case load of patients can be treated on one machine. Obvious disadvantages include a larger capital outlay and running costs, the need to fractionate the radiotherapy owing to radiobiological considerations, an increased risk of patient overdose, as well as the risks associated with any general anaesthetic or sedation that might be required (particularly if a fractionated course of radiotherapy is prescribed). The HDR system tends to contain a single active source, most commonly [192]Iridium, which moves in steps to preprogrammed positions. Each step may have variable dwell times, resulting in the ability to produce a complex and optimal isodose distribution. Typical active source size is in the region of 1 mm in diameter and 4 mm in length (Stout 1996). This is soldered to a stainless steel cable which is mechanically driven in and out of the applicator. Multiple channels can be attached to the source safe, which may then be used to produce interstitial volume implants. Alternatively, the radioactive source may be in the form of a solitary bead, moved into place using compressed air.

The lower dose rate unit offers a more affordable capital outlay, fewer support staff are required, more than one patient can be treated at any one time, and there is better recovery of normal tissue in comparison to the high dose rate option. Lower dose rate units usually contain multiple [137]Caesium sources, and tend to mimic conventional afterloading techniques by using a large number of sources in a linear array, with inactive spacer sources which together may produce differential source activity. Alternatively, source construction may feature a single source which oscillates to produce the same radiation distribution as the linear array described previously.

A pulsed dose rate unit is also now on the market. This uses a high activity [192]Iridium source. By loading the source into the catheter for a few minutes every hour and then retracting back into the safe housing, it mimics an average dose rate similar to that of a low dose rate unit, thereby increasing its diversity of use.

EQUIPMENT DESIGN AND OPERATION

An afterloading unit (see Fig. 8.2) should contain at least the following features:

1. Small radioactive sources.
2. A lead safe to house the retracted sources.
3. A drive mechanism that will take the source from the safe to the catheter/applicator.
4. A control panel indicating source position, and producing a hard copy of the treatment data. This usually incorporates a microprocessor which tracks the source position and controls source release and retraction.
5. A series of applicators, and a dummy source system which tracks along the applicators prior to the release of the active source to verify channel integrity.
6. A uninterruptable power supply, allowing completion of the treatment if the hospital power supply fails, and a failsafe device that will initially retract the source in the event of a power cut. Additional safety interlock systems and emergency stop systems should be present.
7. Dose monitor enabling measurement of rectal and/or bladder doses during gynaecological treatments.
8. An indexer to channel sources into the required linear arrays.
9. An associated 3D treatment planning system.

When the position of the guide catheters has been verified and an isodose distribution has been produced and approved by the clinical oncologist, treatment can commence. The ends of the catheters protruding from the patient are connected to the afterloading unit. The staff then leave the room and the machine is switched on. The patient specific machine parameters will have been pre-programmed into the unit, either by a direct link to the planning computer or by using a floppy disk. Once these have been confirmed at the control panel, the dummy source is sent into the catheter assembly to ensure that the entire transit route is free from obstruction. The sources can then be released from the safe housing, and treatment started. The machine may be interrupted at any point by

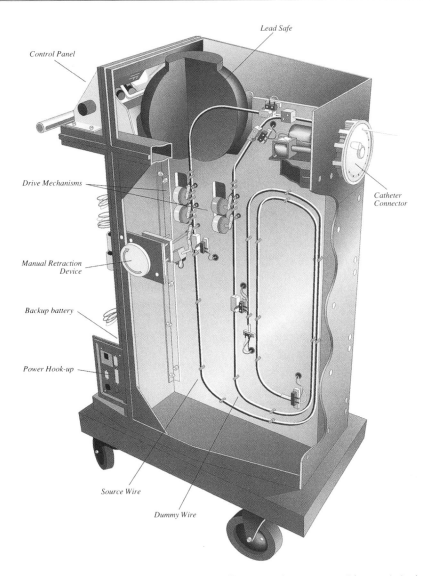

Figure 8.2   A cross-section through a remote afterloading unit (from Omnitron 1991, with permission).

activation of the interrupt switch on the control panel outside the patient's room. Every time this happens the machine records the date and time of the interruption, and the dose given and that remaining to be delivered. Treatment may only be recommended from the control panel.

As the sources travel from the safe housing to the specified position, the patient receives dose. Usually the brachytherapy treatment planning system will calculate the actual isodose distribution solely from the source dwell positions, and

will assume a negligible 'transit' dose. Baskin et al (1993) identified significant transit doses from a ^{192}Ir high dose rate unit under certain clinical situations, and consequently recommend that the isodose distribution be accordingly adjusted.

PROCEDURE FOR PLANNING AND IMPLEMENTING A CLINICAL CASE

The localisation, planning and verification processes undertaken for a brachytherapy patient are very different to those for a patient prescribed external beam radiotherapy. The following stages are usually completed for a brachytherapy patient:

- Definition of the clinical target volume (this is usually established in the operating theatre when the patient is under a general anaesthetic)
- Placement of the guide catheters
- Orthogonal radiographic verification of guide catheter position in relation to the clinical target volume
- Where appropriate, measurement of rectal and bladder dose whilst patient is still under anaesthetic (this is achieved by placing a single but low activity source into the planned source array and recording dose levels)
- Transfer of localisation data to the treatment planning computer
- Reconstruction of catheter positions from orthogonal radiographs, and determination of required prescription point for this particular patient
- For the activity of the sealed sources in question, computer generated optimisation of source position and dwell times to obtain the required isodose at the prescription point
- Production of isodose distribution, and approval from clinical oncologist
- Commence treatment.

 ## LEARNING POINT

The above blueprint of a brachytherapy patient management protocol differs from that of an external beam therapy patient

Questions
What are the implications of this in terms of:

- incidence of treatment errors?
- quality assurance programme?
- student and new staff education?

SPECIFICATION AND CALIBRATION OF SOURCE STRENGTH

Man-made radionuclides of identical shape and size can produce varying dose rates at a specified measurement point. Consequently when new sources are purchased from the manufacturer they arrive with a manufacturer's certificate stating source strength at a specified date and time.

Source strength may be specified in terms of either source activity or radiation output at a stated distance. Historically, radionuclide activity was specified in terms of actual mass of radium in milligrammes. However, in man-made radionuclides mass is not a measure of the radioactivity contained within the source.

Source activity is simply the number of spontaneous radioactive disintegrations that occur per second, a figure normally measured in becquerels (Bq); where 1 curie = 3.7×10^{10} Bq. This is not of much use in the clinical radiotherapy setting, where the dose rate at a point in a medium is of primary interest. Source strength is therefore now commonly specified in terms of radiation output.

The standard unit of radiation output is known as the reference air kerma. This is defined as the air kerma rate (AKR) at 1 metre from the source in free space in units of μ Gy h^{-1} (Williams & Thwaites 1993). This dose rate measurement includes consideration of the radiation attenuated by the source itself, and also the effects of source encapsulation on emitted dose rate.

In terms of calculation of absolute absorbed dose to the patient, the value of reference air kerma then needs to be converted to a dose rate value at a distance of approximately 1 cm (depending upon the chosen dosimetry system) from the source in a tissue equivalent medium. Such mathematical conversions are well described in the texts of Nag (1997) and Williams & Thwaites (1993).

The importance of calibration chains has been reviewed in Chapter 2 and will not be addressed in much detail here. However, it is necessary to recognise that the calibration chain for brachytherapy sources in the UK is not as comprehensive as that for external beam therapy. The National Physics Laboratory have produced calibration figures for ^{192}Iridium use (Sephton et al 1993) with their secondary standard radionuclide calibrator (a well type re-entrant ionisation chamber). These figures allow the user accurately to estimate the reference air kerma value based on the response of the ionisation chamber. Calibration figures are strongly dependent on energy and the type of radionuclide, and NPL continues to work on expanding the range of calibration figures currently available.

DOSIMETRY SYSTEMS

In external beam therapy (as discussed in Ch. 2) there is a range of desirable features of an external beam radiotherapy isodose distribution. It is considerably more difficult to develop such a 'recipe' for an ideal brachytherapy isodose distribution.

As a result of the extremely rapid fall off of isodose lines around a brachytherapy source (see Fig. 8.3) it is difficult to specify a single prescription point where homogeneity of dose is consistent within a limited tolerance range. Additionally, for a number of reasons, it is

not always possible to place the catheters, and therefore the radioactive sources, at the optimal position.

Historically, a number of dosimetry systems existed to allow the user to decide, for a specific radionuclide, exactly how the sealed source must be placed within the patient and how long it must remain there. The systems were developed before the advent of computer aided dosimetry and include:

- The Paterson–Parker or Manchester dosimetry system
- The Paris dosimetry system.

These, and other systems like them, are a series of rules. To deliver a uniform dose to the prescribed plane or volume, details of source geometry, activity, length of implant and type of radionuclide are described. However, owing to the very rapid fall off of dose around a brachytherapy source it is almost impossible to achieve a homogeneous isodose distribution across the planning target volume, as is required in external beam radiotherapy planning (Ch. 2) (documented in ICRU report 50, 1993). With the advent of sophisticated 3D treatment planning computers, capable of rapidly displaying isodose

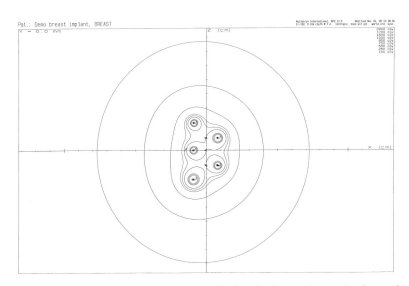

Figure 8.3 The shape of a typical nosode distribution around a brachytherapy breast implant – the five source catheters being viewed end on (by permission of Nucletron®).

lines for any source array, classical dosimetry systems are far less frequently used, particularly with the availability of dose optimisation facilities.

Classical dosimetry systems are still employed in gynaecological applications, where afterloaded source applicators are very similar to the live or manual afterloaded source arrays of old. Caesium needles and iridium wire are also used for a range of other applications, and quite commonly both Paris and Manchester systems can be employed within one cancer centre.

Paterson–Parker (Manchester) system

This was developed by Ralston Paterson and Herbert Parker in the 1930s for the gynaecological application of radium sources. It is also commonly known as the Manchester system of brachytherapy dosimetry. It is now used mainly with ^{137}Caesium needles and tubes.

The system is limited to five different source geometries: linear sources, surface applicators, planar implants, multiple planar or volume implants, and a cylindrical shaped implant. The linear and planar arrays are the ones most likely to be used today, and these source geometries are frequently seen in gynaecology, breast and rectal implants. The rules of the system for planar and linear source patterns are listed below:

- Generally the source array is circular, square or rectangular (Fig. 8.4).
- Each implanted plane is designed to treat a volume of tissue 5 mm either side of it.
- Sources must be used end to end, with inactive ends overlapped to ensure that the gap between adjacent ends does not exceed the distance between the sources and the treated surface.
- Typically squares and rectangular geometries have a treated volume contained within the outermost needles of the array. If it is not possible to produce the desired shape for clinical reasons (e.g. in the case of a needle implant into the anterior two-thirds of the tongue it is often difficult to correctly position the most posterior crossing needle owing to a lack of space), then sources containing differentially loaded activity may be used. These are often called dumbell or club needles.

- With circular source arrays, if the treated area is of a significant size it is sometimes necessary to add additional activity into the centre of the volume in the form of a smaller second circle. A calculation of the ratio of the initial circle diameter to the distance between the sources and the treated plane allows the user to look up whether additional brachytherapy sources are required. If this is necessary, the rules will also state what percentage of activity needs to be placed within the inner circle. Similar rules exist for square and rectangular source arrays.
- Within a parallel array, the needles should normally be 1 cm from each other, but no more than 1.5 cm apart.
- In order to calculate the activity required to deliver the prescribed dose, the source activity needs to be converted into a value of milligrammes radium equivalent. Paterson–Parker tables can then be used to calculate the total activity required, and its dwell time

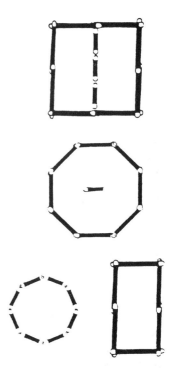

Figure 8.4 Typical Paterson–Parker planar source arrays (from Bomford et al 1993, with permission).

(Clifford Chao et al 1999, Bomford et al 1993, Williams & Thwaites 1993).

• The average dose to the treatment plane at a distance of 0.5 cm from the brachytherapy sources is used as a basis for dose prescription.

Paris system

This system was developed in the 1960s when [192]Iridium became more frequently used. As it is available in wire form, it lends itself for use in non conventional source arrays that do not fit into the 'rule book' scenario of the Manchester system. The implant rules are much simpler, and are summarised below:

• The wires used for implants must be continuous and of uniform activity and length.

• Wire separation depends primarily upon the volume to be treated, but generally they must be equally spaced.

• Crossing wires are not necessary, but the length of each wire must extend 20–30% beyond the tumour volume.

• For volume implants, the wires must be arranged so that the cross-sectional source distribution is either a series of equilateral triangles or squares (see Fig. 8.5).

• The reference point used for dose prescription is 85% of the basal dose rate, the basal dose rate being the average of the dose rates calculated at the minimum dose point in the central transverse plane of the implant (Williams & Thwaites 1993).

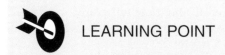

LEARNING POINT

It was previously mentioned that it is not uncommon to see a number of dosimetry systems being used in one radiotherapy centre. Evaluate the clinical implications of this.

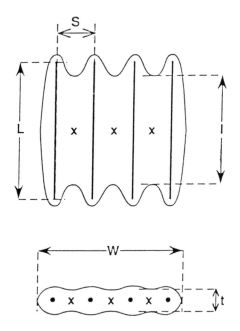

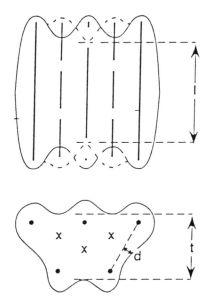

Figure 8.5 The definition of implant dimensions for the Paris system. A single plane implant is shown on the left, and a two plane implant with a triangular arrangement of wire is shown on the right. The reference dose is shown, and the crosses represent the positions of the basal rate calculation (from Williams & Thwaites 1993, by permission of Oxford University Press).

COMPUTERISED TREATMENT PLANNING

The principles of external beam and brachytherapy treatment planning are reviewed in Chapter 2.

QUALITY ASSURANCE

Quality assurance procedures of small sealed source afterloading equipment relate primarily to the functioning of safety procedures associated with the treatment unit, and also to the safe schemes of work that result in the safe and accurate delivery of the brachytherapy treatment itself. Planning computer quality assurance is discussed in Chapter 2.

As reviewed in Chapter 4, a quality assurance programme incorporating daily, weekly, monthly, quarterly and annual quality control tests on the following is required: interlocks, warning lights and alarms, treatment interrupt monitors, patient communication devices, source activity, reproducibility of source positioning, accuracy of dwell time setting, normal termination of treatment and mechanical integrity of the applicators and applicator connections.

A treatment protocol manual containing all of the likely treatment procedures to be carried out on the unit should be kept within the working area. In order for these to work effectively, it is essential that those involved in carrying out the procedures are consulted about the content and scope of each protocol. Additionally it is useful if these staff members are also involved in the regular audit procedures of the treatment protocols.

Clear documentation must also exist regarding the procedures to be followed on the receipt of new small sealed sources, their transient storage conditions prior to being inserted into the brachytherapy unit, acceptable methods of transport within the hospital environment and appropriate methods and routes of disposal for old sources.

ROOM DESIGN

Room design is an interesting issue for brachytherapy applications, mainly because

there are three main types of room which house treatment units such as these:

- Single room on an inpatient ward
- Shared room on an inpatient ward where protection is enhanced by the use of portable lead screens
- Specially designed treatment room, analogous to that required by an external beam treatment unit, usually located within the radiotherapy department (this may be shared with another more frequently used piece of radiotherapy machine, such as a kilovoltage unit).

In almost all scenarios it is important to ensure that there is adequate space in the room for all necessary inpatient equipment and that any nursing procedures required during the course of treatment can be conducted unhindered by space constraints.

Low dose rate equipment emits radiation for many hours, and patients lying in adjacent rooms may reach their public dose limit within a number of days. Consequently wall thickness must be calculated assuming maximum occupancy of all adjacent rooms to ensure the safety of other patients. The room itself may have to be designated as a controlled area as a result of the dose rates when the machine is operating, and so approved communication monitors, interlocks, signs and audible alarms must be installed. However, if the room is shared with another patient, this is not possible, and a definitive area around the patient must be designated as the controlled area, which is then appropriately demarcated with portable shielding. Finally, portable monitors must be available to check all waste and bedlinen which leaves the area to ensure that any identified radiation waste can be dealt with in the recommended manner.

RECOMMENDED READING

Nag S (ed) 1997 Principles and practice of brachytherapy. Futural Publishing, New York
Sephton J P, Woods M J, Rossiter M J, Williams T T, Dean J C J, Bass G A, Lucas S E M 1993 Secondary standard radionuclide calibrator for ^{192}Iridium brachytherapy sources. Physics, Medicine, Biology 38: 1157–1164

Stout R 1996 Intraluminal radiotherapy and its use in lung
cancer. RAD Magazine (April)

Trott N G (ed) 1987 Radionuclides in brachytherapy: radium
and after. British Journal of Radiology, Supplement No. 21

Waksman R, King S B, Crocker I R, Mould R F (eds) 1996
Vascular brachytherapy. Nucletron, The Netherlands

REFERENCES

Baskin K T, Podgorsak M B, Thomadsen B R 1993 Transit
dose components of high dose rate brachytherapy: direct
measurements and clinical implications. International
Journal of Radiation Oncology, Biology and Physics 26:
695–702

Bomford C K, Kunkler I H, Sherriff S B (eds) 1993 Walter and
Miller's Textbook of radiotherapy, radiation physics,
therapy and oncology, 5th edn. Churchill Livingstone,
Edinburgh

Clifford Chao K S, Perez C A, Brady L W 1999 Radiation
oncology: management decisions. Lippincott-Raven,
Philadelphia

International Commission on Radiation Units and
Measurement 1985 Report No. 38. Dose and volume
specification for reporting intracavitary therapy in
gynaecology. ICRU, Bethesda

ICRU 1993 Report No. 50. Prescribing, recording and
reporting photon beam therapy. ICRU, Bethesda

Mould R F (ed) 1989 Brachytherapy 2. Proceedings of the
brachytherapy working conference, 5th international
Selectron users meeting, Netherlands 1988. Nucletron, The
Netherlands

Nag S (ed) 1997 Principles and practice of brachytherapy.
Futural Publishing, New York

National Council on Radiation Protection 1972 Protection
against radiation from brachytherapy sources. Report No.
40. NCRP, Washington

Omnitron International 1991 Omnitron: the new generation
of high dose rate remote afterloaders. Omnitron
International, Houston, Texas

Sephton J P, Woods M J, Rossiter M J, Williams T T,
Dean J C J, Bass G A, Lucas S E M 1993 Secondary
standard radionuclide calibrator for ^{192}Iridium
brachytherapy sources. Physics, Medicine, Biology 38:
1157–1164

Stout R 1996 Intraluminal radiotherapy and its use in lung
cancer. RAD Magazine (April)

Trott N G (ed) 1987 Radionuclides in brachytherapy: radium
and after. British Journal of Radiology, Supplement No. 21

Waksman R, King S B, Crocker I R, Mould R F (eds) 1996
Vascular brachytherapy. Nucletron, The Netherlands

Williams J R, Thwaites D I (eds) 1993 Radiotherapy physics
in practice. Oxford Medical Publications, Oxford

Index